An Illustrated Histo...

MANSFIELD'S RAILWAYS

by

Paul Anderson
and Jack Cupit

IRWELL
PRESS

ISBN 1-903266-15-7

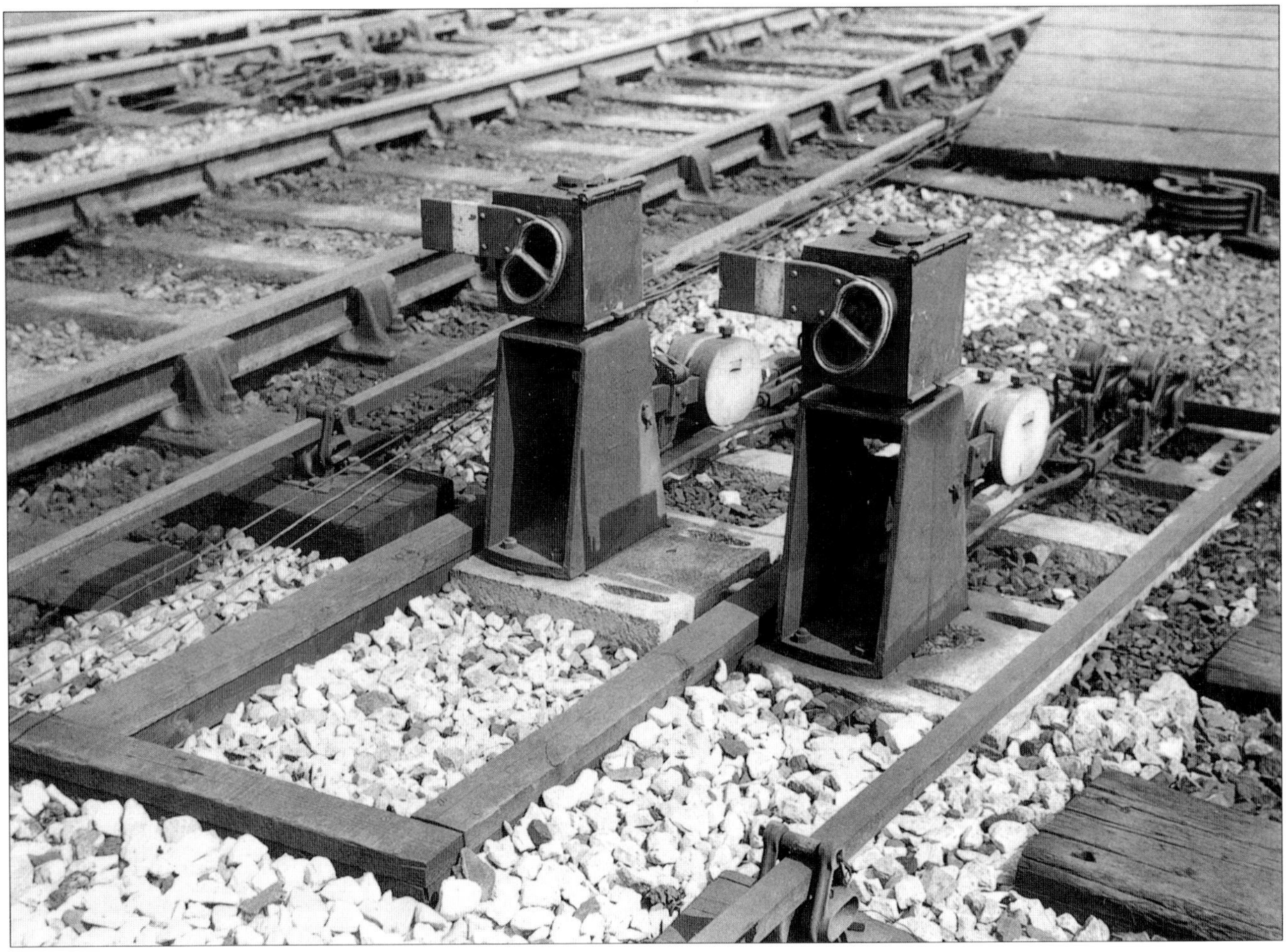

Mansfield Town now has just two through lines with no pointwork to complicate matters. In the past it was very different. These two delightful miniature semaphores at the south end of the station were for shunting movements. They are seen on 10th May 1959. Photograph Jack Cupit.

Front cover. Despite the hilly terrain, tunnels were not a pronounced feature of the railway network around Mansfield. The earliest – and probably the most significant – was Kirkby Tunnel on the Midland line from Nottingham to Mansfield. Stanier 2-6-2T No.40115 approaches the 199 yard bore with a Nottingham Midland-Worksop train on 20th June 1959. Nearby Annesley Tunnel on the Great Central was deeper and considerably longer. Photograph Jack Cupit.

Rear cover. The north end of Mansfield station, seen from Station North signal box on 3rd June 1963. Black 5 No.44658, a Nottingham loco which had spent all of the 1950s allocated to Kentish Town, leaves with a Beeston-Skegness excursion. On the right is the Midland Hotel, which was the Broombank Asylum back in the 1840s when the Midland Railway arrived. Photograph Jack Cupit.

First published in the United Kingdom in 2000
by Irwell Press
59A, High Street, Clophill,
Bedfordshire MK45 4BE

CONTENTS

ACKNOWLEDGEMENTS

The authors have received valuable assistance from many people during the preparation of this book and are indebted to all of them. Special thanks are due to Bill Taylor of Skegby for his meticulous proof reading and helpful comments. Alf Henshaw of Nottingham, Robert Humm of Stamford and Roger Grayson of the Mansfield Chad provided photographs which filled important gaps. Juliet Whitworth of Barrow upon Soar did the exquisite drawings, Sylvia Lee of Kimberley provided useful background books and Pip Bloor of Thurmaston investigated shed allocations. David Clarke of the Mining Records Office at Burton on Trent supplied details of colliery closures, Stuart Oliver of RJB Mining provided up to date information on the coalfield and Peter Whitmore of Thoresby Colliery helped with present day merry-go-round workings. Arthur Cowie, Rail Team Manager at Nottinghamshire County Council supplied facts about the Robin Hood line, the Act of Parliament for which was sought out by Becky Brooks and Gavin Lethbridge of Leicester Reference Library. Volker Döhler of Zwickau clarified the inscription on the German wagon at Mansfield Central. Finally, Jack Cupit in Nottingham wishes to thank his wife Betty for her support, enthusiasm and assistance, while Paul Anderson in Leicester is more than grateful to both of them for their very generous hospitality during the project.

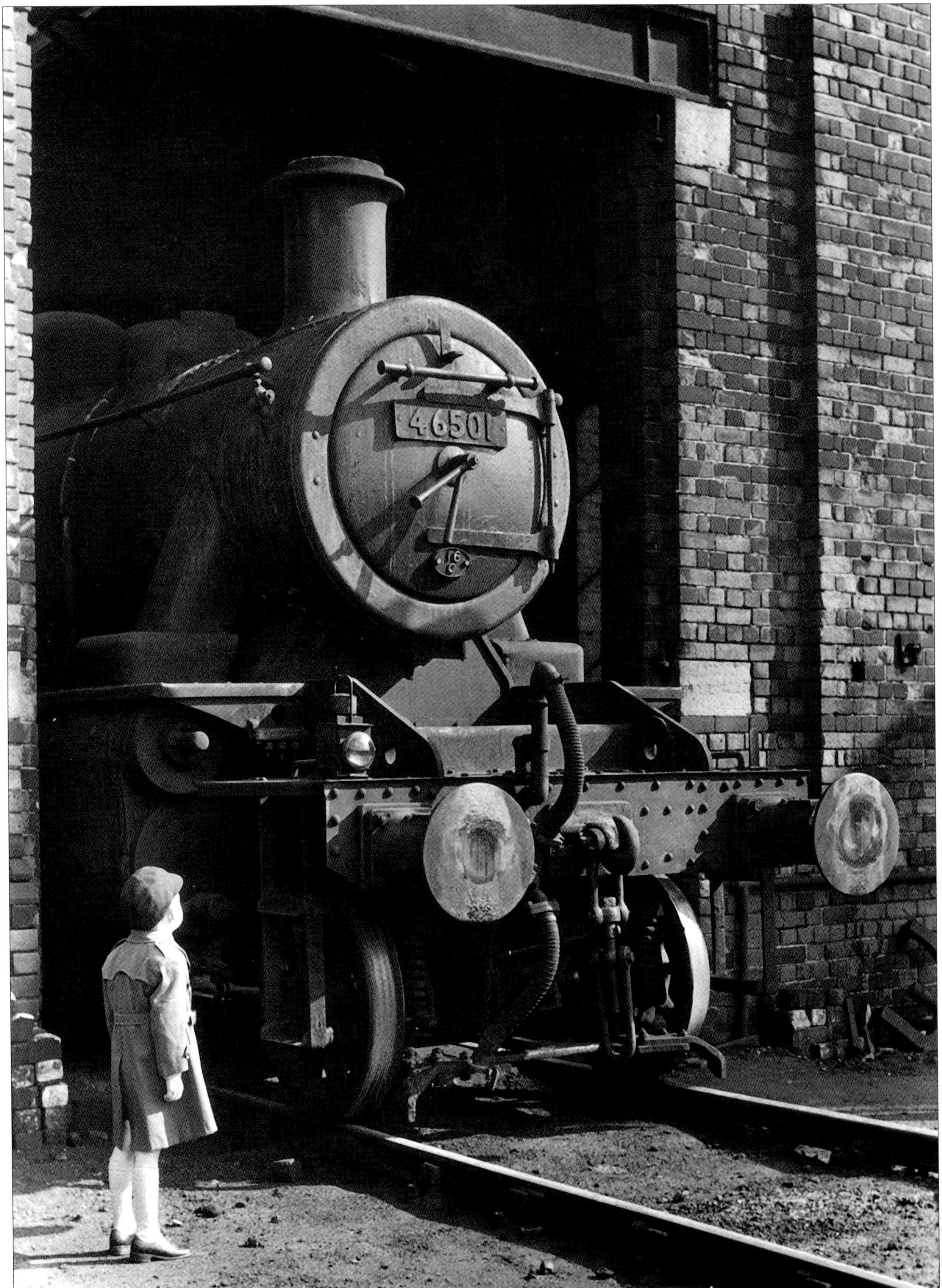

At a time when many small boys still wanted to be engine drivers and it was possible to take a Sunday morning stroll round some sheds with no animosity from staff, young Geoff Cupit gazes up at Ivatt 2MT 2-6-0 No.46501 in residence at Mansfield shed, on 3rd March 1959. This loco, which stood out among the allocation of 2-6-2 passenger tanks and 3F, 4F and 8F mineral engines, was shedded at Mansfield for most of its life, specifically for working the unadvertised workmen's trains to Chilwell Ordnance Depot. Although this scene seemed permanent at the time, much changed over the ensuing forty years. Mansfield lost and regained its passenger services, the shed building has long been incorporated in an industrial complex and Geoff now lectures at Waikato University in New Zealand. Photograph Jack Cupit.

Chapter 1

ROBIN HOOD COUNTRY

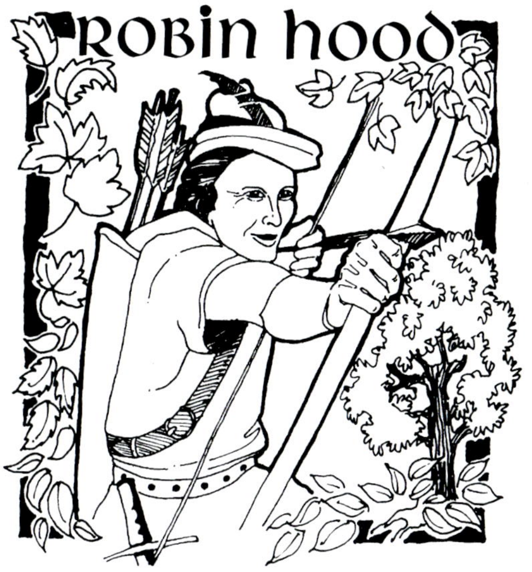

One dank and misty afternoon, the king was enjoying his favourite sport of hunting deer in the Royal Forest of Sherwood. On this occasion he became separated from the party of nobles and attendants and found himself completely lost. Hungry and tired, he stumbled across a watermill owned by John Cockle. Failing to recognise his royal visitor, the miller offered to provide food and shelter for the night, providing he was paid! The king gratefully accepted, without revealing his identity and was 'royally' regaled with copious amounts of ale and venison poached from his own Forest. Furthermore, the host boasted that his family regularly dined on the forbidden meat. Next morning, the hunting party arrived and the miller suddenly realised the status of his guest. As the monarch drew his sword, the hapless artisan fell to his knees, expecting to be beheaded for breaking Forest Law. Instead, the king knighted him Sir John Cockle, ample reward for the hospitality he had shown. That was the origin of King's Mill in the Maun Valley south of Mansfield, so legend has it.

Much, the Miller's son, was a stout yet somewhat witless individual who belonged to the band of men led by that most famous of heroes, Robin Hood. His fellow outlaws included huge and trusty Little John, fat and jovial Friar Tuck, mysterious Will Scarlet and lyrical Alan A'Dale. Beautiful Maid Marian and the evil Sheriff of Nottingham were, of course, an essential part of the adventures. There may well be some basis to the story of the flamboyant 12th century renegades, as it was often related by travelling minstrels during the 1300s. However, the tale was heavily embellished and some of the main characters added, during the romantic Tudor period. Whatever the truth, the saga has made Nottinghamshire famous throughout the world. There is a legacy of place names in the Mansfield area associated with the legend, such as Robin Hood's Hills near Annesley, Friar Tuck's Well at Fountaindale near Blidworth and Robin Hood's Cave at Creswell. The hero's name has also been applied to the reinstated passenger train service through Mansfield, a project which required as much determination as some of those exploits in Sherwood Forest eight centuries ago!

The woodland and heath of Sherwood Forest flourished on Bunter Sandstone, a porous rock which produced acidic soil not really suitable for cultivation. This is one of a series of north-south outcrops in Nottinghamshire and a basic understanding of the geology is essential when considering the landscape, industrial development, spread of coal mining and growth of the railway system in the Mansfield area. Some 300 million years ago, much of Britain was a vast swamp with lush forests which eventually became covered with sediment and compressed to form the Coal Measures. Later, the onset of a drier climate combined with sagging of the earth's crust meant that a clear sea teeming in marine life covered the East Midlands. Thick deposits on the ocean floor resulted in the band of Magnesian Limestone. As the sea retreated, desert conditions encroached about 220 million years ago and a deep layer of Bunter Sandstone, followed by Keuper Sandstone, gradually built up. Because of 'Continental Drift', all this activity took place where Africa now stands. Earth movements meant that these successive layers of rock were tilted down to the east and as a result of relentless erosion, the coal seams are exposed in the west, the limestone outcrops on the Nottinghamshire-Derbyshire border and the sandstone forms a

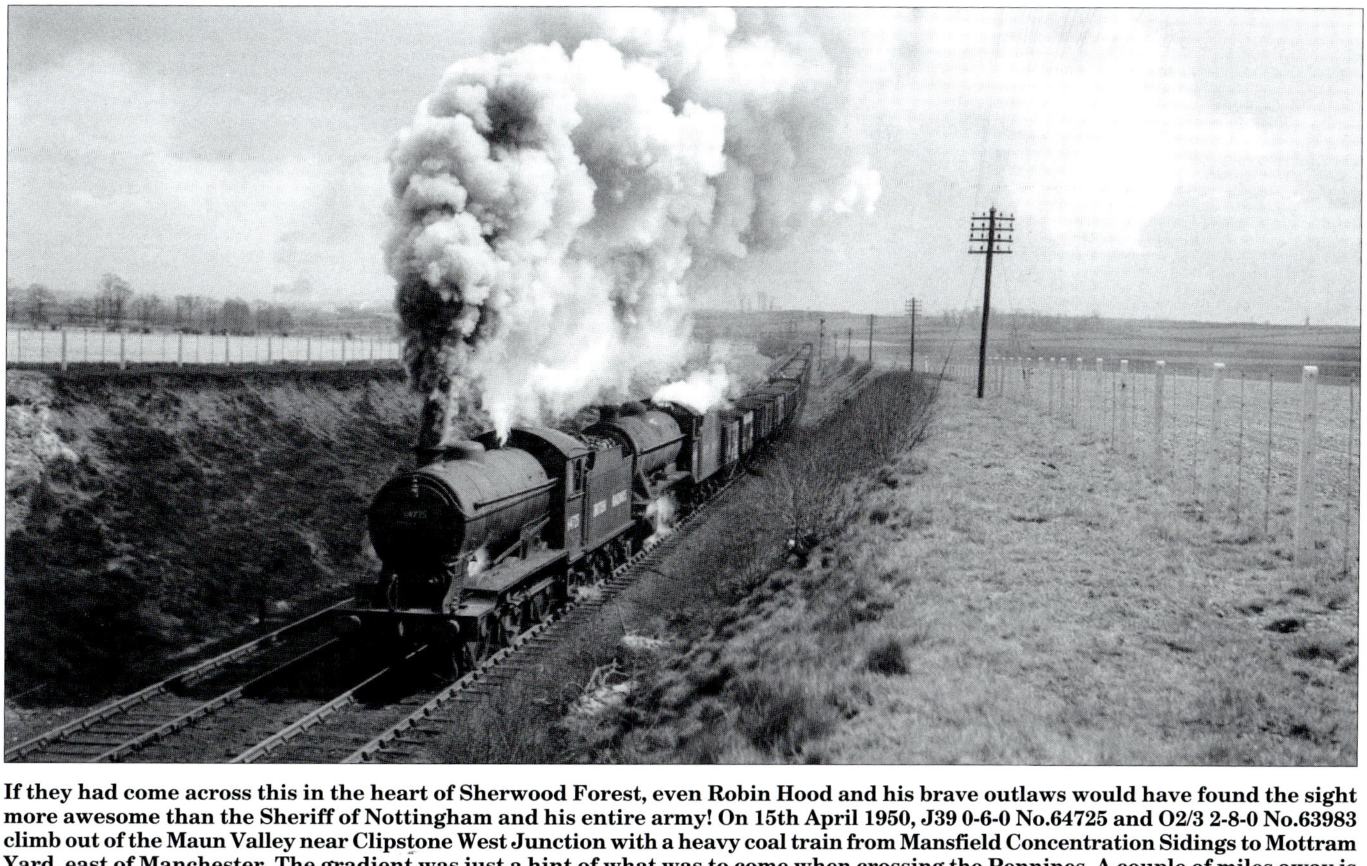

If they had come across this in the heart of Sherwood Forest, even Robin Hood and his brave outlaws would have found the sight more awesome than the Sheriff of Nottingham and his entire army! On 15th April 1950, J39 0-6-0 No.64725 and O2/3 2-8-0 No.63983 climb out of the Maun Valley near Clipstone West Junction with a heavy coal train from Mansfield Concentration Sidings to Mottram Yard, east of Manchester. The gradient was just a hint of what was to come when crossing the Pennines. A couple of miles away is Edwinstowe, where Robin Hood is said to have wed Maid Marian. Photograph Jack Cupit.

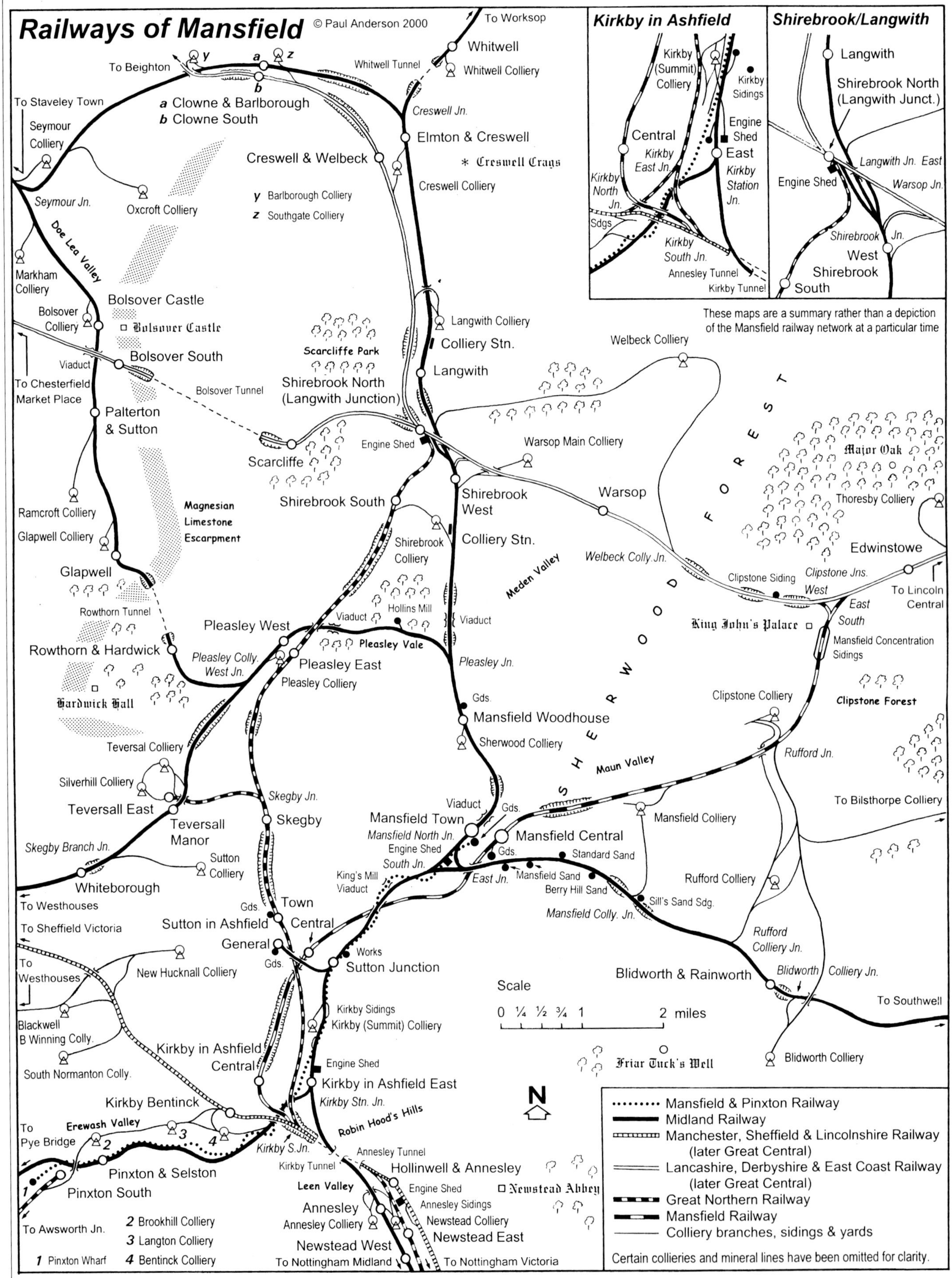
Railways of Mansfield
© Paul Anderson 2000
Kirkby in Ashfield
Shirebrook/Langwith
To Worksop
Whitwell
Whitwell Colliery
Whitwell Tunnel
To Beighton
a Clowne & Barlborough
b Clowne South
y Barlborough Colliery
z Southgate Colliery
To Staveley Town
Seymour Colliery
Seymour Jn.
Oxcroft Colliery
Doe Lea Valley
Markham Colliery
Creswell Jn.
Elmton & Creswell
Creswell & Welbeck
* Creswell Crags
Creswell Colliery
Bolsover Castle
Bolsover Colliery
Bolsover Castle
Viaduct
Bolsover South
To Chesterfield Market Place
Bolsover Tunnel
Palterton & Sutton
Scarcliffe Park
Scarcliffe
Shirebrook North (Langwith Junction)
Langwith Colliery
Colliery Stn.
Langwith
Engine Shed
Welbeck Colliery
Warsop Main Colliery
Shirebrook West
Shirebrook South
Shirebrook Colliery
Colliery Stn.
Warsop
Ramcroft Colliery
Glapwell Colliery
Magnesian Limestone Escarpment
Glapwell
Rowthorn Tunnel
Rowthorn & Hardwick
Hardwick Hall
Pleasley West
Pleasley Colly. West Jn.
Pleasley East
Pleasley Colliery
Viaduct
Hollins Mill
Pleasley Vale
Viaduct
Pleasley Jn.
Meden Valley
Welbeck Colly. Jn.
SHERWOOD FOREST
Major Oak
Thoresby Colliery
Edwinstowe
Clipstone Siding
Clipstone Jns. West East South
To Lincoln Central
King John's Palace
Mansfield Concentration Sidings
Clipstone Forest
Clipstone Colliery
Gds.
Mansfield Woodhouse
Sherwood Colliery
Maun Valley
Rufford Jn.
To Bilsthorpe Colliery
Teversal Colliery
Silverhill Colliery
Teversal East
Teversal Manor
Skegby Jn.
Skegby
Skegby Branch Jn.
Whiteborough
Sutton Colliery
Viaduct
Gds.
Mansfield Town
Mansfield North Jn.
Engine Shed
South Jn.
Mansfield Central
Gds.
Standard Sand
East Jn.
Mansfield Sand
Berry Hill Sand
Mansfield Colliery
Rufford Colliery
Sill's Sand Sdg.
Mansfield Colly. Jn.
King's Mill Viaduct
To Westhouses
To Sheffield Victoria
Gds.
Sutton in Ashfield General
Town
Central
Gds.
Works
Sutton Junction
Rufford Colliery Jn.
Blidworth & Rainworth
Blidworth Colliery Jn.
To Southwell
To Westhouses
New Hucknall Colliery
Blackwell B Winning Colly.
South Normanton Colly.
Kirkby Sidings
Kirkby (Summit) Colliery
Kirkby in Ashfield Central
Engine Shed
Kirkby in Ashfield East
Kirkby Stn. Jn.
Scale
0 ¼ ½ ¾ 1 2 miles
Friar Tuck's Well
Blidworth Colliery
Kirkby Bentinck
To Pye Bridge
Erewash Valley
Robin Hood's Hills
Kirkby S.Jn.
Kirkby Tunnel
Annesley Tunnel
Pinxton & Selston
Pinxton South
Hollinwell & Annesley
Leen Valley
Engine Shed
Newstead Abbey
Annesley
Annesley Sidings
Annesley Colliery
Newstead Colliery
Newstead West
Newstead East
To Awsworth Jn.
To Nottingham Midland
To Nottingham Victoria
1 Pinxton Wharf
2 Brookhill Colliery
3 Langton Colliery
4 Bentinck Colliery
Kirkby (Summit) Colliery
Kirkby Sidings
Engine Shed
Central
Kirkby East Jn.
East
Kirkby Station Jn.
Kirkby North Jn.
Sdgs
Kirkby South Jn.
Annesley Tunnel
Kirkby Tunnel
Langwith
Shirebrook North (Langwith Junct.)
Langwith Jn. East
Engine Shed
Warsop Jn.
Shirebrook Jn.
West Shirebrook
South
These maps are a summary rather than a depiction of the Mansfield railway network at a particular time
Mansfield & Pinxton Railway
Midland Railway
Manchester, Sheffield & Lincolnshire Railway (later Great Central)
Lancashire, Derbyshire & East Coast Railway (later Great Central)
Great Northern Railway
Mansfield Railway
Colliery branches, sidings & yards
Certain collieries and mineral lines have been omitted for clarity.

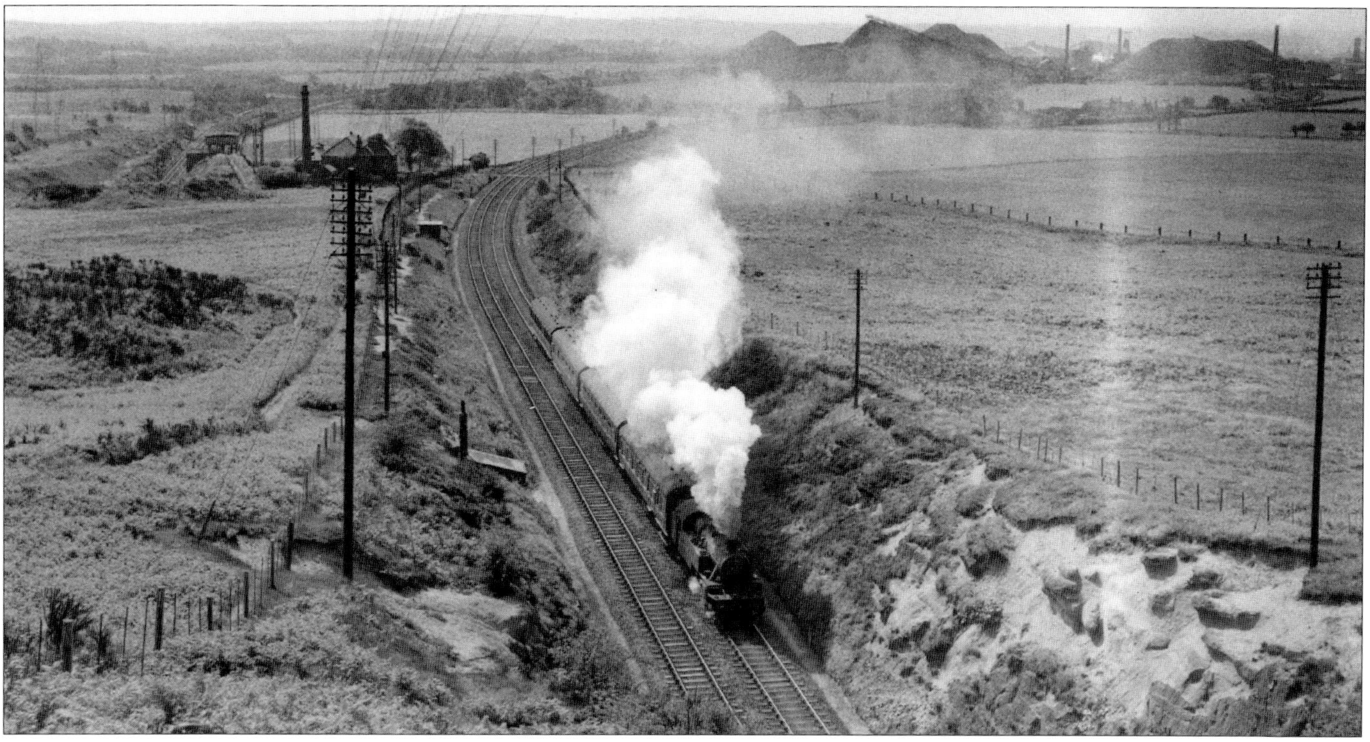

The combination of railways and coal mining had a considerable impact on the landscape of west Nottinghamshire, as illustrated by this view of the head of the Leen Valley from above Kirkby Tunnel on 20th June 1959. With the spoil heaps of Newstead & Annesley Collieries dominating the skyline, a Stanier 2-6-2T pounds up the last few yards of the long climb from Hucknall with a Nottingham Midland-Worksop train. Bunter Sandstone forms the foreground, whilst the Leen Valley pits were sunk through Magnesian Limestone to reach the Coal Measures. Although Annesley loco shed and yard are out of sight, the former Great Central main line just south of Annesley Tunnel can be seen in the left background. Photograph Jack Cupit.

cover to the east. Glacial meltwater carved a passage through the Magnesian Limestone eight miles north of Mansfield, forming the gorge now known as Creswell Crags. At least 45,000 years ago, primitive hunters and gatherers shared the crevices and caves there with bears, bison and wolves. In the last few hundred years BC, Iron Age people built hill forts close to what is now Southwell. The Romans pacified these warring Celts and established undefended farms known as villas, including one north of Mansfield. With the Anglo-Saxon invasion around 600AD, hamlets such as Sutton and Mansfield were created and the powerful kingdom of Mercia emerged. From 800AD, Danish settlers arrived, a lot of new farmland was opened up, and places such as Kirkby, Skegby and Nottingham came into being. Following the Norman conquest of 1066, Mansfield passed into the hands of the king and became the administrative centre for Crown properties over a wide area. In the Domesday Book of 1086 it was noted as having a hundred inhabitants, two churches and a watermill. Sherwood Forest was described as a 'waste' twenty miles long by eight miles wide and courts were held at Mansfield to try poachers under 'Forest Law'. Religious orders began to establish permanent homes in remote areas, Rufford Abbey and Newstead Abbey during 1120 and 1170 respectively, for example. The stage was set for the adventures of Robin Hood, Friar Tuck and the rest of the outlaws!

Away from Sherwood Forest, farming predominated over much of north Nottinghamshire during medieval times and Mansfield officially became a market town in 1229, although trading had no doubt been taking place since just after the Norman conquest. By 1292 there was

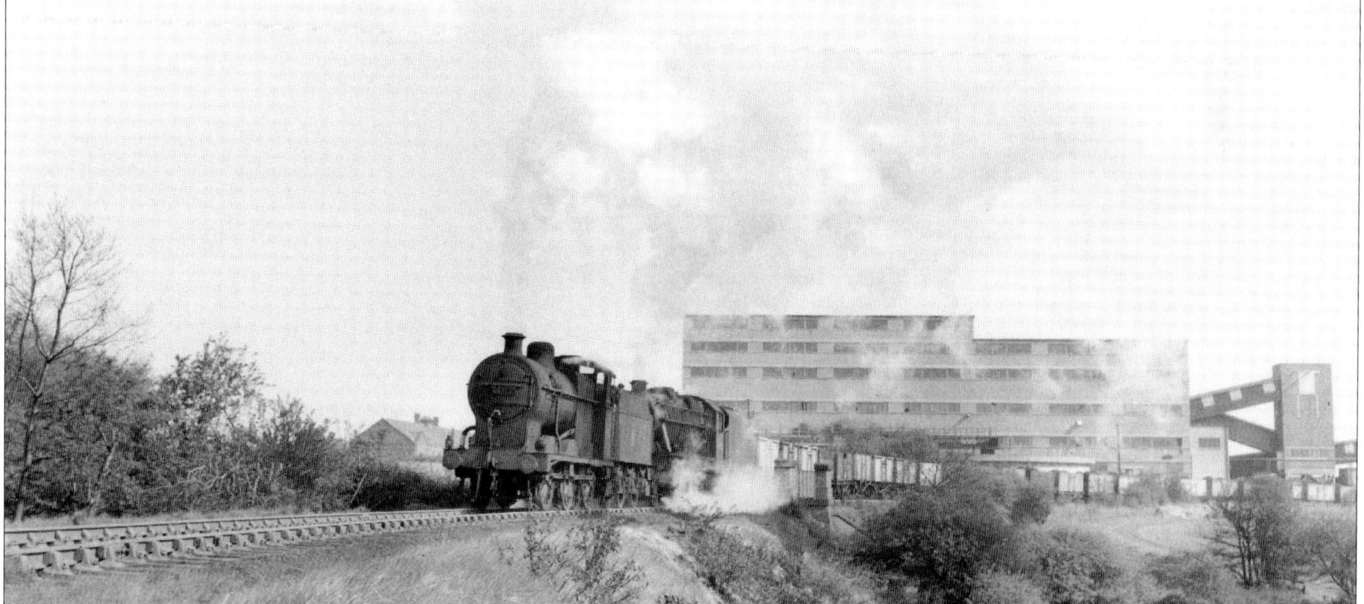

The modern washery at Mansfield (Crown Farm) Colliery forms the backdrop as a 4F 0-6-0 and 8F 2-8-0, both of them Mansfield engines, leave with a trip working for Kirkby Sidings on 2nd May 1959. This highly productive pit was known locally as 'Crownie' and the photographer encountered it at an early age. When his father was working a double shift, the young scholar would deliver essential sustenance (invariably known as 'snap') after school. The thought of an eleven year old wandering around a mine would give a present day Health and Safety inspector nightmares! Photograph Jack Cupit.

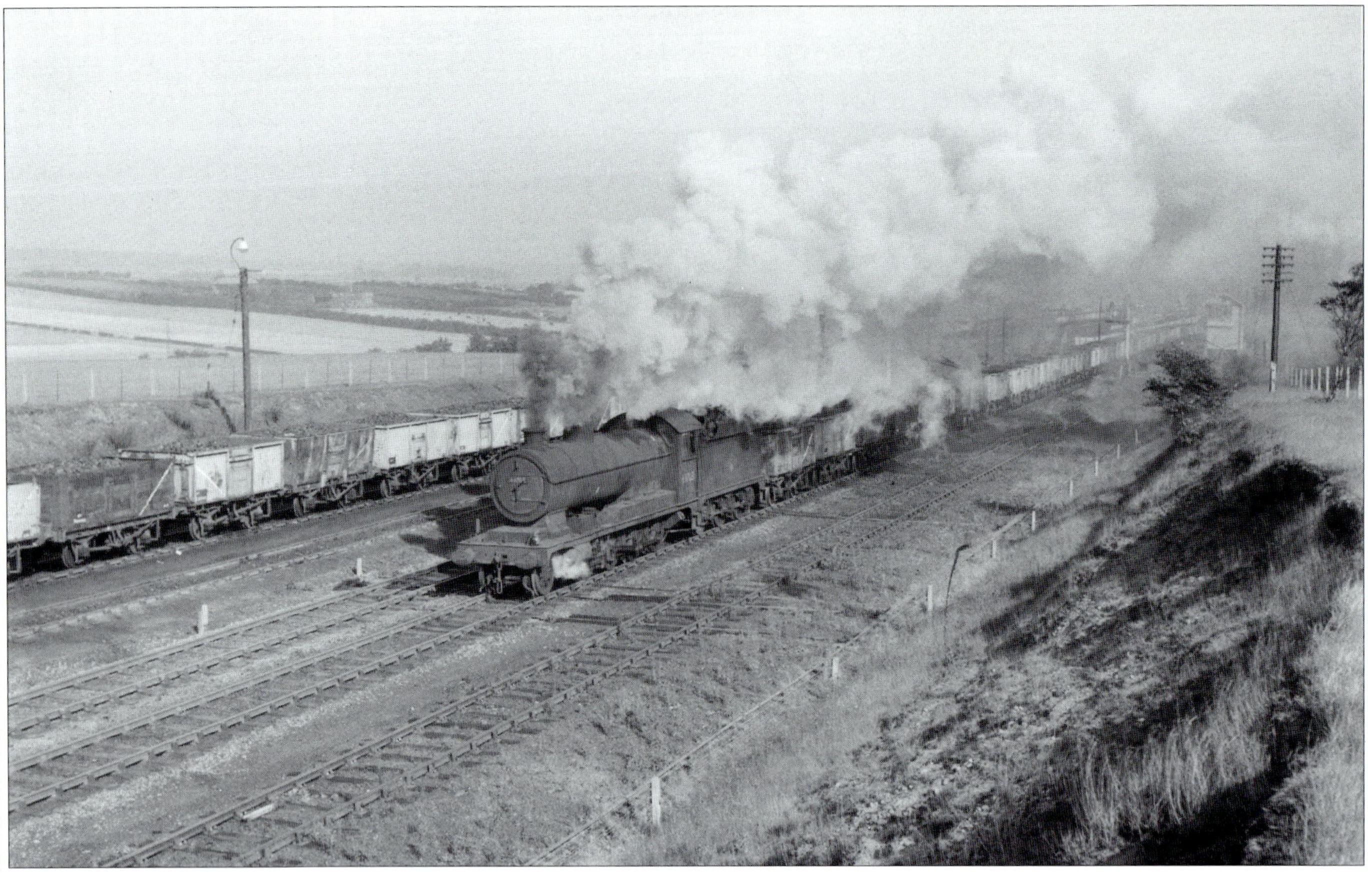

Most of the output from local collieries was worked to the major sorting sidings established by each of the three railway companies serving the Nottinghamshire/Derbyshire coalfield: Toton (Midland); Colwick (Great Northern); Annesley (Great Central). Some traffic went via subsidiary yards at Kirkby in Ashfield on the Midland and Clipstone on the Mansfield Railway. The latter, known as Mansfield Concentration Sidings, was a mere arrow shot from the ruins of King John's Palace, an erstwhile hunting lodge. Class O4/3 2-8-0 No.63703, a long term resident of Langwith shed, draws around fifty empties out of the Concentration Sidings on 29th September 1962. Photograph Jack Cupit.

a fulling mill at Mansfield processing cloth from the wool of Sherwood Forest sheep and during the mid-1300s quarries were supplying stone for Nottingham Castle and local churches. Following the onset of the Tudor dynasty in 1485, Henry VIII's purge of the monasteries saw the dissolution of Rufford in 1536 and Newstead in 1539, both of which were sold to the aristocracy. Mansfield itself consisted largely of timber buildings huddled close together and suffered several fires. In 1546 Coll Davy wilfully started a blaze which devastated the town. She was hanged at the next Assizes. Then in 1591 there was 'a casual fire in Stockwell Gate whereby was burned 150 bays of houses and Old Dunstan's wife'. During the 1600s, much of Mansfield was rebuilt in stone, a century which also saw the development of framework knitting.

For much of the 18th century Mansfield remained a relatively isolated place, the primitive road to Nottingham passing largely through Sherwood Forest where footpads and other outlaws still roamed. In the 1720s Defoe described it as 'a market town but without any remarkables'. However, this was partly put right when the impressive Moot Hall was erected, during 1752. Gradually, Mansfield embraced the industrial revolution. Iron foundries established in the 1780s to make prosaic items such as fireplaces went on to produce decorative lamp posts for London and pillar boxes for the Post Office. From 1782 to 1795 several large cotton mills were built, although at the end of the century there were still around 700 domestic knitting frames producing stockings and gloves. The road to Nottingham was improved after it was designated a turnpike in 1787 and over the next sixty years Mansfield became an important centre for stagecoach services. The principal market place was created between 1823 and 1845, the ornate Bentinck memorial being added in 1849. Mansfield Sand Co began to supply high quality building and moulding sand during the 1840s and Mansfield Brewery was established in 1855, developing a long established and lucrative tradition of malting in the town.

Mansfield's population increased from less than 6,000 in 1800 to over 21,000 in 1900, most of the growth occurring during the last forty years of the century. In the decade from 1900 to 1910, the number of residents almost doubled. Mansfield Woodhouse, Sutton in Ashfield, Kirkby in Ashfield and several other villages in the area mushroomed as well. This transformation was almost entirely attributable to an industry not mentioned thus far – coal mining, of course. The quest for 'black gold' was also responsible for virtually all of the extensive railway network around Mansfield.

Coal had probably been extracted from shallow pits as far back as Roman times, but by the mid-1500s there were several actual mines in the exposed coalfield from Wollaton to Pinxton and Heath, the annual output of around 15,000 tons going to local villages. With its underground drainage sough, horse-driven pumps and horse-operated windlass for raising coal, the Wollaton pit was probably one of the most advanced in the world. Furthermore, in 1604 it gave rise to the first surface railway in Britain. By the late 1700s mines on the Nottinghamshire/Derbyshire border were producing 150,000 tons a year, demand from Mansfield accounting for much of the increase. Newcomen steam engines were replacing horses for pumping water out of the workings and enterprise was firmly in the hands of the landed gentry who could afford to sink substantial pits such as Old Pinxton, opened in 1780. When a waterway between Pinxton and Leicester was established in 1794, there was a much wider market for local coal. Twenty mines were active by 1808 and new hamlets with rows of cottages and non-conformist chapels grew up near them.

The Mansfield & Pinxton Railway opened in 1819 and proved a real benefit to the coalfield. Portland Colliery at Selston, another sizeable project financed by the aristocracy, began to draw coal during 1823. Despite such enterprise, Nottinghamshire pits were relatively backward until the second half of the nineteenth century. They had no ventilation, men rode on buckets up and down the shafts and boys or donkeys were used for haulage underground. When distant markets, notably London, became a lot more accessible with the construction of Midland Railway branches along the Erewash and Leen valleys during the late 1840s, the extraction of coal south west of Mansfield had to improve. Old pits were modernised or abandoned, new

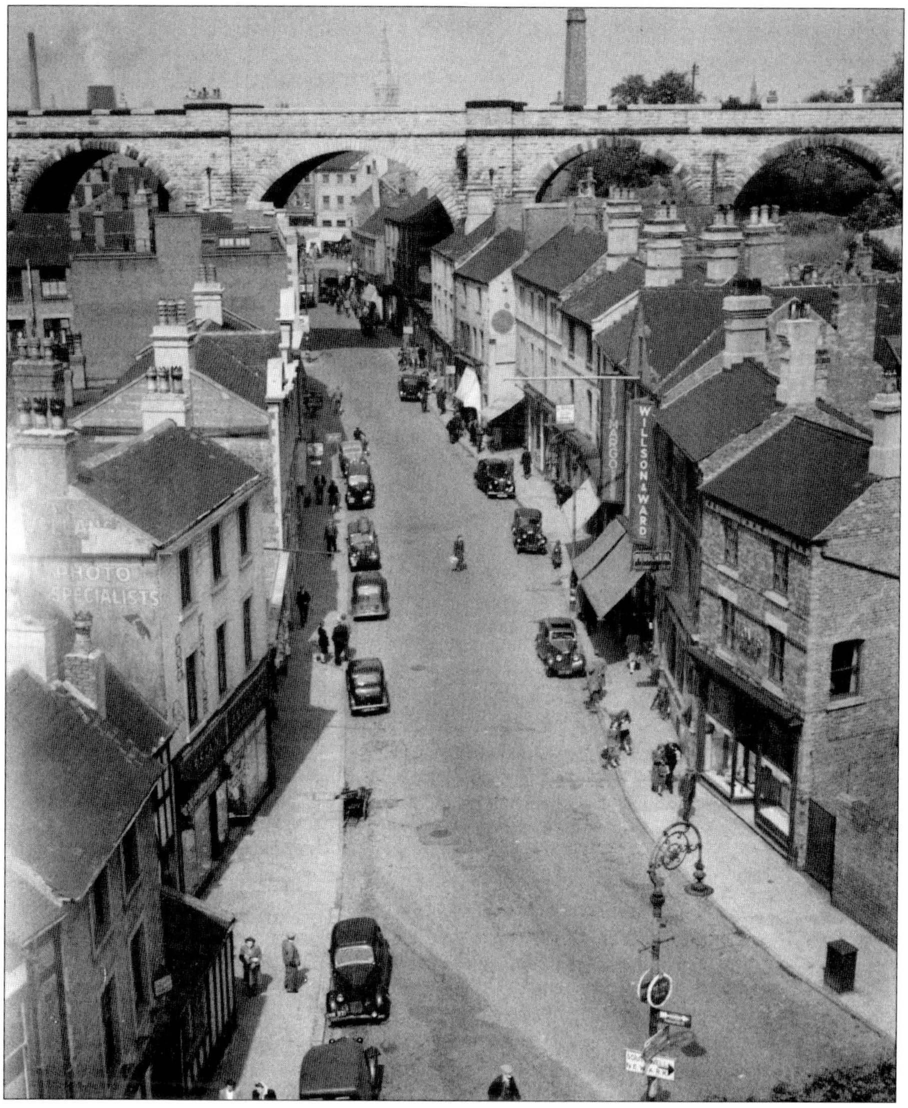

One of the earliest railway viaducts in the country was the 'stupendous bridge of five arches' at King's Mill on the Mansfield & Pinxton. However, the best known viaduct in the Mansfield area is undoubtedly the lofty structure across the town itself, erected in the 1870s to carry the Worksop extension. Seen here from the tower of the ancient parish church on 24th June 1948, it continues to dominate the market place and adjoining streets, and has recently been floodlit by night! Mansfield had two more viaducts, one on each spur of the Southwell branch where they crossed the River Maun to join the main line. Photograph Jack Cupit.

workings were sunk and private companies such as Butterley and Barber Walker became involved. By 1847, Skegby was the last mine dealing in 'landsale' for purely local needs. The lucrative Top Hard seam beneath a covering of Magnesian Limestone was exploited in the Leen Valley by Hucknall Colliery during 1863, followed by Annesley (1865), Bestwood (1872), Linby (1873) and Newstead (1875). Other mines were sunk on the edge of the concealed coalfield west of Mansfield, namely Teversal (1868), Sutton (1873), Silverhill (1875) and Pleasley (1877), Midland branch lines being built to serve them. These new collieries featured innovations such as furnace ventilation and cages for miners ascending and descending the shafts.

Investment in mining then stagnated, largely because of a severe recession which persisted for most of the 1880s. Eventually the economy had recovered and new pits were sunk at Kirkby Summit (1887), Bolsover (1891), Warsop (1895), Kirkby Bentinck (1896) and Creswell (1896). Other railway companies successfully challenged the Midland's monopoly of coal traffic in the Mansfield areas during this period, the outcome being lines built by the Manchester, Sheffield & Lincolnshire (later Great Central), the Lancashire, Derbyshire & East Coast and the Great Northern. A boom following the Boer War saw deeper mines at Sherwood (1903) and Mansfield Crown Farm (1905) being sunk further east through the Bunter Sandstone as well as the Magnesian Limestone. Even deeper shafts were necessary for Rufford (1913) and Welbeck (1915) at the onset of World War One. The spread of mining into Sherwood Forest gave rise to the Mansfield Railway, the coalowners' line.

Between the two World Wars, five mines opened in Sherwood Forest: Clipstone (1922), Blidworth (1924), Ollerton (1927), Bilsthorpe (1928) and Thoresby (1928). Apart from Bevercotes, an isolated development during the early 1960s, this proved to be the end of a feverish century of colliery openings around Mansfield. By 1938, the Nottinghamshire/Derbyshire coalfield was the most efficient in the country, with no less than 70% of coal cut by machine. During the late 1940s, a hundred pits were at work, the last eight to be built employing 13,000 men between them. Throughout the 1950s and 1960s, collieries provided ample traffic for the railways, as illustrated in this book, but wholesale mine closures during the 1980s and 1990s led to fundamental changes in the economy and transport requirements of the Mansfield area.

Before reading about the origins, developments and mixed fortunes of Mansfield's unique and fascinating rail way network, enjoy this 'taster' in the form of a few of Jack Cupit's personal recollections:

'Seemingly, Mansfield was not the best birthplace for anyone with an interest in railways. When it came to

Geological Cross Section of the Coalfield (Diagrammatic)

© Paul Anderson 2000

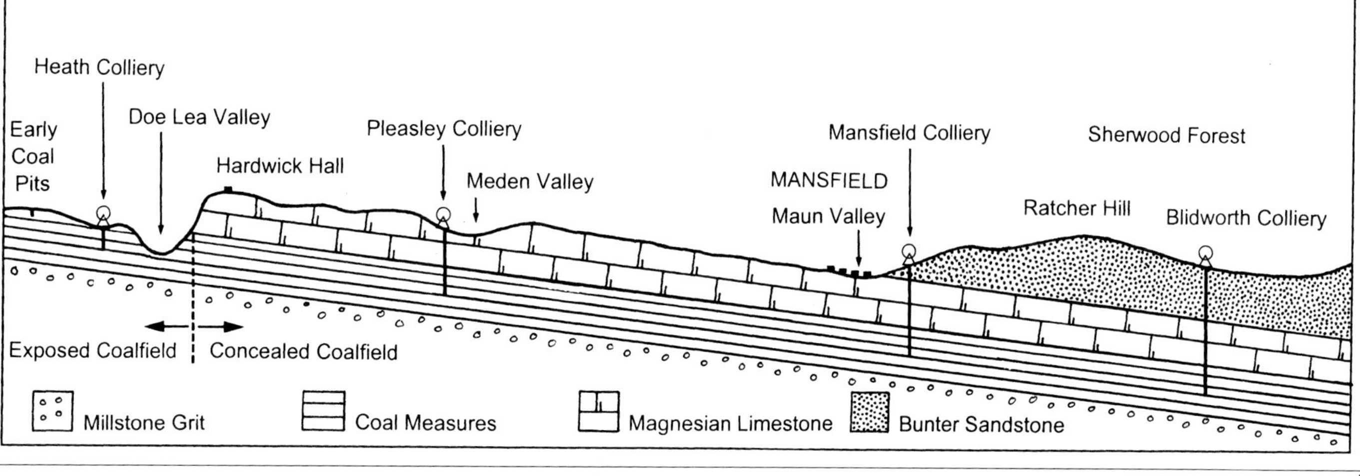

Gresley and Stanier Pacifics, Pullmans and named expresses, Deltics and even smart new diesel multiple units, the town was a non-starter for enthusiasts, such things being unknown in the Maun Valley. But Mansfield had a lot going for it at the nitty-gritty level. Unlike most places, it had two lines of great contrast – one very early and one very late in the railway story, one carrying traffic for nearly two centuries and still with us, the other with a full working life of less than forty years and gone virtually without trace. The older of the two was intensely local, yet had more traffic, an engine shed (an ideal venue for Sunday morning walks) and numerous private branches serving mills, sand quarries and chemical works. The younger line brought glimpses of the wider railway world, including fish from Icelandic waters, timber from the Baltic and the glory of the Leeds-Bournemouth express. So, for a boy with a natural interest in railways, perhaps Mansfield was not such a bad place to be born and grow up in!

'I attended Newgate Junior School, the playing field of which lay beside the Mansfield Railway just east of Central station. A 'temporary' extension in the form of a large wooden hut stood next to the line and I was fortunate to spend a year in the outermost of the two classrooms, the domain of Miss Richardson. Undoubtedly, the highlight of the school day was just before lunch break, around 11.45am, when the up Leeds-Bournemouth express passed within a few yards of the window. Headed by an ex-Great Northern large-boilered Atlantic, the train had just three coaches, one or two of which were in a green the like of which the young scholar had never seen. To a collier's son brought up in mid-Nottinghamshire during the early 1930s, the Southern Railway was very remote.

'Senior school days brought a different aspect of the railway. High Oakham School was just over a mile from home and the route to it lay for the most part within sight of the Southwell branch which carried the output of several large collieries. There was a bridge over the exchange sidings of a private branch from a sand quarry, which had its own motive power in the form of an 0-4-0ST EMPRESS. It was an introduction to the industrial railway – all part of a good education!

'When I was a youngster, the favourite family picnic venue was Edwinstowe. There was cricket on an attractive village green, but a wander through the forest to the Major Oak and to hide in the hollow tree where Robin Hood is said to have hidden too was a must. In those far-off days there was no Visitor Centre, no funfair, no rangers and no car parks. The journey from Mansfield was usually made by bus, there being no Sunday trains, but on Bank Holiday Mondays there was a train and that added much to the day. From Mansfield Central the outward journey was by a local service, but a homeward bound Skegness excursion made a special stop at Edwinstowe for the return journey and provided the opportunity of travelling in corridor stock behind an engine sporting express headlamps.

'Mansfield Central station was a gaunt, dismal and draughty place with wooden platforms and stark waiting rooms, thinly populated and reeking of fish. The down side platform was built on stilts over the embankment and it was easy to lose pennies intended for the sweet machines through cracks between the planking. The station was well away from the middle of Mansfield and the entrance faced away from the town, as if Central had turned its back on the place it was built to serve. The platforms were connected by a subway and long tiring flights of steps. Yet for at least one youngster it had an air of promise, for our annual pilgrimage to the East Coast for a week's holiday began here. There were also occasional day trips on the 10.23am Skegness Sunday only excursion, which ran for the duration of the summer timetable. It was a long day, the return from the seaside being about 8pm. On the last occasion we used this train, the journey back was made in the dim twilight of blue painted light bulbs – it was late August 1939 and the lamps were, indeed, going out all over Europe.

'My early working days were spent within sight and sound of the Midland, just north of the viaduct. Being based upstairs in the bindery was something special, for a clear view could be had of the continuous procession of coal trains headed by 3Fs, 4Fs and 8Fs pounding their way over the town on the way to Kirkby yards where most mineral traffic was sorted. The coal continued to move at night. One abiding memory is of lying awake in the small hours listening to an 8F struggling to re-start with a full load, having been checked at Station North's home signal high on the viaduct. With greasy rails and the whole train hanging on the draw bar because of the 1 in 132 gradient, it was a sound never to be forgotten and proof that all was well with the world! There were passenger trains, too, slotted into the endless stream of coal. The 10.28am and 4.10pm to Sheffield sported LNER teak coaches hauled by an LMS loco, tangible evidence of a long-forgotten compromise.

'The Midland station was a proper station. It had an overall roof, three platforms, a footbridge, a bookstall and, to the delight of most small boys, red painted vending machines dispensing thin bars of Nestlé milk chocolate. There was also an

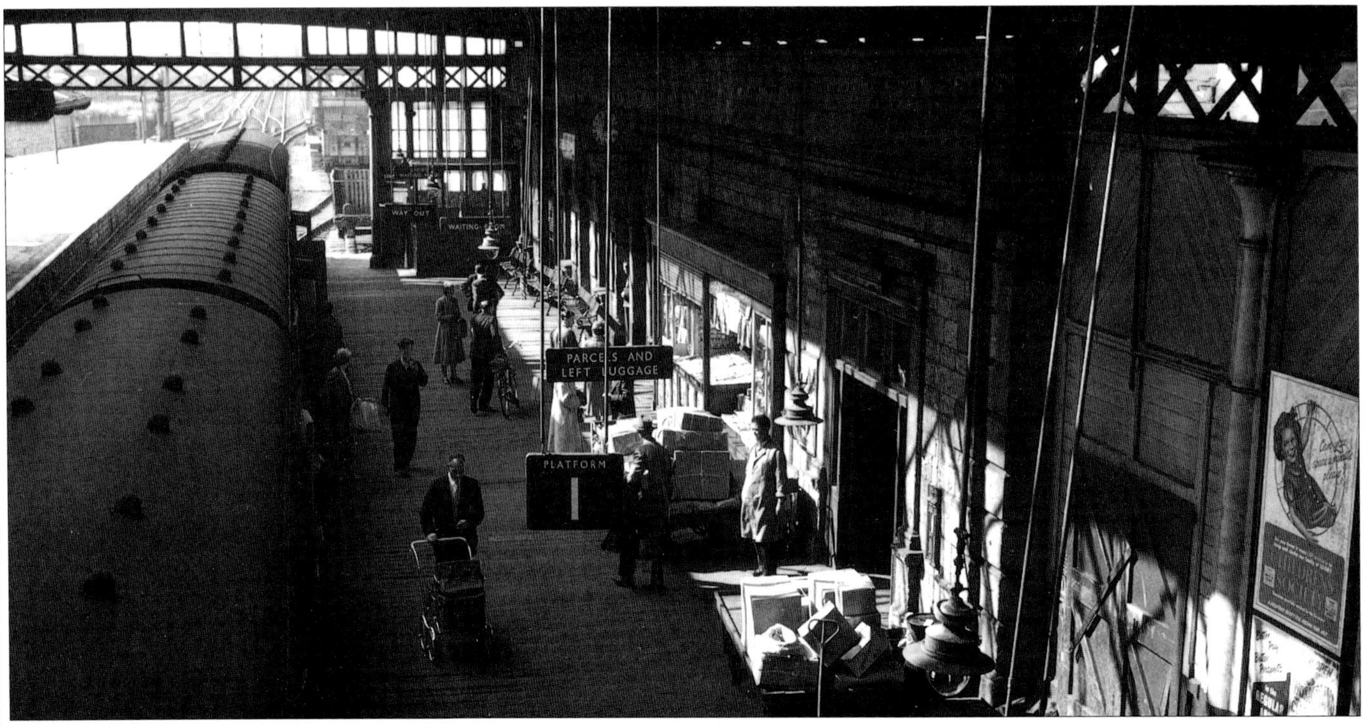

With its overall roof and deep end screens, Mansfield Town was quite a cosy station. In this animated view from the footbridge on 8th September 1953, people with assorted paraphernalia including shopping bags, suitcases, a bike and a pram leave a Nottingham Midland-Worksop service at platform 1. The well stocked bookstall, proliferation of benches, barrows of parcels and boxes of pigeons suggest a bustling passenger train business, but the abiding memory is of an endless procession of mineral trains, filling the place with smoke, steam and a delicious never-to-be-forgotten smell! Photograph Jack Cupit.

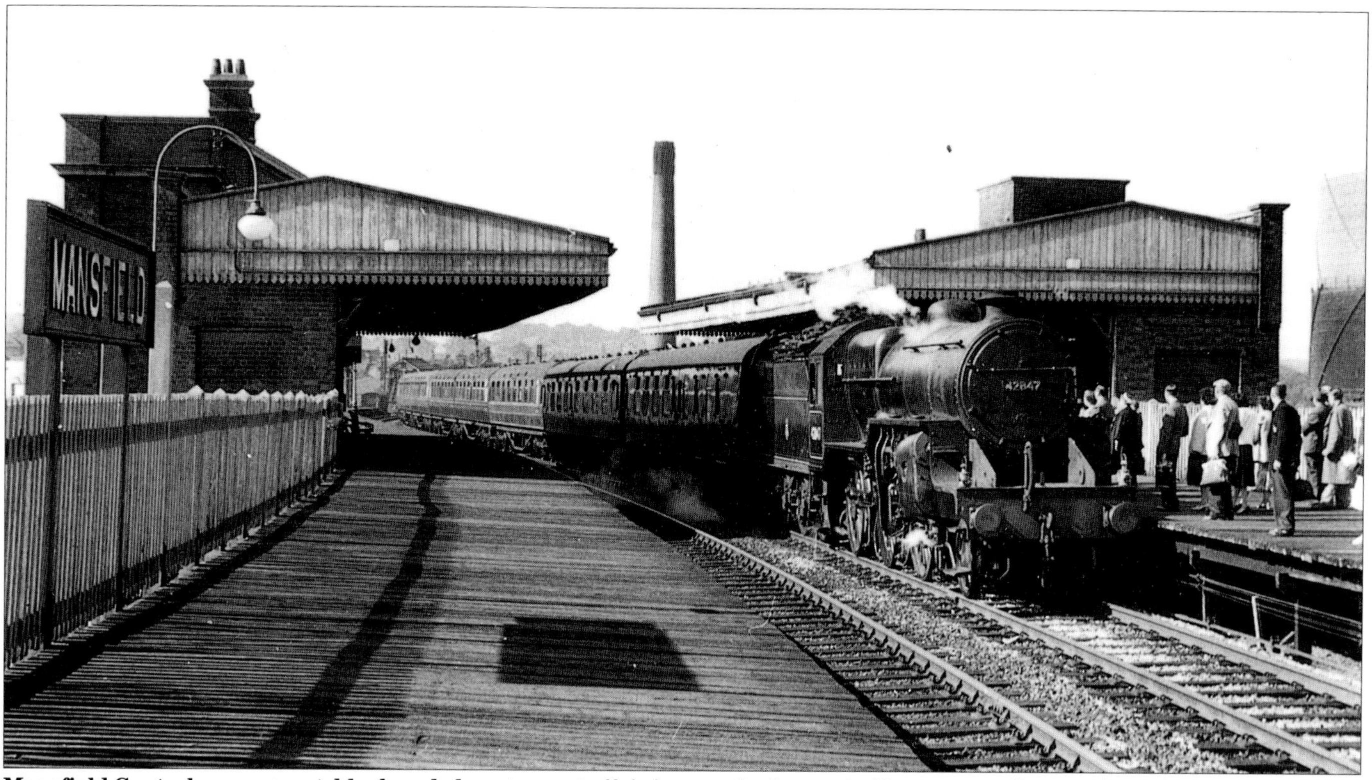

Mansfield Central was a gaunt, bleak and almost secret affair in a workaday part of town, some distance from the bustling market place. Situated on an embankment and very susceptible to inclement weather, it always had a temporary feel about it. Indeed, regular passenger services lasted for less than forty years. However, through goods traffic was very varied and this was the station for the seaside. On 2nd August 1959, Annesley 'Crab' No.42847 pulls into Mansfield Central with the 9.33am Sunday excursion to Mablethorpe on the Lincolnshire coast. Photograph H.B. Priestley.

old drinking fountain with a chained cup, although the water always tasted of rusty iron! In true Midland tradition there were a couple of signal boxes to handle no more than a dozen points between them. The station was high above the town, entailing a stiff climb for prospective passengers. Then, having breathlessly bought a ticket, the cry 'Any more for Nottingham?' prompted a final sprint over the footbridge. This, then, was the station remembered for family visits to Bulwell from an early age to regular commuting before closure in 1964.

'At many lineside locations, there is often one spot which commends itself to railway observers above all others, and the Midland at Mansfield had such a place. It was a footbridge just south of Mansfield North Junction box which gave a magnificent panoramic view of almost all the Midland installations in the town. The bridge led to Cinderella Walk, the local name for a path to the shed and it was boarded, so keeping out most of the wind. To the north lay the station, extensive sidings and the goods yard which incorporated the original Mansfield & Pinxton Railway Portland Wharf. The yard was the haunt of Mansfield's pilot engines, latterly Nos.41712 and 41844, vintage Midland tanks, one of which pottered around the sidings for most of the day. To the south of the bridge lay the carriage sidings, complete with an old Midland railway Pullman Car body which served as the mess room. The bridge is still there, as is Cinderella Walk and the engine shed, albeit in industrial use. Double track survives, as does the old station building alongside the new Robin Hood line facilities, but the rest has gone. On those sunny Saturday afternoons long ago, we basked in the warmth and thought it would be there forever – the sharp bark of exhaust, the sight of labouring steam, the clank of buffers and the sound of block bells in the signal box heralding yet another train.'

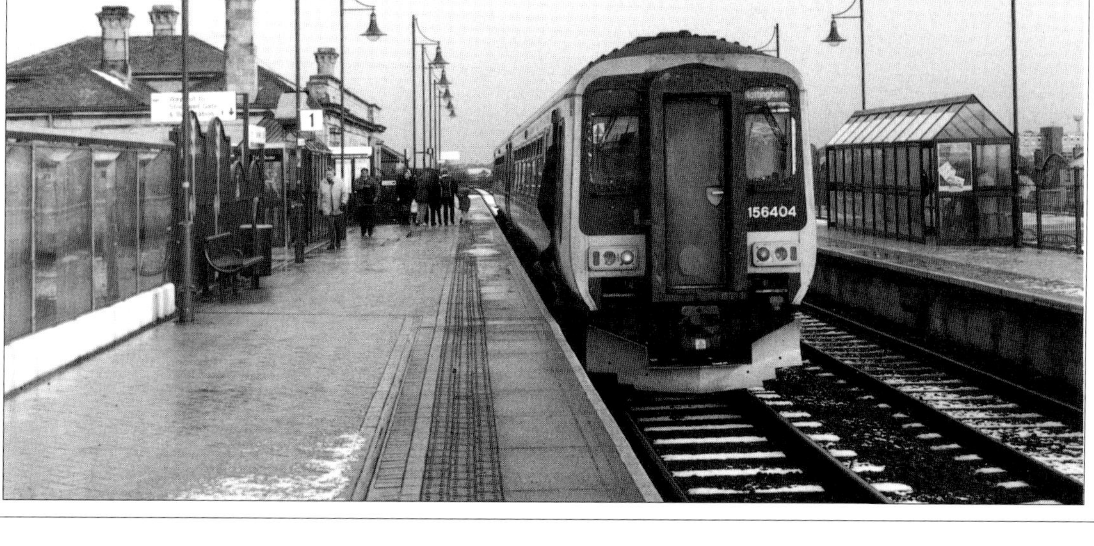

Fortunately, this book is not just a celebration of Mansfield's remarkably varied railway network when coal was king. It is also about the restoration of a passenger service after an absence of thirty years, the largest project of its type ever undertaken in Britain. Sprinter 156 404 forming the 11.18 from Nottingham to Worksop calls at Mansfield on 15th December 1999. The Robin Hood line now generates around 3,000 journeys a day and the Midland building at Mansfield was refurbished during 2000 as an integral part of the station. Photograph Paul Anderson.

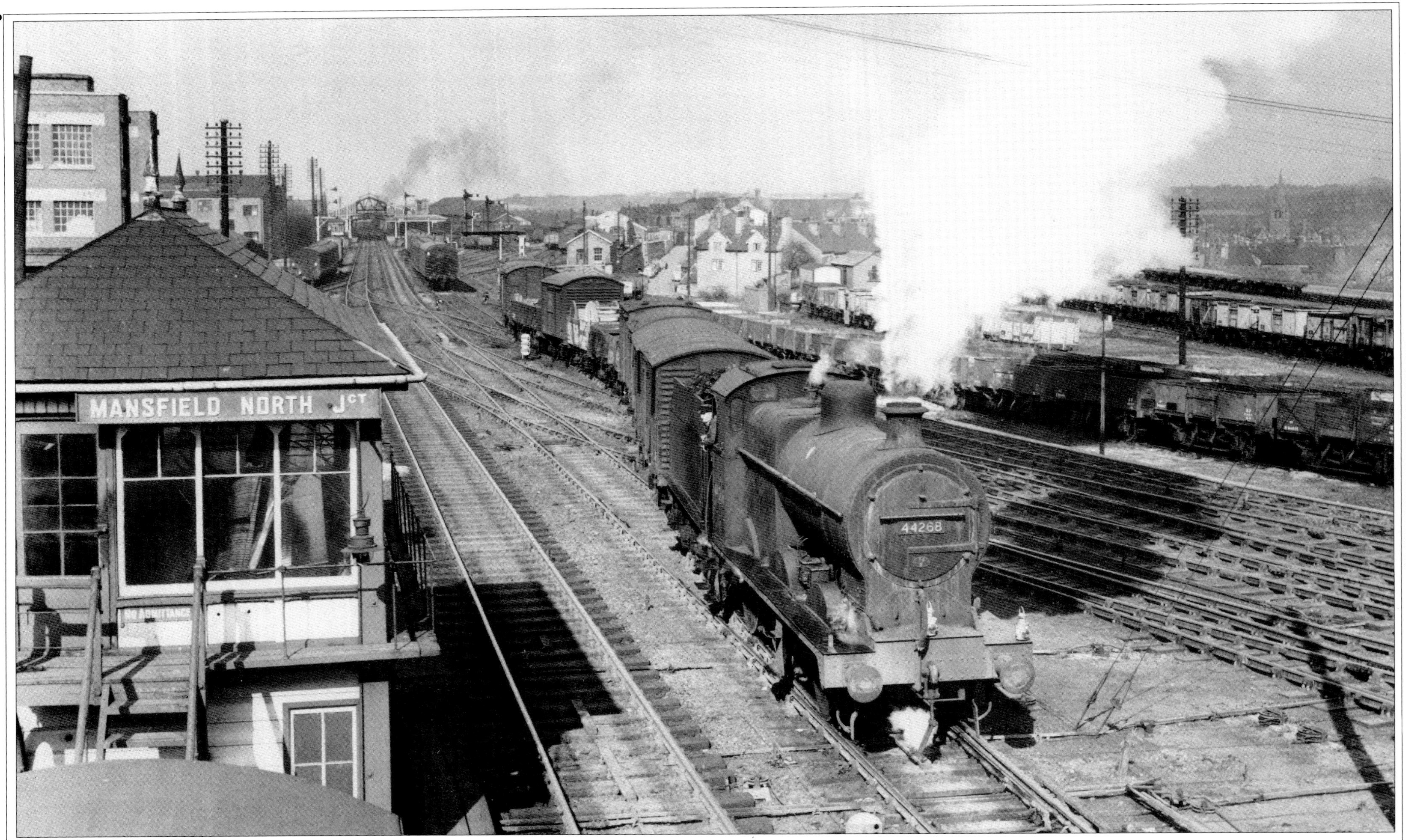

On 28th April 1962, Fowler 4F 0-6-0 No.44268 of Kirkby in Ashfield shed guides the afternoon Mansfield-Nottingham goods out of the yard past Mansfield North Junction signal box. From this viewpoint, on the footbridge to Cinderella Walk, three distinct phases of Mansfield's railway development could be appreciated. The 1819 Mansfield & Pinxton terminus was on the site of the large warehouse beyond the nearest signal post, while the 1849 passenger terminus was above the box van flanked by open wagons towards the end of the goods. On the left, smoke rises from an 8F 2-8-0 with a coal train awaiting the road through the 1872 station. Photograph Jack Cupit.

Chapter 2

MANSFIELD & PINXTON

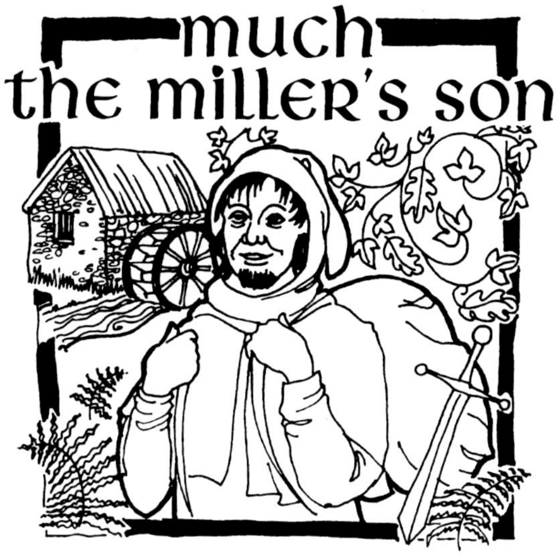

Way back at the dawn of the seventeenth century, when Sir Francis Drake's maritime exploits were still fresh in the mind and England had yet to endure the traumatic Civil War, Huntingdon Beaumont had a problem. He worked the highly productive coal pits at Strelley, some three miles west of Nottingham, but the rutted cart track to town seriously hampered trade. However, less than two miles to the south, there was a thriving wharf where the output of other local pits was sold. This was at Wollaton which had a good road to Nottingham. Beaumont was at the forefront of coal mining technology and decided to lay a row of parallel timber baulks down the slope from his collieries to the busy landsale site. Horses began to haul coal wagons with flanged wooden wheels over the Wollaton 'Rayleway' in 1604 and continued to do so for about fifteen years. A similar, though less spectacular, development took place in Shropshire during 1605 and there was even a plan to extend the Wollaton line down to the navigable River Trent. The transport revolution that changed Nottinghamshire, Britain and the rest of the world had made its first tentative steps.

For over a century the construction of wooden wagonways was largely confined to the North East where chauldrons of coal rumbling down to staithes on the Tyne and Wear eventually became an everyday sight. Nevertheless, by 1750 primitive railways were a familiar feature of coalfields throughout Britain. The development of inland water transport led to a huge increase in the number of wagonways, built as feeders. It all happened very quickly. Between 1775 and 1800 no less than 252 miles of canal and river navigation work was completed or nearing completion in Nottinghamshire, Derbyshire and Leicestershire – and this total did not include improvements to 67 miles of the Trent. Typical of the harmonious association of waterways and horse railways was the Chesterfield Canal, which opened in 1777 and extended for 46 miles from the River Trent to Chesterfield. Before long it was served by at least seven wagonways in the Staveley area, originating at collieries, ironworks and a glassworks.

Despite this phenomenal expansion of water transport during the last quarter of the eighteenth century, Mansfield missed out. In fact the town was destined to remain the largest in the East Midlands without a canal or navigable river. By virtue of their location on the exposed coalfield, lesser places to the south west were far more fortunate. The Erewash Canal reached Langley Mill in 1779 and within a decade an extension northwards was being discussed. Iron furnaces at Butterley, limestone quarries at Crich, cotton mills at Cromford and miles of untapped coal seams in the Erewash Valley offered great potential. There was also the prospect of traffic from towns such as Matlock, Belper, Alfreton and, of course, Mansfield. The 14½ mile Cromford Canal opened in 1794 and was paying a very healthy 10% dividend to shareholders twenty years later.

At Pye Hill, just short of the daunting 1¾ mile Butterley tunnel through the Derwent watershed, a 2½ mile branch headed up the Erewash headwaters to Pinxton. It too opened during 1794, stimulating coal production and pointing the way towards Mansfield. Indeed, an extension to the town was considered in 1803 but it would have been a difficult project and nothing came of the idea. By 1809, local coalowners were talking of building a railway to provide the necessary link, the Cromford Canal already having numerous feeder wagonways serving collieries and quarries. Incidentally, a line at Pinxton lower pit still had

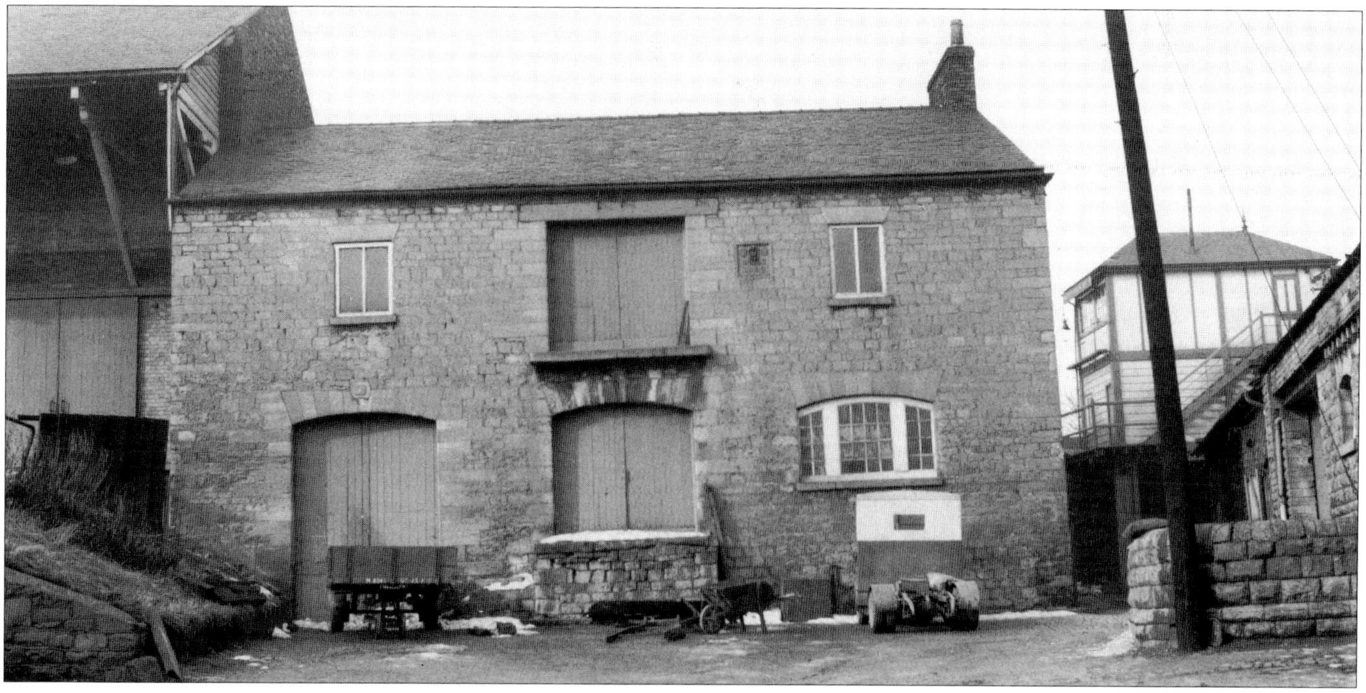

Simple, sturdy and very functional overall, the Mansfield & Pinxton warehouse at Portland Wharf in Mansfield nevertheless displayed some features of note. The well proportioned dressed stone lintels above the windows and ground floor doorways were reminiscent of contemporary Georgian town houses. There was also a date stone incorporating the Prince of Wales feathers, the reason for this being a mystery. The large structure on the left is a Midland Railway goods shed dating from the 1870s; Mansfield Station North signal box on the Worksop extension stands at a slightly higher level, and stables for railway horses are on the extreme right. This historic Mansfield & Pinxton building, seen here on 13th February 1954, remained in use under Midland, LMS and British Railways ownership. Photograph Jack Cupit.

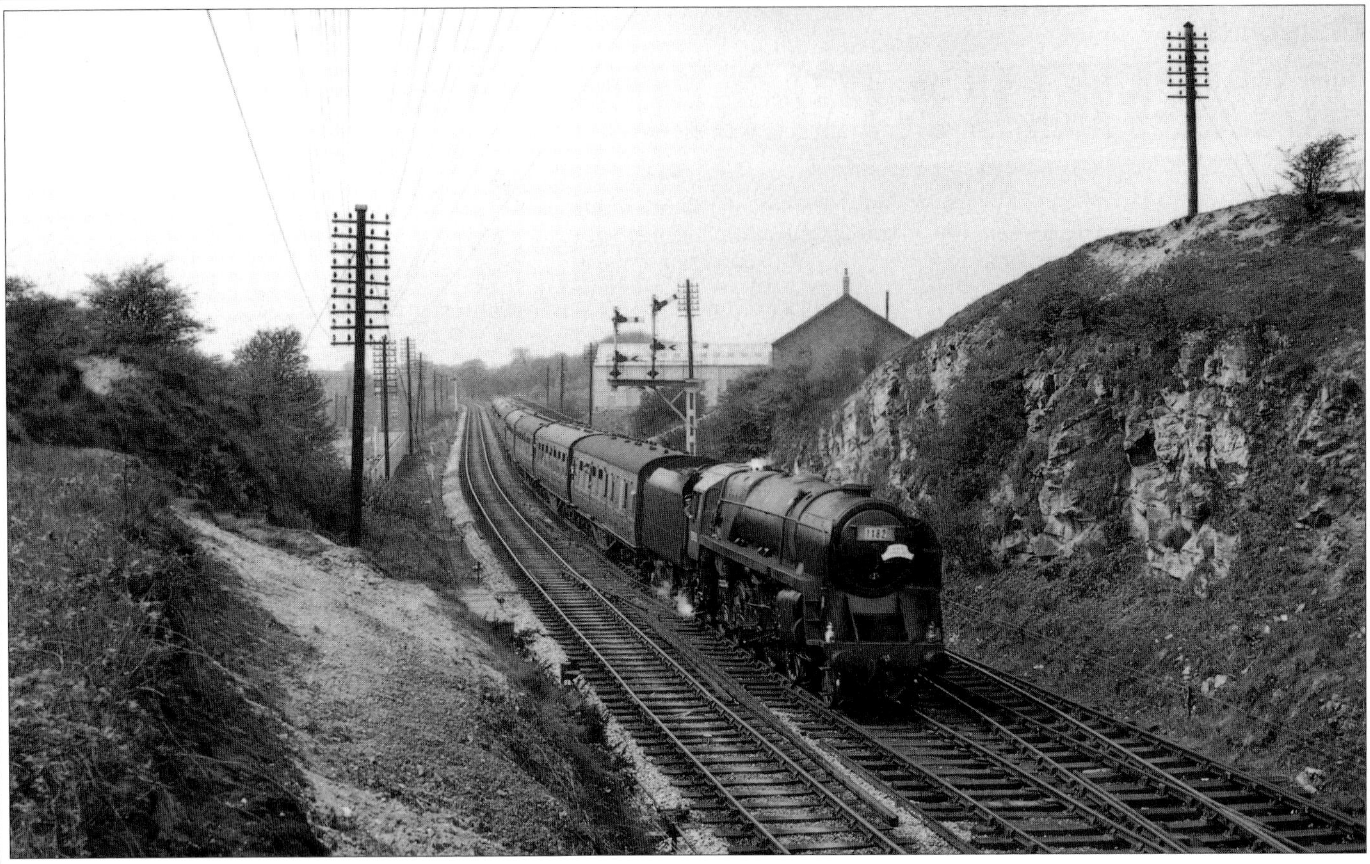

Wherever possible, the Mansfield & Pinxton went round obstacles rather than tackling them with expensive earthworks, so deviations were made later in order to avoid the more severe curves. On 8th May 1965, Saltley 9F 2-10-0 No.92155, hauling a Birmingham New Street-Doncaster special, approaches Mansfield South Junction through a substantial cutting opened up in 1872. The original trackbed over King's Mill viaduct came in from the right, beyond the rear of the train, then headed off to the left, behind the nearest telegraph pole, round this limestone spur on the side of the Maun Valley. The points on the right gave access to a siding leading to King's Mill viaduct, an arrangement resulting from the changes of 1872. Photograph Jack Cupit.

wooden rails as late as 1808. Although plans for the Mansfield & Pinxton Railway were deposited in 1813, with the intention of applying for an Act of Parliament the following year, a prolonged debate about which type of track to use caused some delay. Plateways, where the rails rather than the wheels had flanges, were in fashion. Eventually there was general agreement to use conventional rails, so progress could be made at last.

The Mansfield & Pinxton was granted its Act of Parliament on 16th June 1817, the sixteenth public railway company to be authorised (the first was the Surrey Iron Railway of 1801). Work commenced on the eight mile formation from Pinxton Basin to Bull's Head Lane in Mansfield at the beginning of July and never ceased to be a source of fascination for local residents, it seems. On 13th April 1819,

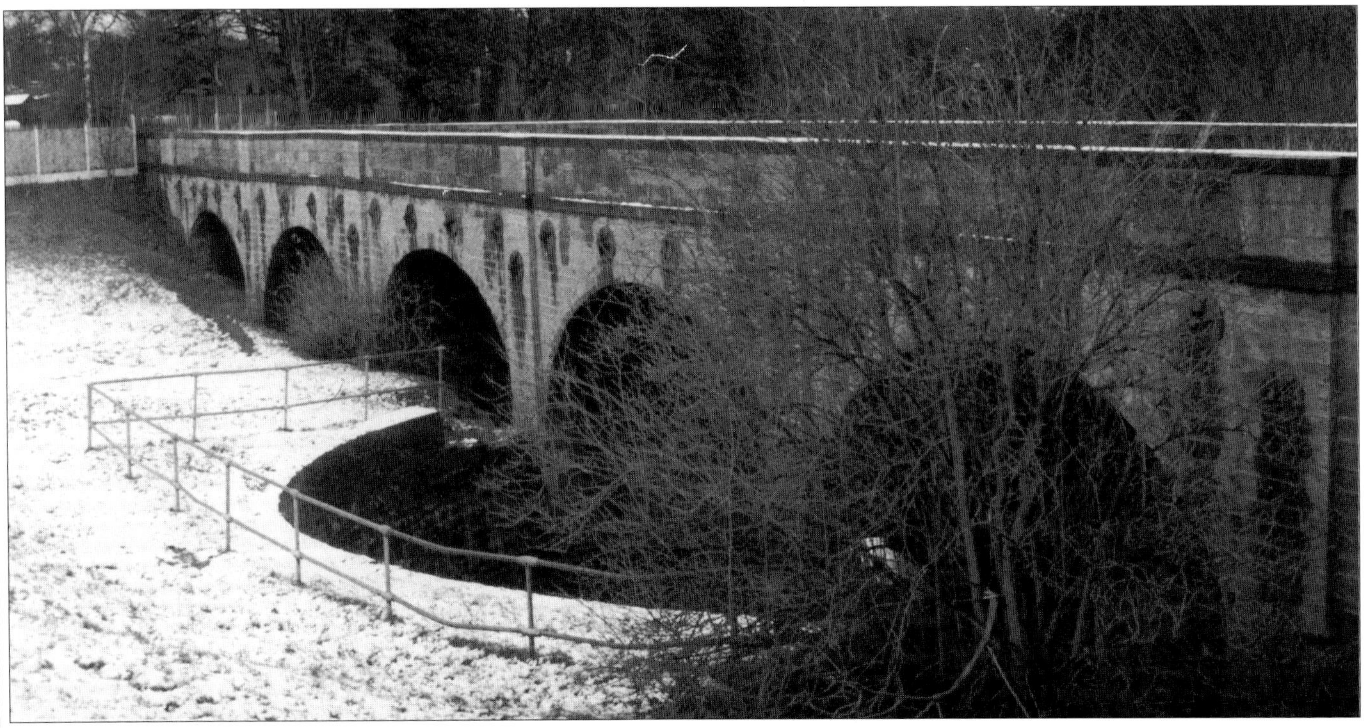

Limestone for the splendid five-arch viaduct at King's Mill was provided by the same Derbyshire quarries that supplied the sleeper blocks. A date stone, similar to that on the Portland Wharf warehouse, was incorporated above the crown of the centre arch. Looking as fine as ever on 15th December 1999, over 180 years after trains first used it, the structure still spans a wooded gorge-like stretch of the River Maun. Two sidings, part of the main line until 1872, remained across the viaduct until early British Railways days. Photograph Paul Anderson.

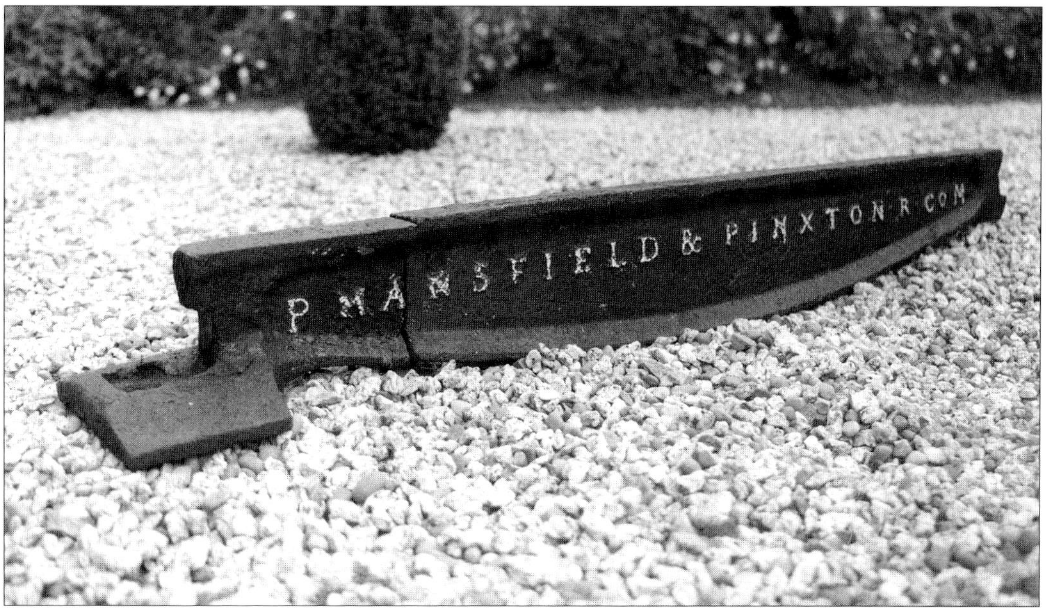

At least one Mansfield & Pinxton rail has found a good home. It is seen here in preservation on 4th August 1999. Note the unusual interlocking joint, involving a flat base at one end of each section. This incorporated a hole for the iron spike which secured the rail to its own stone sleeper and also provided a bed to receive the adjoining length. In addition to the company name, every rail had 'M' and 'P' cast into it, to denote which way to lay it – towards Mansfield and Pinxton respectively. Photograph Paul Anderson.

church bells began ringing early, people flocked in from villages up to eight miles away and the first wagon of rail-borne coal from Pinxton Colliery trundled into Mansfield at 9am. Ten more arrived during the afternoon amid hearty celebrations and 'a good band of music from Sutton in Ashfield long provided for the occasion.' Much ale and good beef was consumed at inns throughout the town and a pile of coal was ceremoniously set on fire in the market place where it burned away merrily all night. The Mansfield & Pinxton Railway was in business!

For nearly thirty years horses hauled sturdy chauldron wagons along the line. The company never possessed any steam engines, although they had been around since 1804 when Trevithick's pioneering locomotive first creaked along the new Penydarren tramway in South Wales. The Crich tramway, which fed the Cromford Canal, was the scene of experiments by William Brunton's 'Patent Steam Horse' during 1813. This remarkable contraption pushed itself along on grasshopper type legs at 2mph, hardly a match for the horses in terms of speed! It was soon dispatched to the North East where several lumbering machines were already terrifying the timid peasantry and showering fields with cinders in their endeavours to move ever increasing amounts of coal. During 1840 the Pinxton company considered using steam engines, but horse traction continued and Mansfield had to wait until August 1849 before seeing its first locomotive.

The Mansfield & Pinxton was double track throughout, and laid to a gauge of 4ft. 4in. Each rail was 3ft. long and over 55,000 of them were cast by Oakes of Alfreton. They were spiked to stone sleeper blocks which came from Whatstandwell Quarry in the Derwent Valley. Had locomotives been introduced, heavier track would have had to be deployed. In terms of engineering work, the line represented a transition stage between wagonways, which were usually laid directly on the ground, and trunk railways of the 1830s and 1840s with their spectacular structures.

Pinxton Basin, at the end of the Cromford Canal branch, was just less than 300ft. above sea level. The wharf, warehouse and exchange sidings were accompanied by the *Boat Inn*, which no doubt saw some lively times when trade thrived. From here, the Mansfield & Pinxton climbed steadily up the Erewash Valley past several collieries, their output keeping the railway busy. Near Kirkby in Ashfield the Erewash headwaters have cut fairly deep clefts in the western slopes of Robin Hood's Hills. As a result, the railway had to negotiate some very undulating country by a series of sharp curves and a substantial embankment at Grives Wood. Although horses had to slog up this section with heavy loads, the usual practice was to let gravity serve for the descent to Pinxton. Kirkby summit, just above 500ft. lay on featureless ground close to Kirkby Hardwick – a medieval hall where Cardinal Wolsey reputedly stayed on his fateful last journey to Leicester Abbey.

East of Sutton in Ashfield the line entered the Maun Valley and began to lose height. Below King's Mill (an old water-powered flour mill) it crossed the river by means of a five-arch viaduct. This fine structure was beautifully executed in chiselled blocks of pale greyish-cream stone and had more than ample breadth for double track. After a couple more curves the railway had a straight run into Mansfield, where it terminated somewhat below 400ft. on a low hill within sight of the market place. The yard was known as Portland Wharf and it boasted a two-storey warehouse incorporating large loading bay doors on both floors.

Although the Mansfield & Pinxton was originally envisaged as an extension of the Cromford Canal, it seems that the waterway company took little interest in the railway. Indeed, by far the greatest traffic flow in later years was coal from pits alongside the lower part of the line to the foundries, mills and domestic hearths of Mansfield. The amount of stone conveyed was less than expected, mainly because of the expense of carrying it forward by canal. Nevertheless, one of Britain's most famous landmarks – the Houses of Parliament – was rebuilt during the mid-1830s using limestone transported over the Pinxton line. Mansfield dispatched its renowned moulding sand to local ironworks via the railway and received wagons of metal for its foundries. Bricks, lime, timber, slate and assorted agricultural produce made up the remaining traffic. But for every chauldron wagon carrying these miscellaneous cargoes, seven were loaded with coal – a hint of things to come, so far as Mansfield's railways were concerned.

A passenger service of sorts was inaugurated in 1832 by the landlord of the *Boat Inn* at Pinxton. The horse-drawn carriage, no doubt a fairly rudimentary vehicle, ran to and from Mansfield on Thursdays for the weekly market. It may have lasted for a few years but seems to have expired by the early 1840s. Otherwise the line continued to carry coal in its antiquated way. As described in Chapter 3, the Mansfield & Pinxton eventually became embroiled in the relentless growth of the national railway network and was incorporated in the Codnor Park-Mansfield route, opened by the Midland Railway in 1849.

Some of the severe curves were abandoned at that time. The embankment in Grives Wood, looking like a prehistoric earthwork, is a relic of the original trackbed. Other sections of the 1819 formation were relaid with modern track but later closed, again as detailed in Chapter 3. However, they continue to exude some of the character of the horse wagonway. At Kirkby in Ashfield, just below the Robin Hood line station and near the *Railway Inn*, a surfaced track falls away gently past a hillside. With a little imagination, horses pulling chauldron wagons can be seen here. Undoubtedly the most wonderful place of all is King's Mill viaduct, overlooking the tranquil, wooded Maun Valley. It was here that the ceremonial procession into Mansfield assembled over 180 years ago, the horse-hauled train preceded by a flag bearing the motto *'By Perseverance We Have Obtained.'*

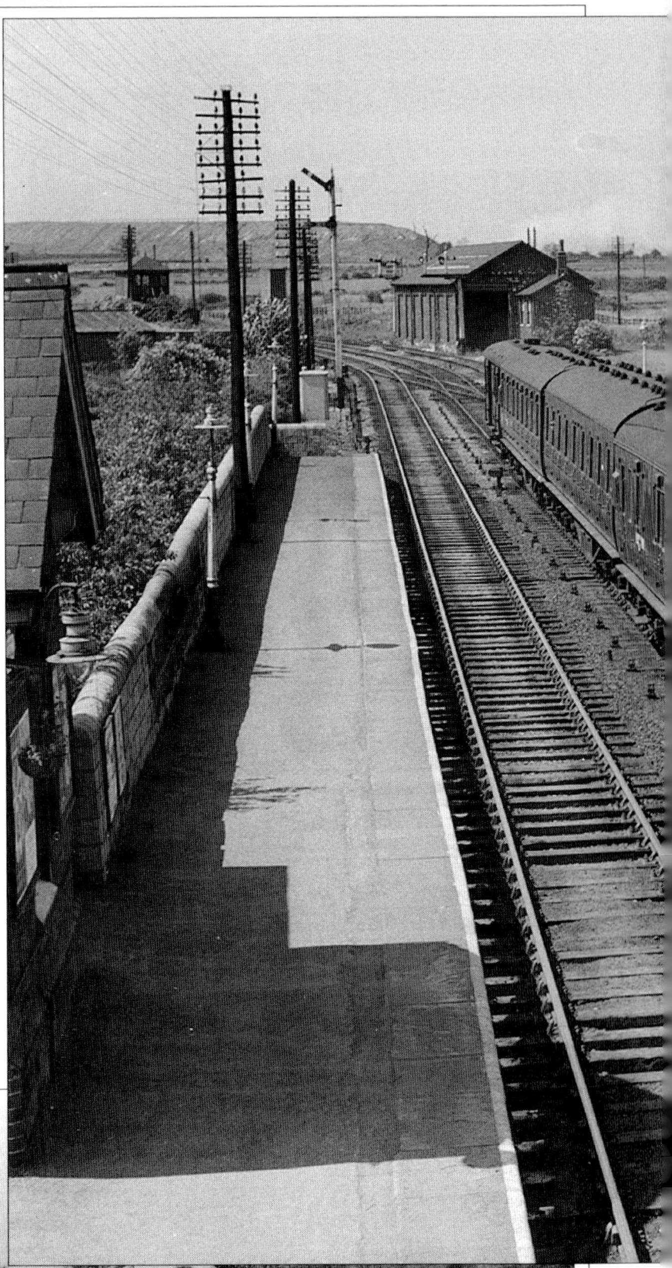

Right. Some sections of the original Mansfield & Pinxton alignment are still used by present-day Robin Hood passenger services. One such stretch is that through the outskirts of Sutton in Ashfield. On the beautiful sunny morning of 20th June 1959, Stanier 3MT 2-6-2T No.40168 of Mansfield shed pulls into Sutton Junction with a Nottingham-Worksop service. Although the station buildings date from 1893, the platform wall on the left is built of stone sleeper blocks from the wagonway. The spoil heap of Kirkby (Summit) Colliery forms the left backdrop. Photograph Jack Cupit.

Below. Sharp curves abounded where the Mansfield & Pinxton threaded the Erewash headwaters in the vestigial folds of Robin Hood's Hills. Even when the Kirkby deviation opened in 1892, the sinuous nature of the trackbed was perpetuated. On 29th April 1957, Nottingham-based Stanier 5MT 4-6-0 No.44841 leads the Saturdays only Clowne-Blackpool service down the 1 in 60 from Kirkby in Ashfield. The rough ground to the left of the train marks the original wagonway alignment, whilst the earthworks in the left background belong to the long-abandoned Great Northern Leen Valley Extension north to west spur. Photograph Jack Cupit.

Bottom right. Kirkby in Ashfield's Stanier 8F 2-8-0 No.48101 eases an up mineral working into Kirkby Loaded Sidings on a fine spring afternoon in April 1955. The train is trip 172 from one of the local collieries further north. This was the highest point on the Mansfield & Pinxton line and inspired the name of Kirkby (Summit) Colliery, which was on the left behind the camera. The bridge in the background carried the driveway to Kirkby Hardwick. There was a sand quarry siding here in Mansfield & Pinxton days. Photograph Jack Cupit.

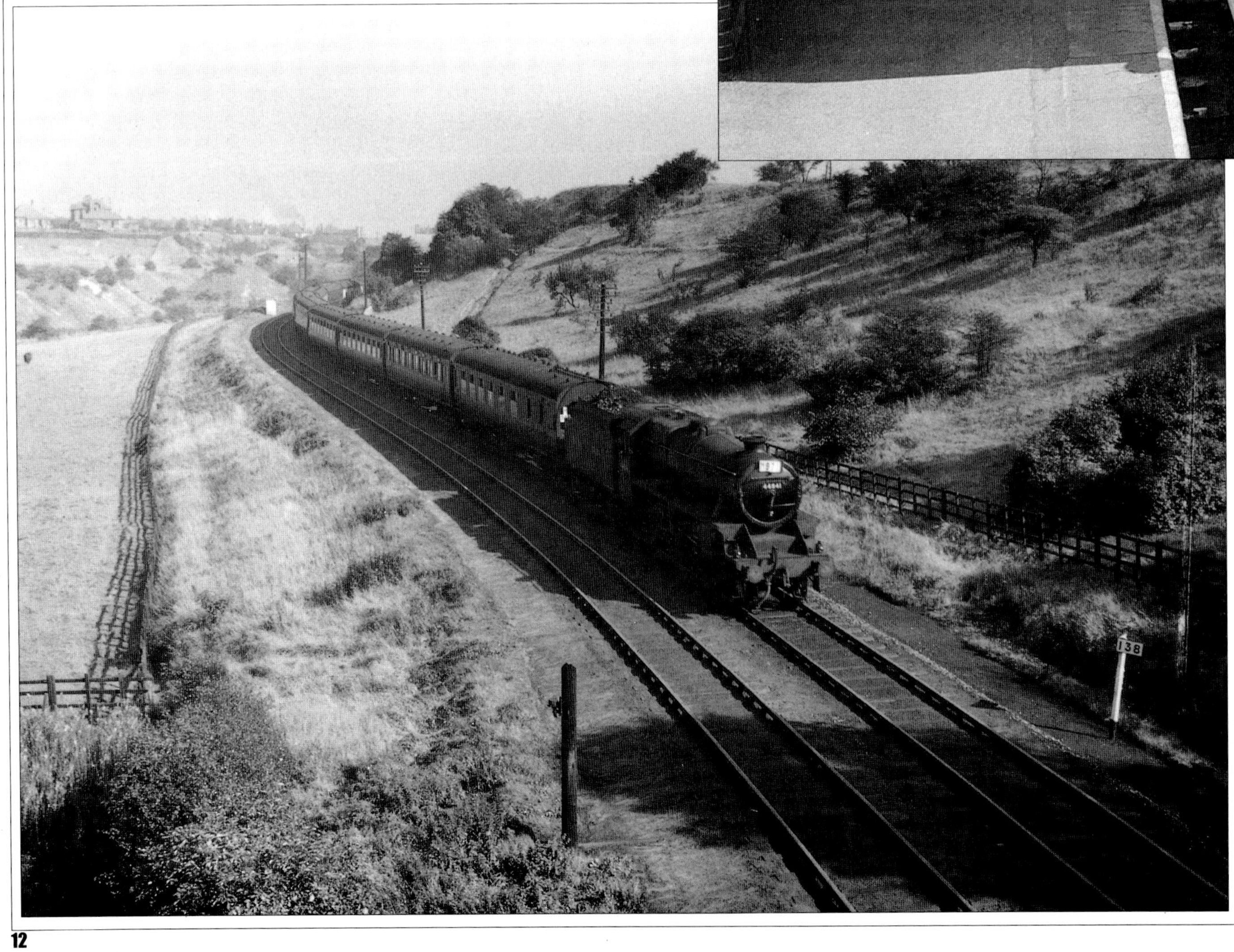

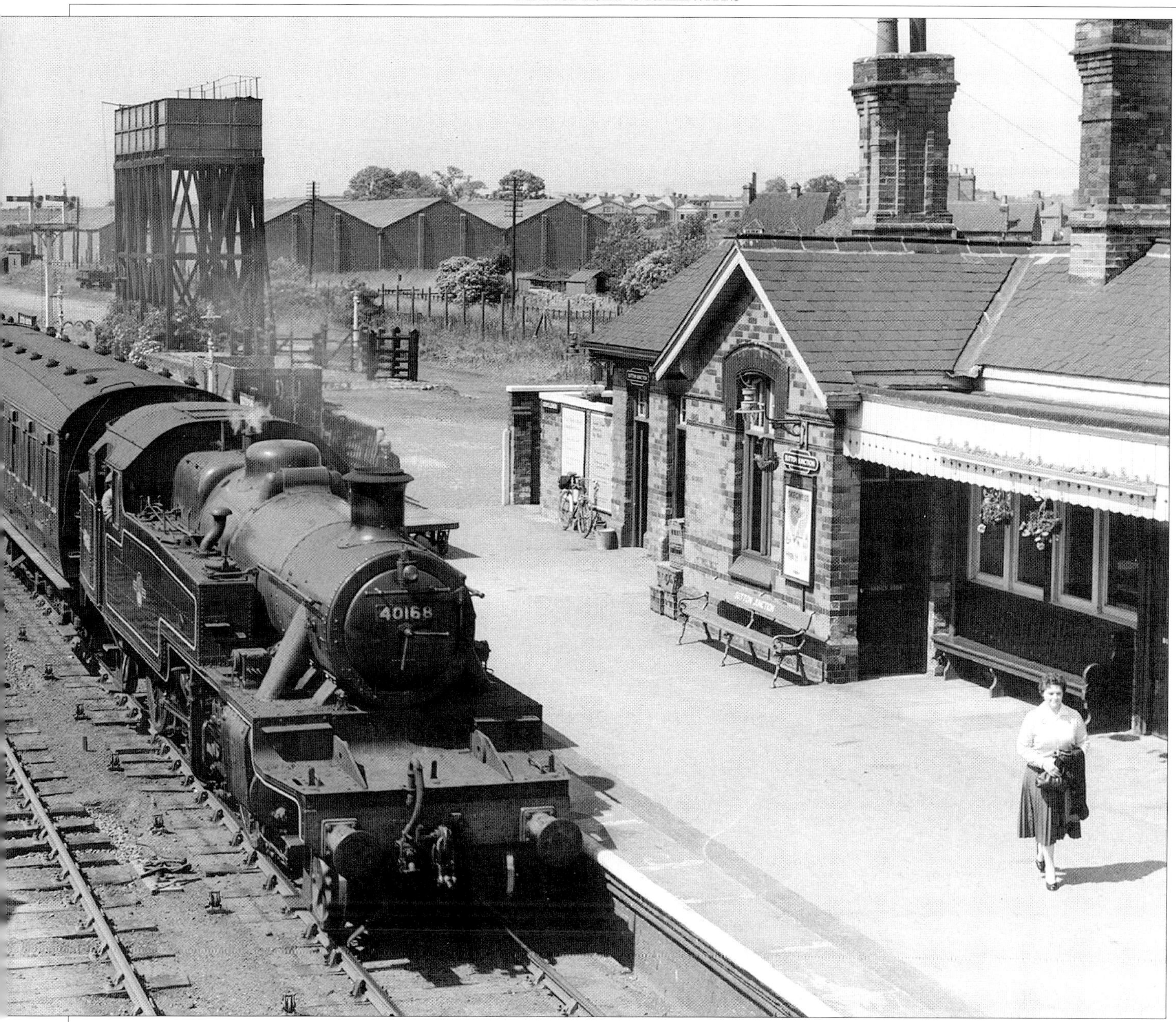
40168

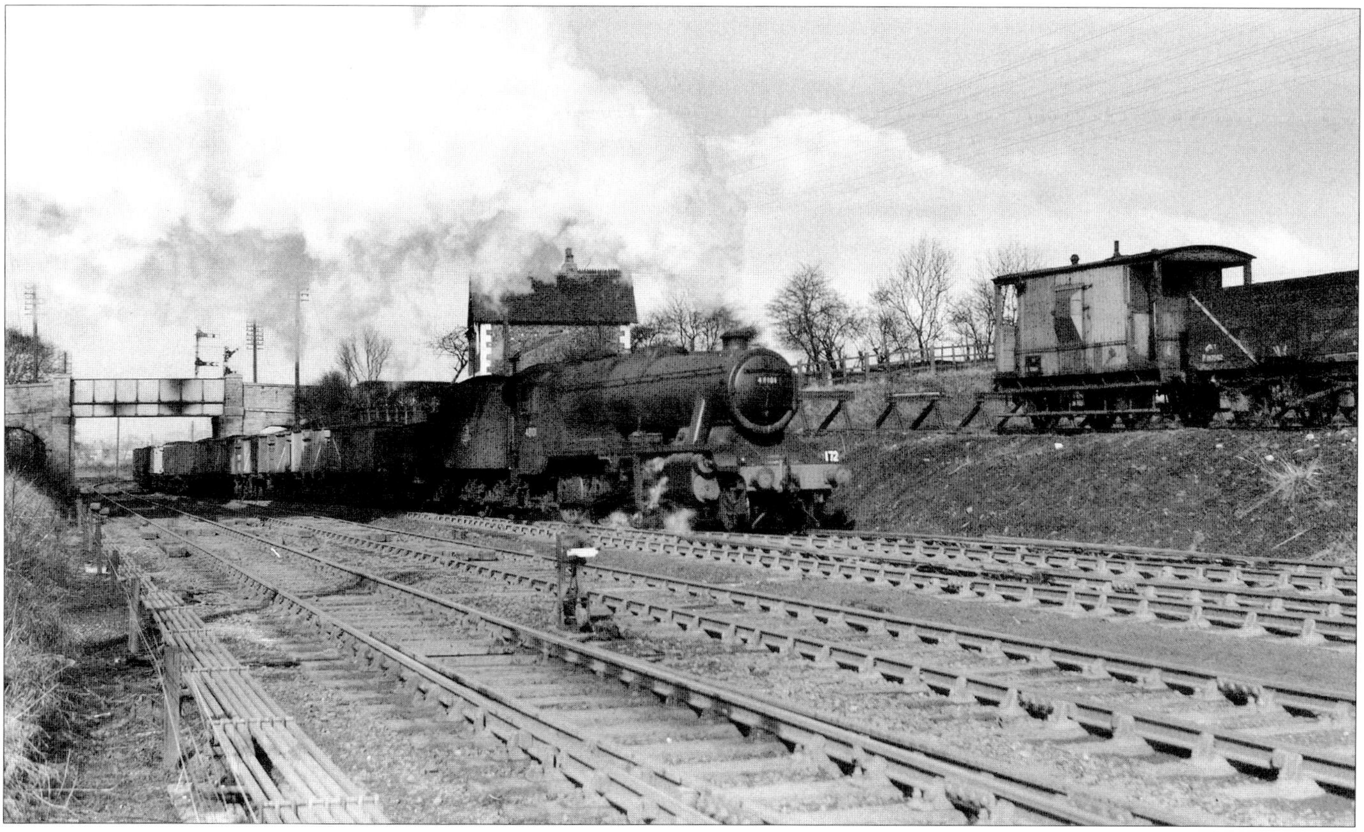

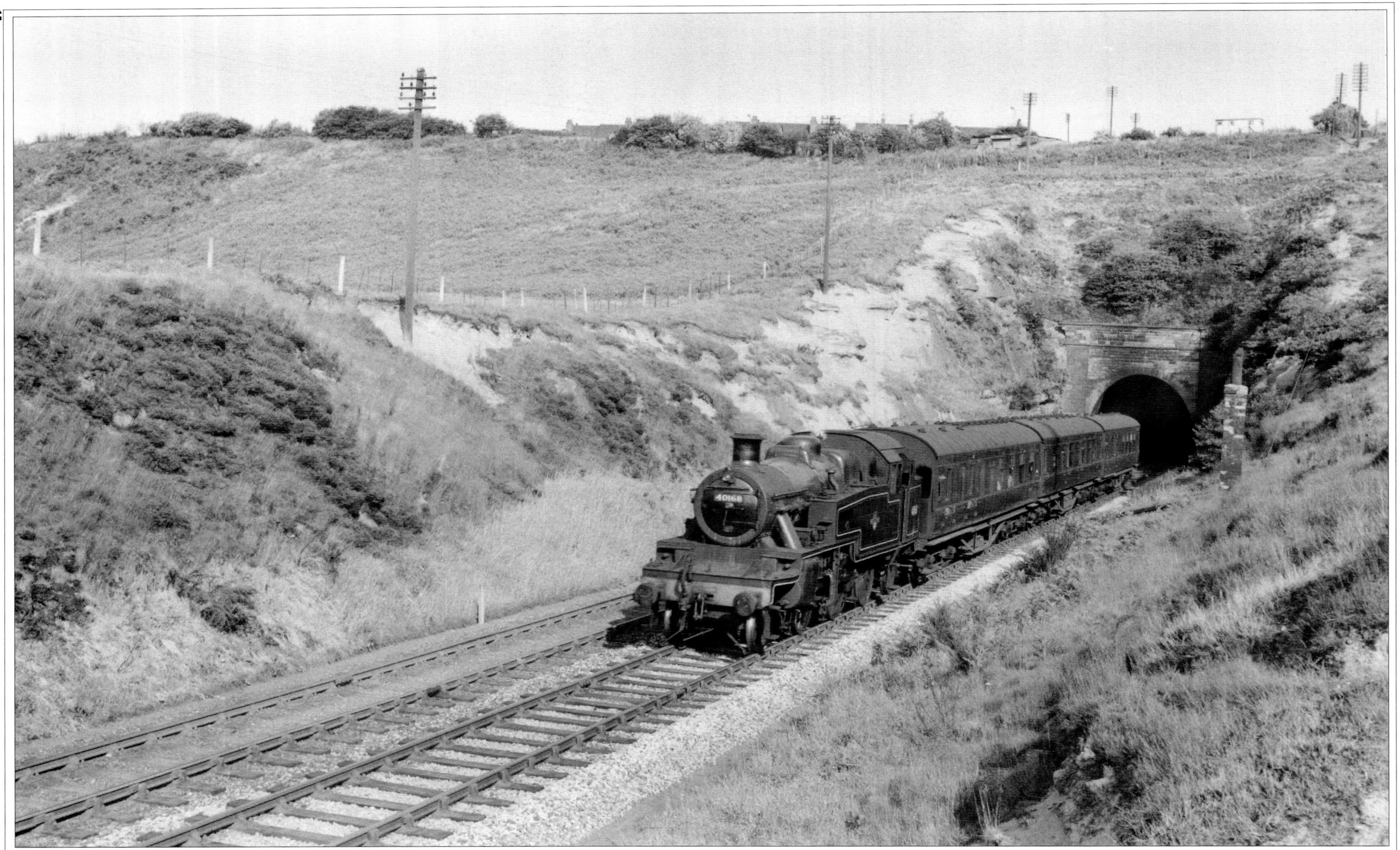

Byron's 'Hills of Annesley, bleak and barren' looked almost inviting in early morning sunshine as Stanier 3MT 2-6-2T No.40168 drifted out of Kirkby Tunnel into the Leen Valley with a Mansfield Town-Nottingham Midland train on 20th June 1959. Mansfield shed was proud of its little passenger tanks and kept them in very good condition. This viewpoint on the southern slope of Robin Hood's Hills is almost above the Great Central's Annesley Tunnel, which is exactly five times as long as the Midland excavation. Photograph Jack Cupit.

Chapter 3

THE MIDLAND ARRIVES

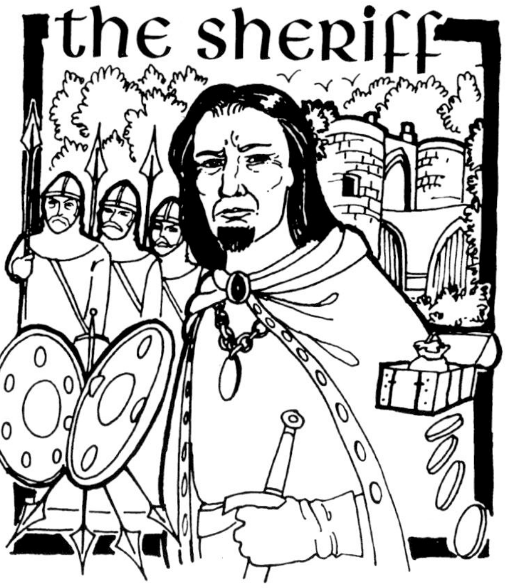

The Mansfield & Pinxton Railway led an isolated, almost naive, existence until the mid-1840s, although there had been a previous occasion when promoters with grandiose ideas appreciated its strategic importance, as noted below. Meanwhile, rail transport was undergoing a series of revolutionary developments akin to the advance of computer technology in recent decades. Despite being much celebrated as the world's first proper railway, the Stockton & Darlington of 1825 was essentially a traditional 'waggonway' employing horse traction over iron rails laid on stone blocks. However, it brought together three established yet disparate threads – namely, a public company, steam locomotives and advertised passenger services. Even before it was completed, men of vision saw great significance in this local line of the North East and the first ripple of railway speculation began.

Without a doubt, the main outcome was the Liverpool & Manchester Railway. It opened in 1830 and proved that it was possible to lay rails through daunting terrain, that steam locomotives had tremendous potential and that trade between major commercial centres could be revolutionised. Several lesser lines emerged as well, including the Leicester & Swannington – but more of that later. The Liverpool & Manchester was a phenomenal success and gave rise to a serious bout of railway mania during the mid-1830s. Consequently, a number of trunk routes were in operation by 1840, including the London & Birmingham Railway and, indeed, most of the present day West Coast line between Euston and Lancaster. During 1833 a company with the somewhat bloated title 'Midland Grand Junction Railway' wooed the Mansfield & Pinxton as part of its ambitious plan to connect Sheffield, Chesterfield and Mansfield, but the scheme proved abortive. Nevertheless, two lines which were to have a bearing on the development of the coalfield were successfully completed.

The first was the Midland Counties Railway, opened between Derby and Nottingham in 1839 and from the mid-way point at Trent Junction to Loughborough, Leicester and the London & Birmingham route at Rugby the next year, 1840. Far more heavily engineered was the North Midland Railway between Derby, Chesterfield, Rotherham and Leeds. It too opened during 1840 and featured a series of beautiful neo-classical station buildings – a far cry from Portland Wharf warehouse at Mansfield! Together with the Birmingham & Derby Junction Railway of 1839, these companies shared a large through station at Derby. Unfortunately there was bickering between the partners and the two southern companies eventually embarked on an all-out price

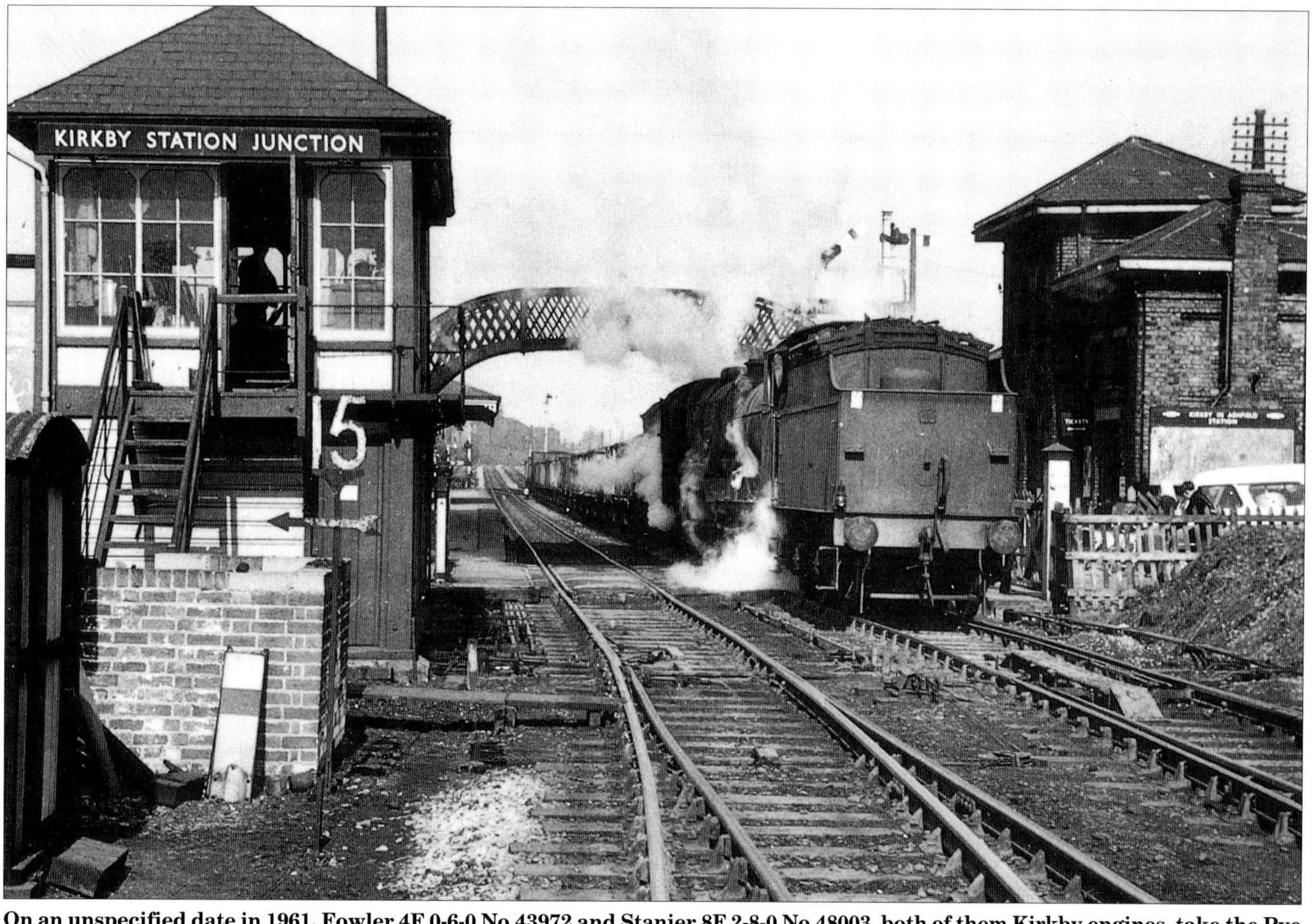

On an unspecified date in 1961, Fowler 4F 0-6-0 No.43972 and Stanier 8F 2-8-0 No.48003, both of them Kirkby engines, take the Pye Bridge line at Kirkby in Ashfield with a Kirkby Sidings-Toton Yard coal train. Double heading was to provide extra brake power on unbraked, loose-coupled mineral trains going down the upper Erewash Valley. The distinctive station building and later Midland Railway features such as the signal box, footbridge and crossing gates dominated the centre of East Kirkby, a township which owed its very existence to coal mining and railways. Photograph H.B. Priestley.

war. Proverbial heads were knocked together by George Hudson, the self-styled 'Railway King', and all three amalgamated to form the Midland Railway, on 10th May 1844.

By then, many railways had become excellent investments and there happened to be an abundance of capital on the London money markets. Just 37 Acts for new lines were passed in 1844, but during 1845 Parliament had to deal with 224 serious contenders out of a staggering 1,400 proposals, some of them frankly ludicrous. Many of the schemes came to fruition, one of the first being the Nottingham-Lincoln route via Lowdham, Rolleston and Newark on Trent. Work began on this 33-mile Midland branch in October 1845 and proceeded at such a frenetic pace that the official opening took place within 10 months, on 3rd August 1846.

The haste was understandable. George Hudson controlled the whole chain of railways from Berwick upon Tweed to Rugby via Newcastle, York and Derby, thus monopolising Anglo-Scottish traffic between Euston and Edinburgh over the only route available at the time, but one of the Mania schemes was the London & York, which would have siphoned off much business. The Lincoln extension was a bid to claim territory and ward off the rival. Hudson's efforts were in vain, as the direct East Coast route in the form of the London & York (by then referred to as the Great Northern Railway) was authorised a week before trains began running on his Lincoln branch. The main line from Doncaster to London King's Cross opened in stages, culminating in the Retford-Peterborough section through Newark and Grantham during 1852. By this time 'King' Hudson had fallen from grace in a spectacular manner, but his Nottingham-Lincoln line with its delightful Italianate and *cottage orné* station buildings remains much as built over 150 years ago.

Now for Mansfield's first conventional railway, or more correctly railways, as the lines from Nottingham and the Erewash Valley were authorised separately, despite being virtual contemporaries and very much inter-related. Both schemes stemmed from the promotional turmoil of the mid-1840s and, to some extent, were a response to threats from rival concerns. Bringing Midland trains to Mansfield was a complex business, involving a fair amount of parliamentary time and not a little intrigue. In a way, the story begins well before the Mansfield & Pinxton opened.

From 1794, navigable water extended all the way from Pinxton to Leicester and that town soon became a lucrative market for Erewash Valley coal. Leicestershire mines, relying on carts for transport, could not compete and were plunged into a deep recession. Eventually a solution was found, in the form of the Leicester & Swannington Railway, the first part of which opened on 17th July 1832. Erewash mine owners had failed to secure a reduction in canal tolls, thus the famous meeting at the *Sun Inn*, Eastwood, on 16th August 1832 when it was decided that a railway from Pinxton to Leicester was the only answer. In effect, this would have been an extension of the Mansfield & Pinxton line.

The coal producers could not raise sufficient capital and, prompted by the success of the Liverpool & Manchester, turned to Lancashire, a rich source of railway finance. But the northern men had a much broader vision and envisaged the Midland Counties Railway (as the project had become) as part of the national network. It still included a branch to Pinxton, but the North Midland (also before Parliament) saw this as a threat, especially as there was talk of an extension to Chesterfield. The choice was simple: either the Erewash line was dropped or the Bill would be lost. Consequently, the Midland Counties Act of 21st June 1836 excluded a vital section of route which had brought the scheme into being in the first place. The frustrated colliery proprietors continued to lobby for a line, but were consistently thwarted by railway politics. Early in 1844 they took matters into their own hands and formed the Erewash Valley Railway.

Any jealousy between the North Midland and Midland Counties evaporated overnight when the Midland Railway was formed in May 1844. At first, the new company was preoccupied by the threat posed by the London & York and the need to strengthen its position by acquiring existing lines. However, it could not ignore a small but potentially important independent branch line in its heartland, so the Erewash company was purchased and an Act obtained for the railway in 1845. Traffic from Long Eaton Junction to Codnor Park commenced on 6th September 1847. At long last the coal owners had their railway, but the prime aim of serving Leicester was lost in the mists of time.

Having gained parliamentary approval for its Erewash Valley line, the Midland began to take an interest in the Mansfield & Pinxton Railway and also recognised the need for a direct Nottingham-Mansfield route. It was not alone. In November 1845, two companies backed by the London & York set their sights on Nottinghamshire. The Boston, Newark & Sheffield was to pass through Southwell and Mansfield, while the Not-

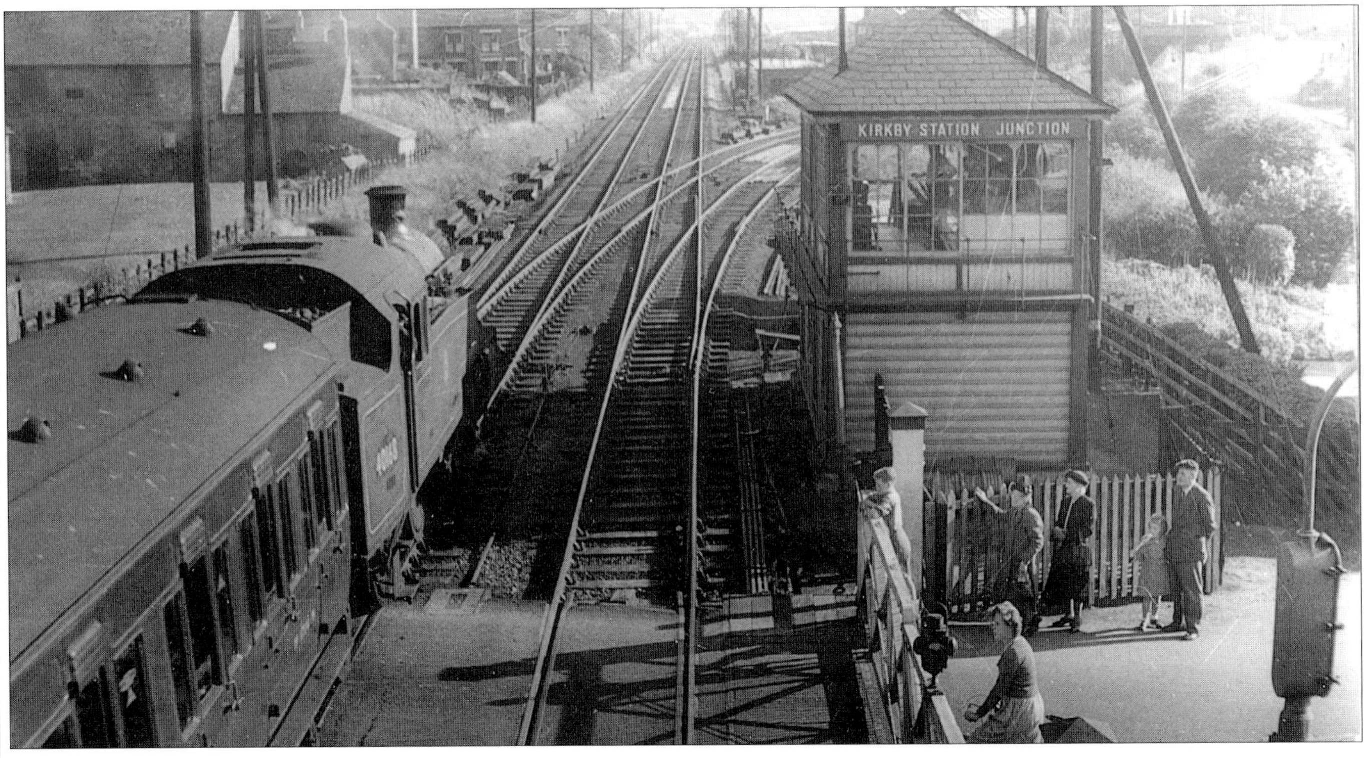

Seen from the station footbridge, Stanier 2-6-2T No.40168, originally a Bournville engine, heads out of Kirkby in Ashfield towards Kirkby Tunnel with a Mansfield-Nottingham train, on 2nd September 1955. In time-honoured fashion, we can ascribe a variety of feelings to the people waiting at the crossing; a boy has clambered eagerly on the gates, a little girl clings to her granddad, the elderly women look on contentedly and the young woman on the bike is irritated by the delay. The Pye Bridge line drops steeply down to the right. Photograph H.C. Casserley.

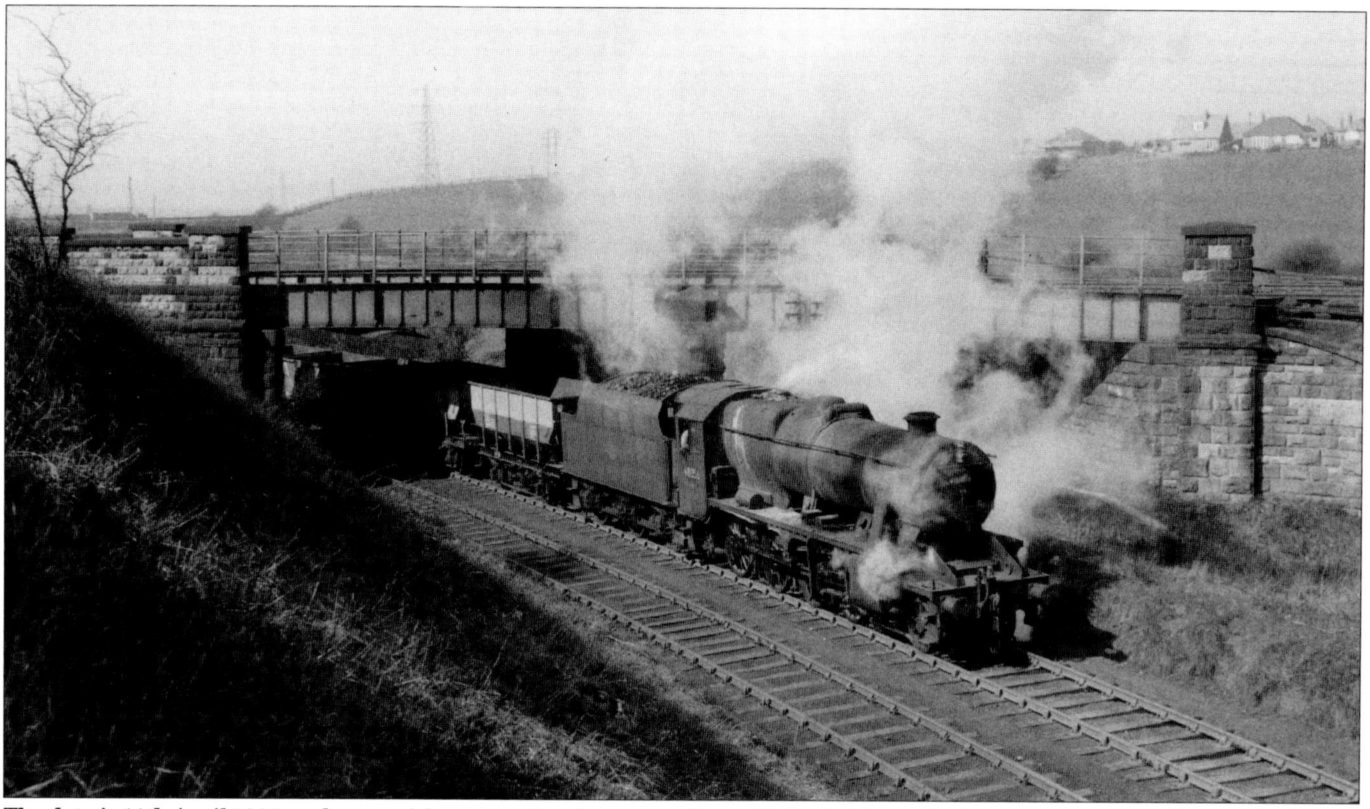

The date is 11th April 1964, and even with a train of coal empties, Toton 8F No.48056 needs plenty of steam to tackle the climb from Pinxton to Kirkby in Ashfield. With a combination of greasy rails and adverse signals, engines often struggled on the 1 in 75 gradient and sharp curve round to the Nottingham-Mansfield line a few hundred yards to the right of this view. In fact, with much slipping and copious eruptions from the chimney, trains could take as long as ten minutes to clear the level crossing at East Kirkby. The Great Northern Leen Valley Extension crosses the bridge in the foreground, whilst the Mansfield Railway occupies the distant embankment. Photograph Jack Cupit.

tingham, Mansfield & Midlands Junction would incorporate the Mansfield & Pinxton tramway. These two organisations were so confident about their prospects that they jointly purchased the Mansfield & Pinxton the following year. Conflict was inevitable as a meeting of Midland shareholders in January 1846 had already decided to build lines from Codnor Park to Clay Cross (on the former North Midland) and from Nottingham to Mansfield, the latter utilising part of the Pinxton Railway.

Parliament favoured the Midland plans, an Act for the Nottingham-Mansfield railway (initially connecting with the Mansfield & Pinxton north of Kirkby in Ashfield) being passed on 16th July 1846. There was a fairly lethargic start, as contracts were not sought until March 1847. Meanwhile, the unfortunate custodians of the tramway were in a dilemma, for they did not have parliamentary approval either to work it or sell it!

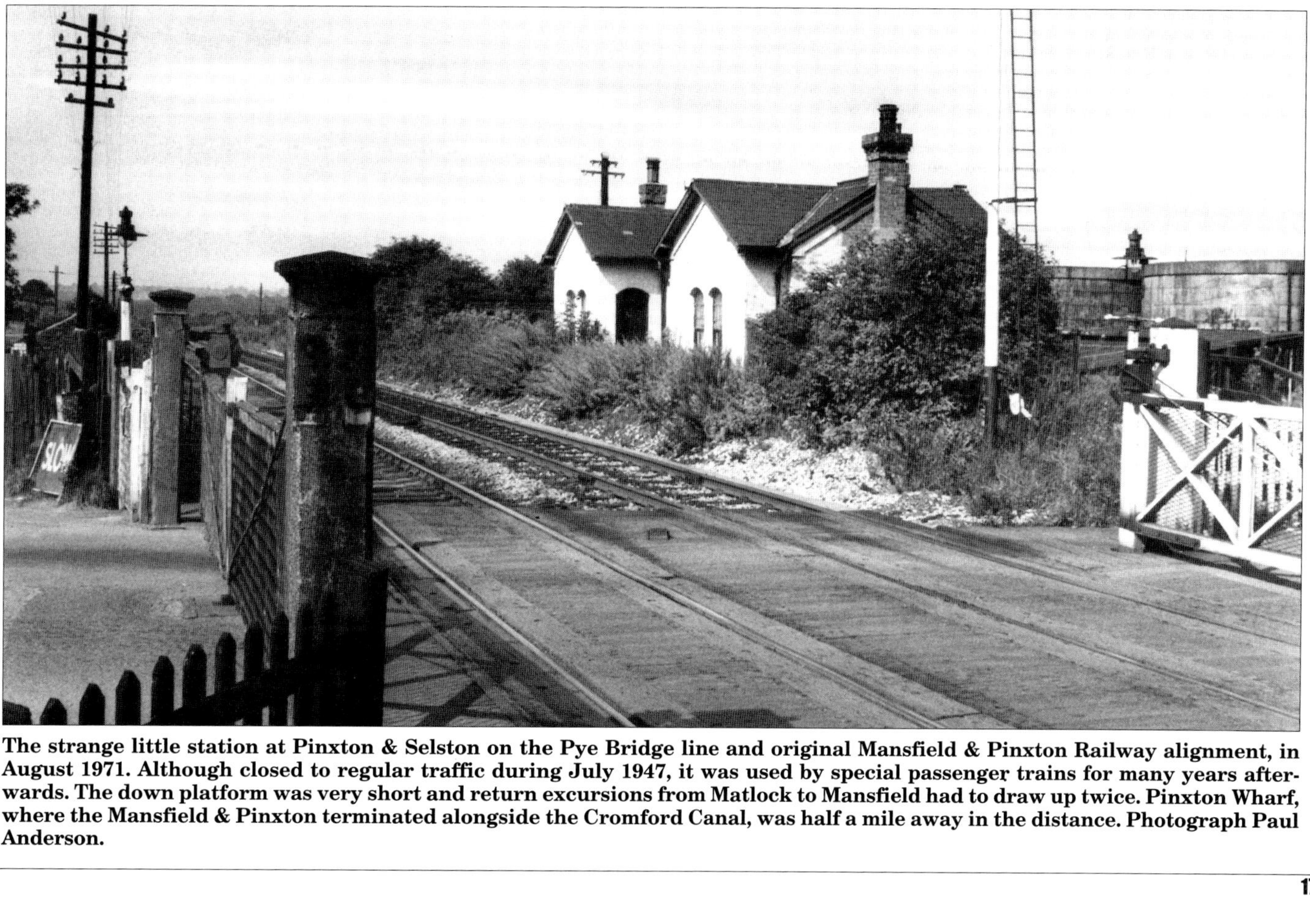

The strange little station at Pinxton & Selston on the Pye Bridge line and original Mansfield & Pinxton Railway alignment, in August 1971. Although closed to regular traffic during July 1947, it was used by special passenger trains for many years afterwards. The down platform was very short and return excursions from Matlock to Mansfield had to draw up twice. Pinxton Wharf, where the Mansfield & Pinxton terminated alongside the Cromford Canal, was half a mile away in the distance. Photograph Paul Anderson.

Matters were confounded even further when the Midland acquired its Mansfield & Pinxton and Erewash Valley Extension Act on 9th July 1847. This sanctioned the purchase of the tramway and its incorporation in a line between Codnor Park and Mansfield. Tenders were sought for the erection of Mansfield station and conversion of the old horse-operated line in September 1847, but ownership of the latter remained a problem. The issue was finally resolved on 15th February 1848, when the Mansfield & Pinxton was amalgamated with the Midland and immediately dissolved, its erstwhile proprietors comforted by a batch of Midland shares.

Once the contract had been awarded, progress on the Nottingham-Kirkby line was fairly rapid. The main task was a tunnel through Robin Hood's Hills, the abrupt sandstone ridge known to Byron of nearby Newstead Abbey as 'the hills of Annesley, bleak and barren' Work was completed in July 1848 and navvies were treated to a dinner at the *Blue Bell* in Annesley Woodhouse to celebrate the event. The line passed its government inspection and opened without ceremony on 2nd October 1848. A timetable of three weekday trains each way was announced, with departures from Nottingham at 8.10am, 12.10pm and 6.20pm. Northbound services were allowed 45 minutes, while southbound trains took 40 minutes, reflecting the gradients. There were two return services on Sundays.

The opening coincided with Nottingham Goose Fair week and trains were heavily used, although the *Nottingham Journal* rightly predicted that this level of patronage could not continue in view of the unacceptably high fares. A two-compartment horse-drawn carriage was constructed at Derby Works to provide connections to and from Mansfield over the northern part of the Pinxton tramway. With a touch of astute foresight, the Midland provided no less than twenty daily services between Kirkby and Nottingham during Fair week. Unfortunately, the horse coach was completely overwhelmed by the demand for transport to Kirkby. Most people had to walk to join the steam trains, a trek which hardly endeared the residents of Mansfield to the new railway.

Meanwhile, work on converting the Pinxton tramway into a fully fledged railway was progressing well. On 24th August 1849 a contractor's locomotive visited Mansfield and received a lot of attention from locals, many of whom enjoyed a free ride in the empty wagons it had come to collect. Midland directors arrived in a first class carriage on 17th September, to view the new terminus, and the official inspection took place on 25th September. The Kirkby-Mansfield section was deemed to be in good shape, but the Codnor Park line was missing several crossing gates and even some short lengths of track, earning the company a mild rebuke. Workmen putting finishing touches to Mansfield station on Sunday 7th October also met with disapproval, this time from one of the occupants of Broombank Asylum, which overlooked the terminus. His main thrust was that 'Napoleon was a great man, but a Sabbath breaker, and was subdued by his enemies!'

Mineral workings over the Codnor Park line and passenger services from Mansfield to Nottingham commenced on 9th October 1849. One report indicates that a large crowd watched the first train, but the *Nottingham Journal* reported that there was little interest and 'the only sign of approval or disapproval was the braying of an ass.' Departures from Mansfield were at 9.00am, 12.45pm, 3.00pm and 6.20pm, the journey taking 55 minutes. The *Nottingham Journal* really seems to have had it in for the Midland, describing the railway as 'one of the most ill-constructed in the kingdom.' It added that 'engines have been off the line in the station yard at Mansfield several times since the opening on Tuesday week.'

Having left the former Midland Counties route within sight of Nottingham Castle, Mansfield trains followed the River Leen through Lenton, Radford, Basford, Bulwell and Hucknall. Beyond here, steadily rising ground required an arduous four mile climb at 1 in 79 past Linby and Newstead to Kirkby Tunnel. This modest 199 yard bore through Robin Hood's Hills effectively marked the transition from south to north Nottinghamshire. Featureless ground led to Kirkby in Ashfield, or, more accurately, the location where the Victorian township of East Kirkby eventually grew up. Just north of here, the line adopted the course of the Pinxton tramway past Sutton in Ashfield and across King's Mill viaduct to Mansfield, mainly on a falling gradient of 1 in 151. The length of the journey from Nottingham to Mansfield was about 17½ miles.

Most station buildings were of a pleasant Tudor-gothic style, and the one at Lenton even had buttresses similar to a medieval church. Kirkby in Ashfield, however, consisted of a vaguely Italianate two-storey block featuring a pyramidal roof with very prominent eaves, slightly

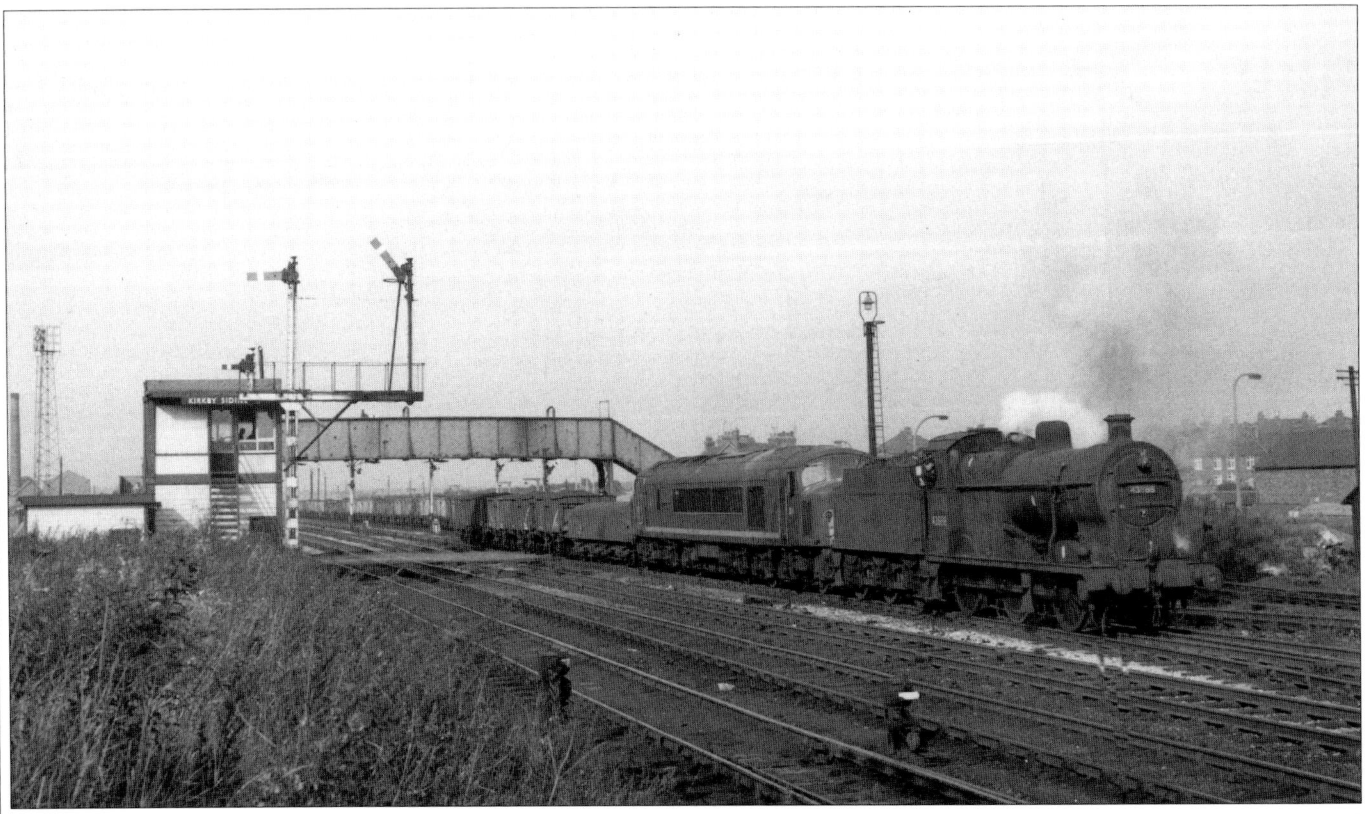

During the transition from steam to diesel traction, this lengthy Kirkby-Toton coal train had very mixed motive power as it passed Kirkby Colliery Sidings signal box, on 14th August 1963. Kirkby 4F No.43888 pilots Toton's Derby/Sulzer type 4 No.D1 SCAFELL PIKE, complete with brake tender. Just visible in the right background, the houses of Low Moor Road were home to numerous miners and railway workers. Photograph Jack Cupit.

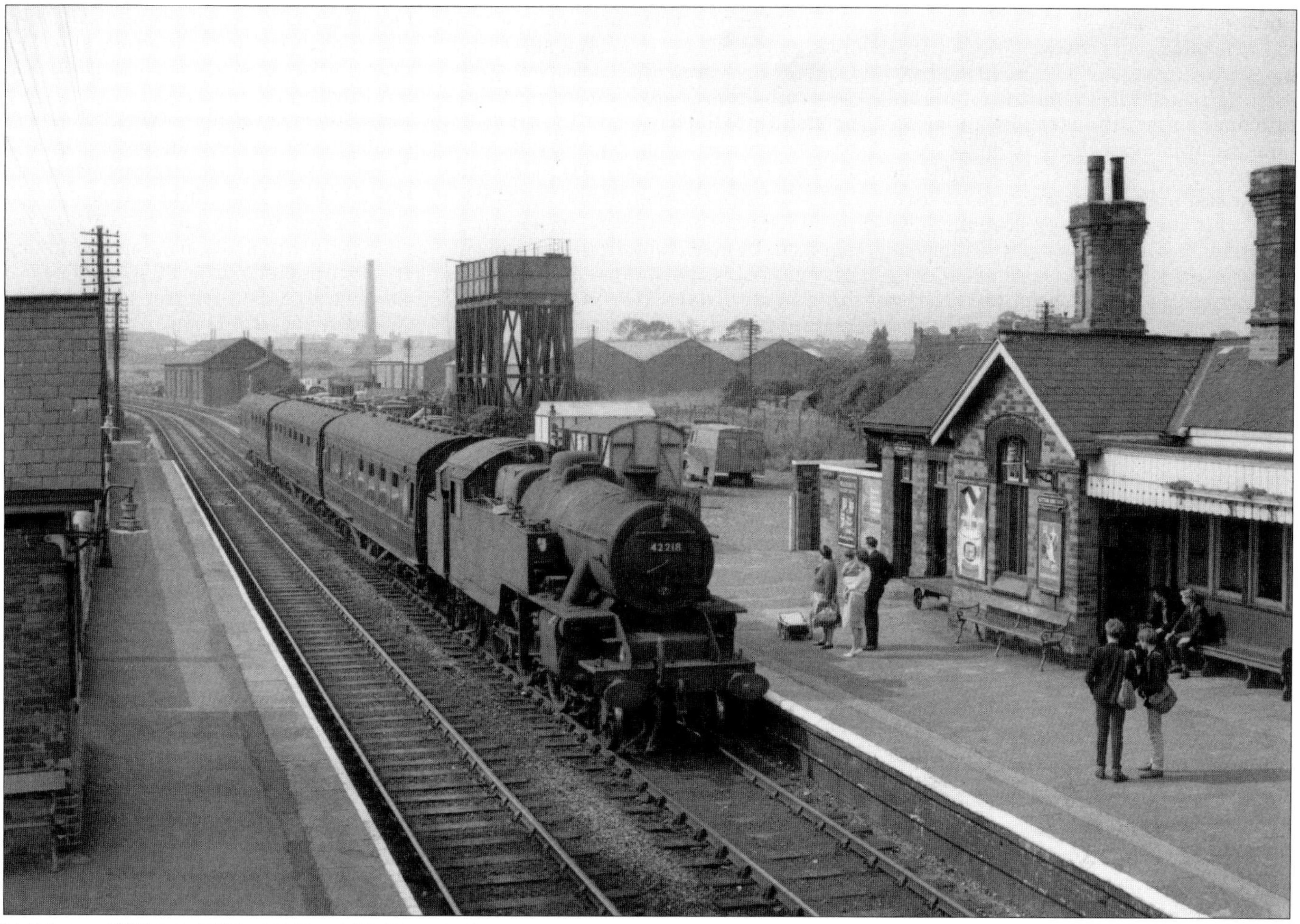

Fairburn 4MT 2-6-4T No.42218, of Kirkby shed, arrives at Sutton Junction with a Nottingham Midland-Worksop train on 14th September 1963. Although the original station house, a rather plain structure, survived further down the platform, the neat building in this view dates from 1893 when the short branch to a terminus nearer Sutton in Ashfield town centre opened. Connecting services ran from a bay on the down side, occupied by a goods van in this picture. Photograph Jack Cupit.

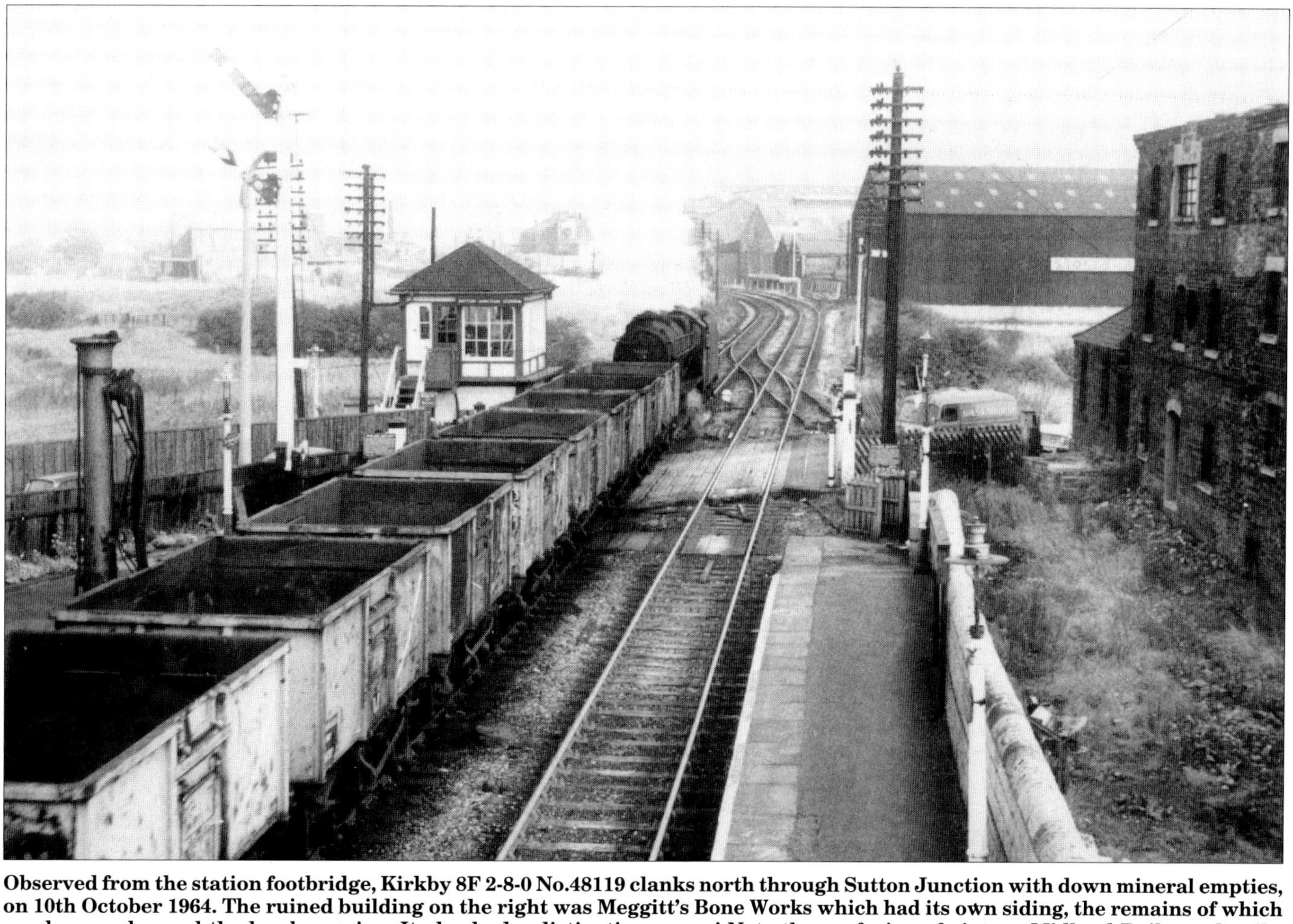

Observed from the station footbridge, Kirkby 8F 2-8-0 No.48119 clanks north through Sutton Junction with down mineral empties, on 10th October 1964. The ruined building on the right was Meggitt's Bone Works which had its own siding, the remains of which can be seen beyond the level crossing. It also had a distinctive aroma! Note the profusion of vintage Midland Railway details, including lamps, fencing and the water column. Photograph H.B. Priestley.

protruding brickwork at the corners and round headed doors and windows. Its single-storey appendage had a hipped roof. Although somewhat reminiscent of certain stations on the Nottingham-Lincoln line, the building was devoid of the style and ornamentation of Hudson's days. In fact, rather ironically, it had much in common with Great Northern stations such as Spalding and Bardney, on the Lincolnshire Loop. Mansfield terminus was in the same style, but was attached to the original Mansfield & Pinxton warehouse. The dozen or so crossing houses tended to be simplified versions of the stations.

The Codnor Park-Mansfield railway climbed gently up the Erewash Valley to join the old tramway formation east of Pinxton basin. Although the line largely traced the course of the horse tracks beyond this point, two particularly sharp curves north of Kirkby Woodhouse were replaced by a more or less straight alignment involving some earthworks in 1849. The gradient steepened to 1 in 94 then 1 in 75 along this stretch. A Mansfield-Nottingham passenger service via Codnor Park and Long Eaton commenced on 1st November 1851, but the three trains each way on weekdays and two on Sundays took 1 hour 40 minutes for the circuitous journey. A station was provided at Pinxton & Selston and it was quite remarkable – not for its aesthetics, but for its overall concept. Matching single-storey pavilions connected by a transverse section, forming an H-shape in plan, anticipated the Midland's widely-adopted standard design by sixteen years. Originally so contentious, the highly desirable Erewash Extension from Codnor Park and Pye Bridge to Clay Cross (on the former North Midland line) opened in 1861. Later, there were improvements to the old Mansfield & Pinxton route as well. On 25th February 1872, a new alignment north of Sutton in Ashfield came into operation, eliminating a curve near Hamilton Hill and the erstwhile tramway formation across King's Mill viaduct. Most of the latter remained in use as a siding serving King's Mill itself, with access from the Mansfield direction. From 15th August 1892, the junction between the Codnor Park line and the Nottingham-Mansfield tracks was immediately south of Kirkby in Ashfield station, rather than half a mile to the north. Trains were diverted over a new spur involving a deep cutting and gradients as steep as 1 in 60. It seems that the main reason for the project was to improve communications for passengers from Pye Bridge and Pinxton to East Kirkby. The station at Kirkby in Ashfield consequently became a junction and new waiting rooms featuring cantilevered canopies typical of current Midland practice were provided on each platform. The northern part of the old trackbed was retained as sidings for Summit Colliery.

With pits in the Pinxton area becoming increasingly productive and seven new collieries transforming the Leen Valley into an industrial area during the 1860s and 1870s, the Midland's Mansfield lines saw a massive increase in coal traffic. There was also the relentless march of deep mining from the Nottinghamshire/Derbyshire border towards Mansfield itself. Inevitably, other railway companies were eager to tap this bonanza of black gold. As a result, the Midland found its coveted territory threatened by the Manchester, Sheffield & Lincolnshire from the north and the Great Northern from the south and east. A successful response came during 1865 in the form of the Mansfield Lines Act which sanctioned extensions to Worksop and Southwell, as well as a new through station at Mansfield and the Sutton in Ashfield deviations mentioned above.

Rival companies eventually established themselves in the Mansfield area, as described in later chapters. Despite this competition, the Midland went from strength to strength and gained a fair proportion of its prosperity from Nottinghamshire coal. Passenger services based on Mansfield multiplied as new lines opened, no less than eight routes operating out of the Midland station in the halcyon days just prior to World War I. Engine sheds were found at Mansfield and Kirkby in Ashfield, numerous sidings served collieries, factories and other industrial premises, and Kirkby yards dealt with the relentless flow of coal wagons. An outline of traffic, both passenger and goods, is given in the next chapter. The demise of the Nottingham-Mansfield passenger service is lamented, and its reinstatement celebrated , in Chapter 10.

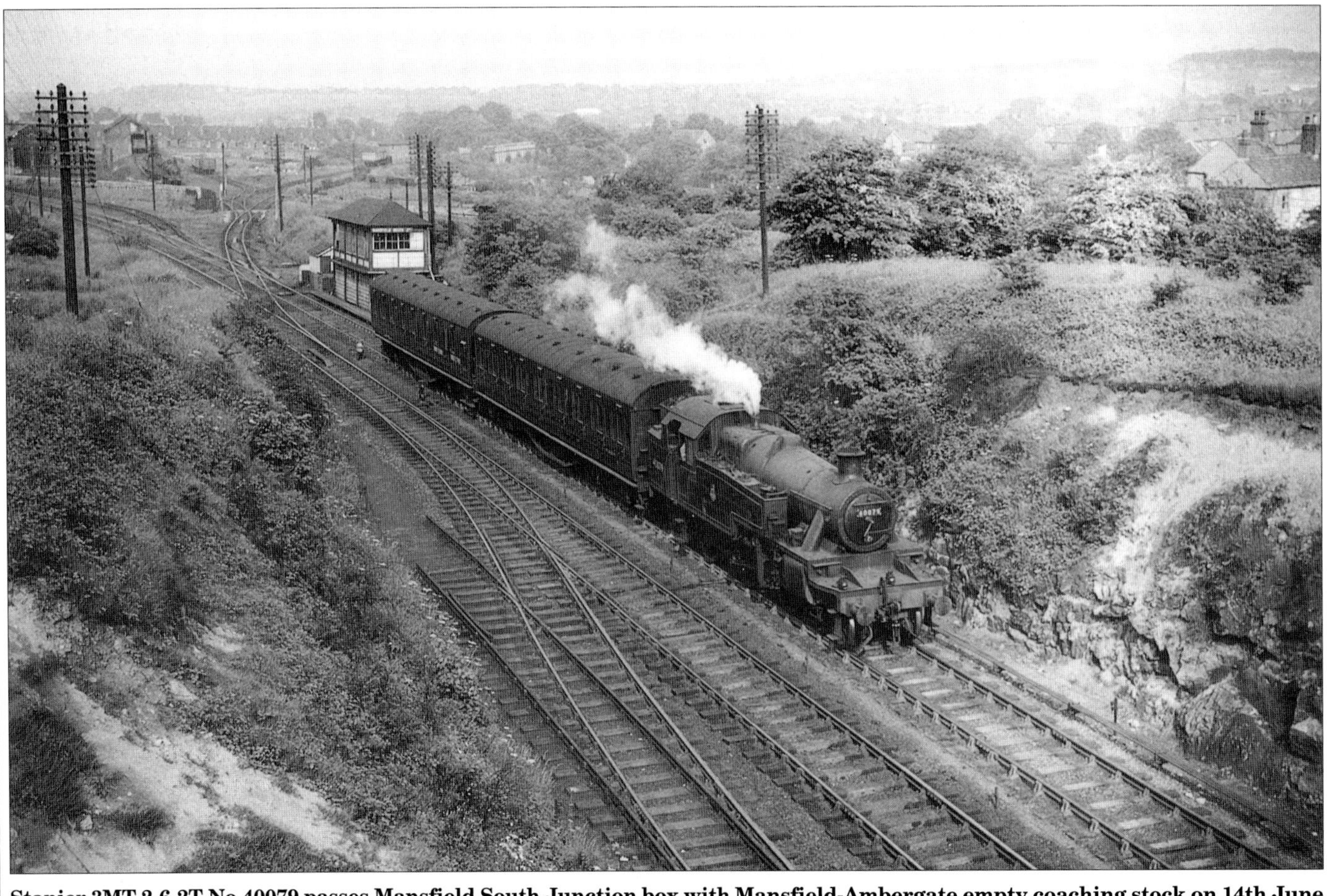

Stanier 3MT 2-6-2T No.40079 passes Mansfield South Junction box with Mansfield-Ambergate empty coaching stock on 14th June 1958. The shed is in the left background, adjacent to the east-south curve of the Southwell branch. For over twenty years the line from Sutton in Ashfield followed the old Mansfield & Pinxton alignment at this point; the train is on the 1872 deviation which was designed to eliminate sharp curves and provide easier access to the newly opened Southwell route. The original course ran parallel to the stone wall near the engine shed and passed behind the high ground to the right. Photograph Jack Cupit.

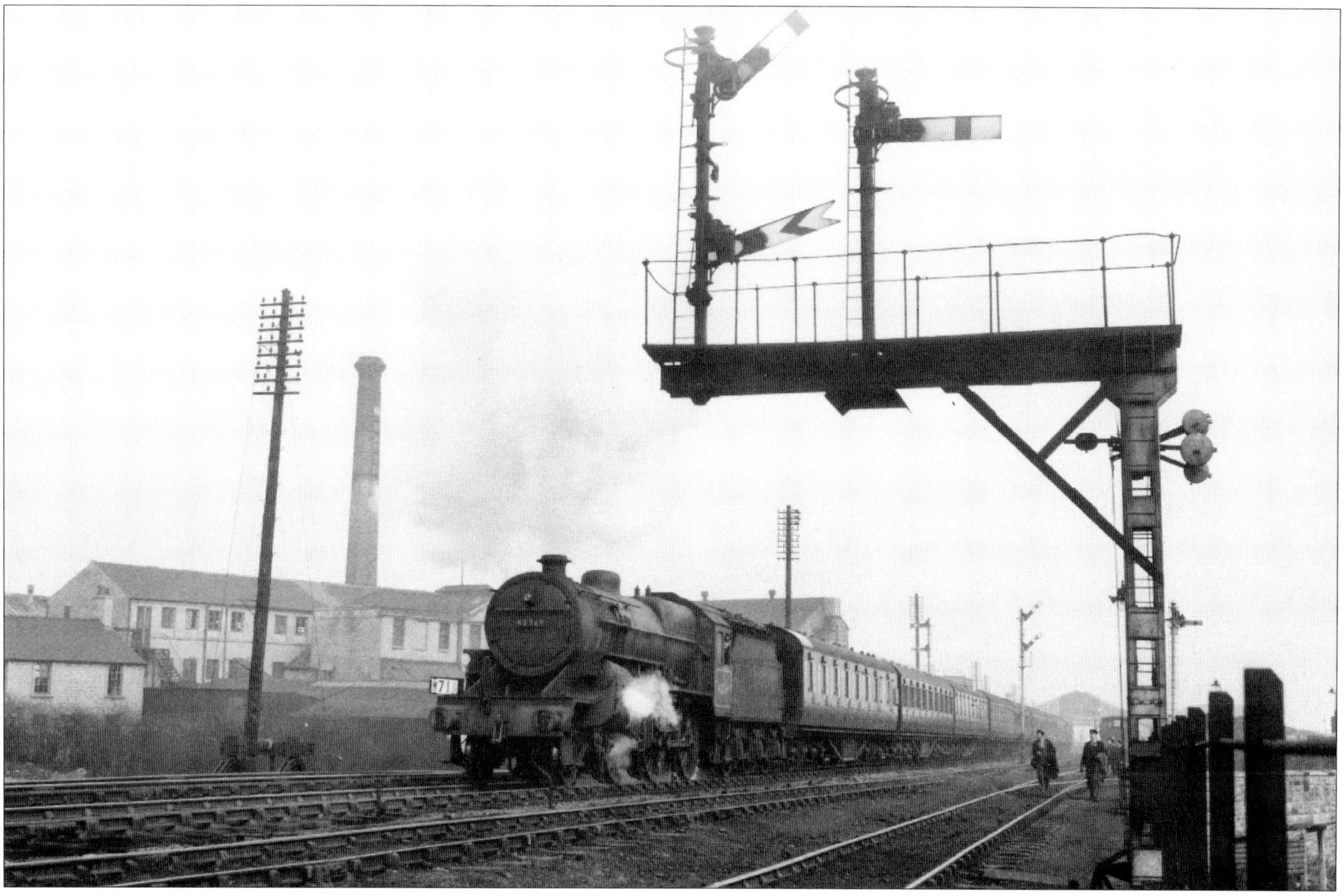

On 2nd March 1957 a Mansfield-Derby excursion, with Nottingham 'Crab' No.42769 in charge, passes Mansfield North Junction where the single track north to east curve of the Southwell branch went off and had its own bracket signal. The former Cash's textile mill behind the train was one of numerous industrial establishments in the Mansfield area having its own siding. Photograph Jack Cupit.

Standard 5MT 4-6-0 No.73142, a Rowsley engine, leaves Mansfield with the 4.00pm evening excursion to Matlock, on 23rd April 1962. Signalling features strongly in this view of the south end of the station. On the left is Station South box, one of five Midland cabins in Mansfield. From left to right, the semaphores control the up main from platform 2, bay platform 3 and a siding. At the end of the platform are two miniature signals used for engines reversing into the station. Photograph Jack Cupit.

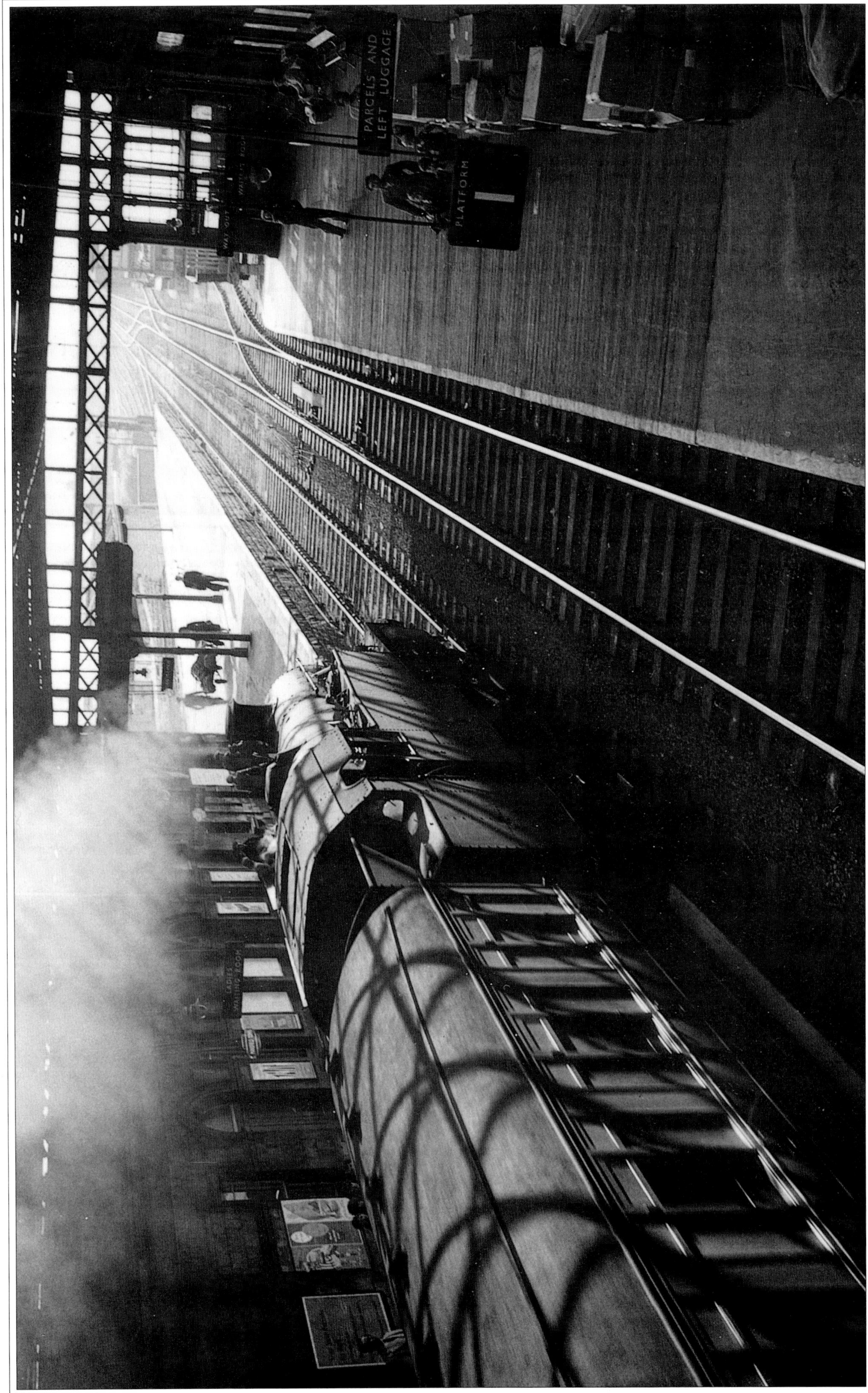

An atmospheric view of Mansfield Town station on 8th September 1953, as a Worksop-Nottingham Midland train arrives behind the local shed's Stanier 3MT 2-6-2T No.40079. The station had a good vantage point in the form of a footbridge within the train shed. Platform 1 on the right was much shorter than Nos.2 and 3 on the left. Photograph Jack Cupit.

Chapter 4

ON TO WORKSOP

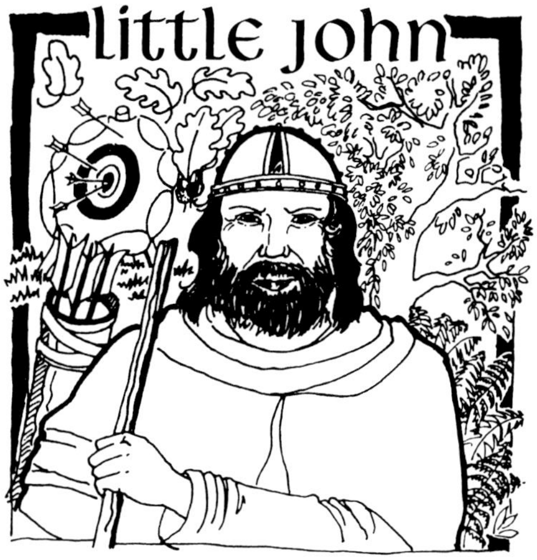

During the first three decades of its seventy-eight year existence as an independent company, the Midland Railway was obsessed with territorial gains. Initially there were a couple of eastward thrusts to counter the embryonic Great Northern, namely the Nottingham-Lincoln and Leicester-Peterborough lines. Around the same time, the existing route from Birmingham to Gloucester and Bristol was acquired. With dogged determination and far from modest expenditure, the Midland eventually made it to London, Manchester and Carlisle. In the original heartland a number of branches and connecting lines opened; Little Eaton to Ripley and Pye Bridge to Clay Cross, for example.

None of this helped Mansfield very much. The town certainly benefited from its railways to Nottingham and the Erewash Valley, but nevertheless suffered from the lack of a through route. Passengers and commercial traffic to Retford, Worksop and Sheffield had to go a very long way round by rail, or use the highly unsatisfactory roads. A line connecting these important towns opened three months before trains began running from Nottingham to Mansfield, but over 25 years elapsed before the much needed Mansfield-Worksop link became a reality. To some extent, the Midland was forced into building the line because of threats from rival companies, although massive untapped coal reserves beneath the intended course certainly provided an incentive. Again, it is necessary to delve back into history to set the scene.

One of the most ambitious projects resulting from the success of the Liverpool & Manchester was the Sheffield, Ashton-under-Lyne & Manchester Railway, authorised in 1837 but originally planned under another title back in 1831. The prize was lucrative business between Lancashire and South Yorkshire, which had developed thriving textile and metalworking industries respectively. However, there was a daunting barrier in the form of a particularly inhospitable stretch of the high Pennines. The line picked its way through Millstone Grit moors with their veneer of bleak peat bogs and breached the watershed by means of the notorious Woodhead Tunnel. Such was the scale of the task, that through services between Manchester and Sheffield had to wait until 1845.

By this time the Railway Mania had erupted and an extension eastwards was inevitable. The Sheffield & Lincolnshire Junction Railway, which planned to lay tracks through Worksop and Retford to Gainsborough, received the go ahead on 3rd August 1846. Meanwhile, the Great Grimsby & Sheffield Junction had been formed to provide a connection with the North Sea Coast. All three railways form-

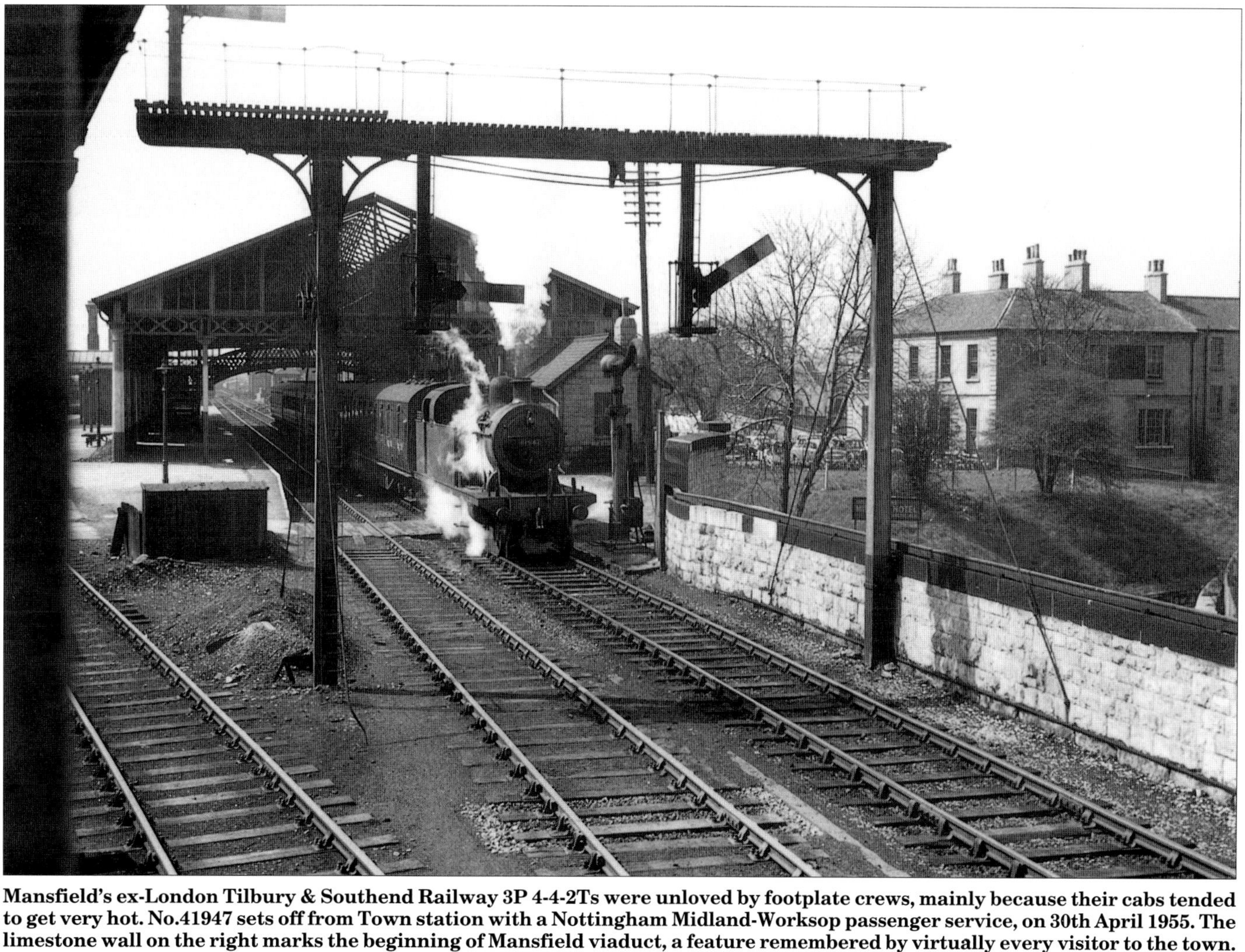

Mansfield's ex-London Tilbury & Southend Railway 3P 4-4-2Ts were unloved by footplate crews, mainly because their cabs tended to get very hot. No.41947 sets off from Town station with a Nottingham Midland-Worksop passenger service, on 30th April 1955. The limestone wall on the right marks the beginning of Mansfield viaduct, a feature remembered by virtually every visitor to the town. Photograph Jack Cupit.

ing the revolutionary chain of communication between Manchester and Grimsby (one a reality, the others still on paper) amalgamated on 27th July 1846 and the Manchester, Sheffield & Lincolnshire company was born. This gritty northern child soon grew up and became established as a result of its mining and manufacturing hinterland. Eventually it became a thorn in the side of the Midland, at Mansfield, Nottingham, Leicester and even London – but that story belongs to later chapters.

The Sheffield-Gainsborough line opened on 17th July 1849. No doubt in deference to the Duke of Newcastle's great house at Clumber, just four miles away, the MS&L spent a lot of money on Worksop station. Built of pale grey Steetley stone, its very long frontage was a remarkable interpretation of the Jacobean style. Besides a variety of gables, there were rich embellishments including strapwork, medallions, rusticated pilasters (fixed columns with projecting blocks) and a broken pediment above the entrance. Somewhat strangely, the proportions and positioning of the windows detracted from the overall elegance.

With ready access to South Yorkshire collieries, the MS&L probably only cast the occasional idle glance towards the Derbyshire coalfield at first. It was a different matter with the Great Northern. Having established itself as a major trunk route from London to the north by the late 1850s, the company began to look for other districts to exploit, particularly those rich in minerals. The Erewash Valley was tempting, but physical access would be difficult and no doubt the Midland would put up a good fight. However, that part of the Dukeries between Mansfield and Worksop had untapped reserves of coal and, as yet, no railways.

Despite its adventures involving Manchester and London, the Midland had to address the prospect of having a stranger in its midst. Consequently, plans for a Mansfield-Worksop line were drawn up in 1859, though the proposed alignment was very different to the one eventually built. It left the existing branch near King's Mill, passed well to the west of Mansfield town centre then headed north-eastwards to Langwith Mill, near Cuckney. After negotiating the little gorge at Creswell Crags, the route made for Belph, Steetley and finally the MS&L at Shireoaks. The scheme was presented to Parliament in 1860, but was soon withdrawn because of opposition from the Duke of Portland and Duke of Newcastle, who objected to it infringing on their estates at Welbeck and Clumber respectively. An incidental bonus of this failure was that heavy coal trains would never disturb the prehistoric cave dwellings at Creswell Crags, recently proposed as a World Heritage Site.

This Midland initiative woke the MS&L from its slumber and from the summer of 1860 territorial rivalry was rampant in north Nottinghamshire. Both the Midland and MS&L introduced Bills for a Mansfield-Worksop line during the 1861 session, the Great Northern deciding to make mischief by supporting the MS&L venture. By mutual consent, these schemes were withdrawn as well, and in November 1861 the Midland promised the MS&L running powers to Mansfield. All went quiet for a while, understandable in view of the Midland's commitment to its London Extension from Bedford to St. Pancras and ambitions to reach Carlisle, to become the third Anglo-Scottish trunk route.

Exploitation of the Coal Measures north of Mansfield was becoming increasingly likely, however, and both the MS&L and Great Northern were still eager to muscle in on the area. In February 1864 the Midland board expressed concern over 'other parties at work' and set about resolving its dispute with the Dukes. This was duly accomplished and the landowners then declared their support for a re-routed Mansfield-Worksop line. Plans were drawn up, but the Great Northern re-entered the fray by promoting a Mansfield & Retford Railway. The Midland was in no mood to grant further running powers and opted for a straight fight. Fortunately, Mansfield's industrialists were wholly behind the Midland scheme and Parliament decided in favour of it, while rejecting the line from Retford. Besides sanctioning the Worksop route, the Mansfield Lines Act of 5th July 1865 authorised a new passenger station in Mansfield and the railway to Southwell, which is described in Chapter 5.

The extension to Worksop adopted a far more direct course than that proposed in 1860. Firstly, rather than avoid the pronounced hollow drained by diminutive Lady Brook, the railway would stride purposefully across it on a viaduct dominating Mansfield town centre. Further north, a succession of cuttings through Magnesian Limestone was required where ridges got in the way. Finally, instead of keeping to low ground in the vicinity of Creswell Crags, a tunnel was to be driven under Bakestone Moor near Whitwell. Unfortunately, the country was in the grip of a trade recession during the late 1860s and the Midland had already

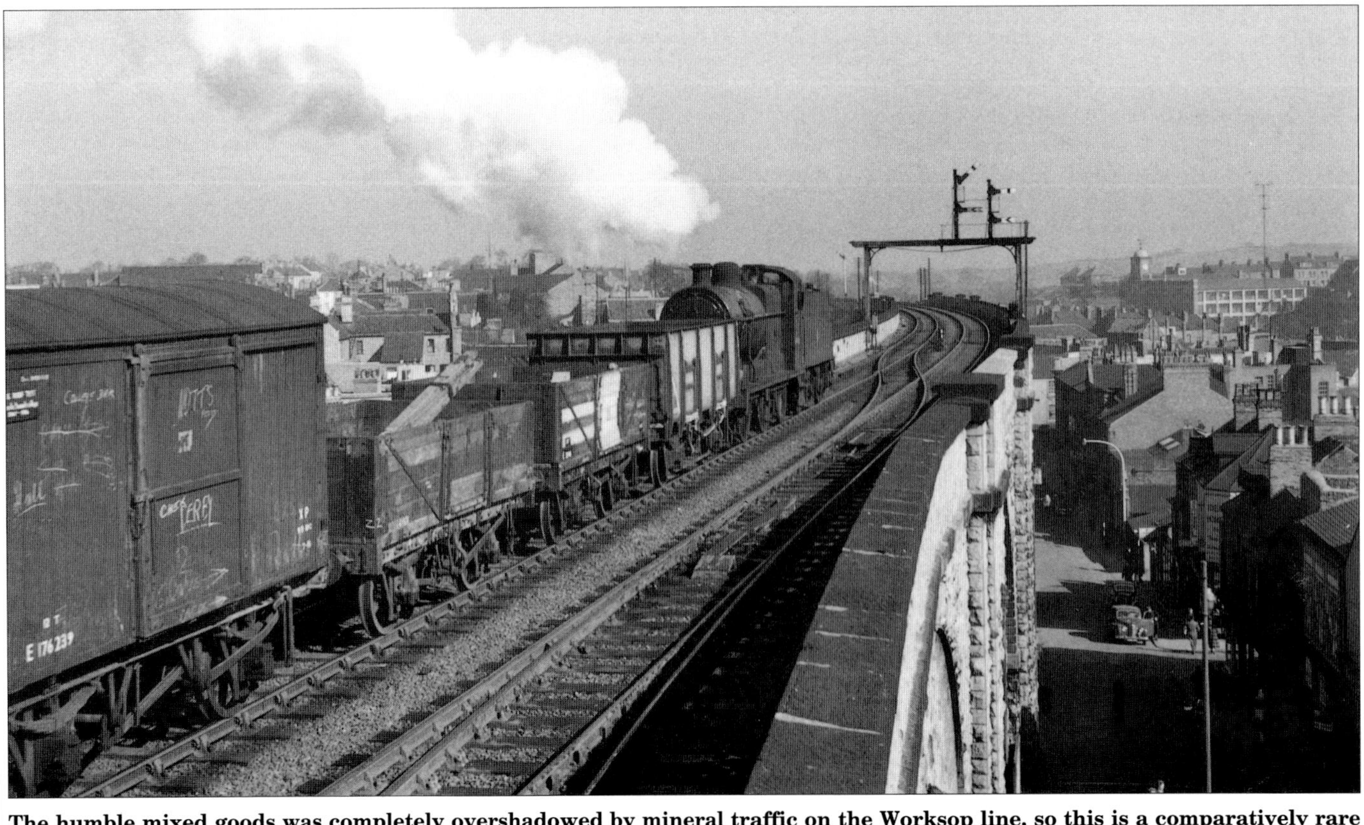

The humble mixed goods was completely overshadowed by mineral traffic on the Worksop line, so this is a comparatively rare view. Ex-LMS 4F 0-6-0 No.44415, which spent its entire BR existence allocated to Mansfield shed, sets off with the down pick-up on 11th March 1956. The large building with the domed tower, to the right of the signal gantry, was a metal box making factory. White Hart Street in the foreground was created by the railway works and named after a hotel demolished when the viaduct was built. This inn was originally the home of Dame Cecily Flogan, one of Mansfield's benefactors. Photograph Jack Cupit.

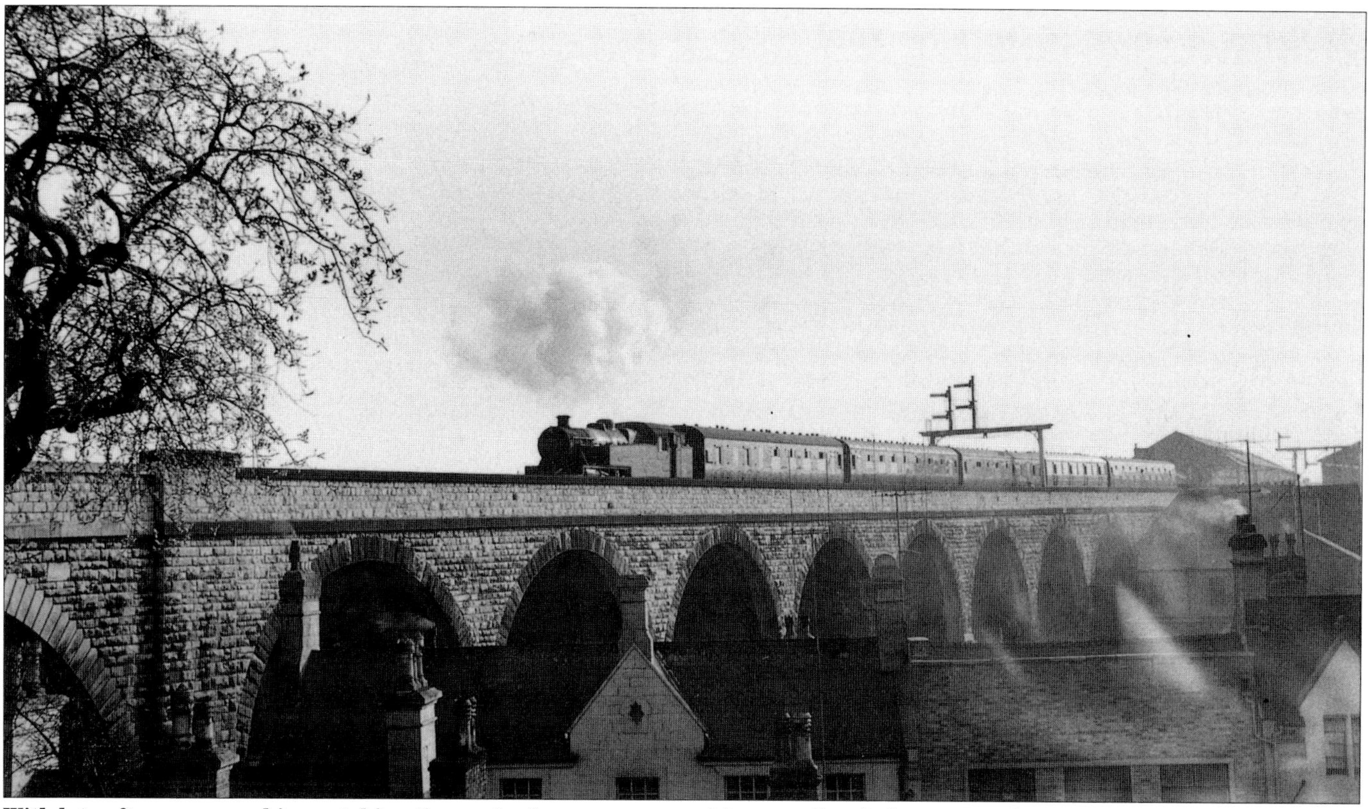

With late afternoon sunshine catching the smoke from numerous chimneys, the viaduct across the Ladybrook valley is seen from the north west on 23rd March 1961. Stanier 2-6-2T No.40142, a late transfer from Kentish Town to the Midlands, leaves Mansfield with a Nottingham Midland-Worksop train, comprising three corridors of LMS design, an ex-LNER Gresley vehicle and a BR Standard bringing up the rear. Photograph Jack Cupit.

spent a lot of money on the line to St. Pancras. Accordingly, Mansfield had to wait even longer than expected for its new outlet.

Tenders were sought at the end of January 1869 and work finally began in June 1870. The large cutting at Langwith was tackled first, and blocks of limestone from this excavation were used to build up the piers of Mansfield viaduct. Whitwell tunnel caused all manner of problems, despite its modest length, for the tough rock proved very difficult to crack and required seemingly endless charges of gunpowder. It was eventually completed in December 1874. Meanwhile, the Southwell line had opened for passenger traffic in spring 1871 and for eleven months the trains used Mansfield's original terminus. The new through station opened on 1st March 1872, but for over three years it, too, functioned as a terminus.

Passenger traffic over the Mansfield-Worksop route commenced on 1st June 1875. Over 150 people took a trip on the first train, about a hundred of them trav-

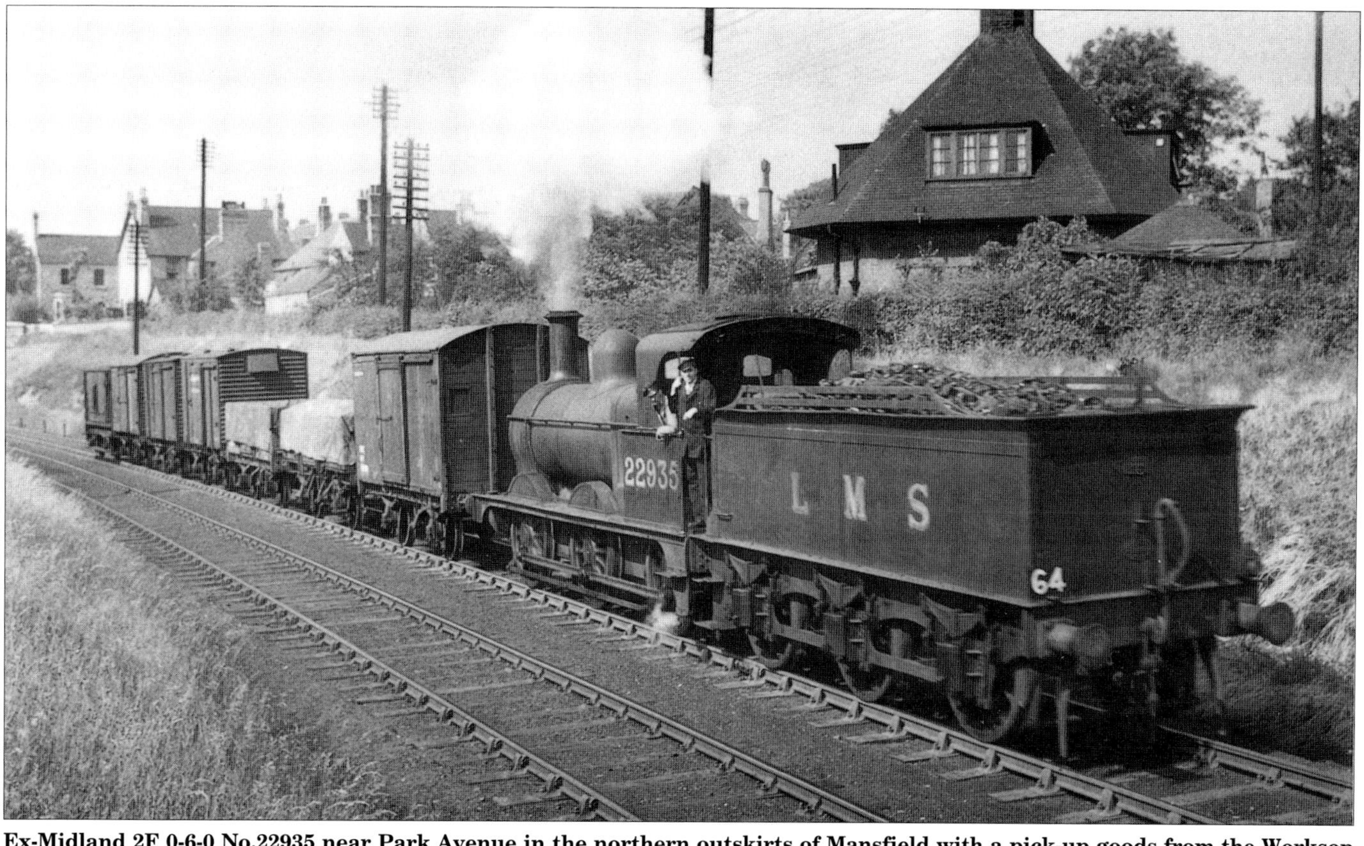

Ex-Midland 2F 0-6-0 No.22935 near Park Avenue in the northern outskirts of Mansfield with a pick-up goods from the Worksop direction, 24th June 1948. Although apparently in good condition, the engine was withdrawn soon afterwards. Photograph Jack Cupit.

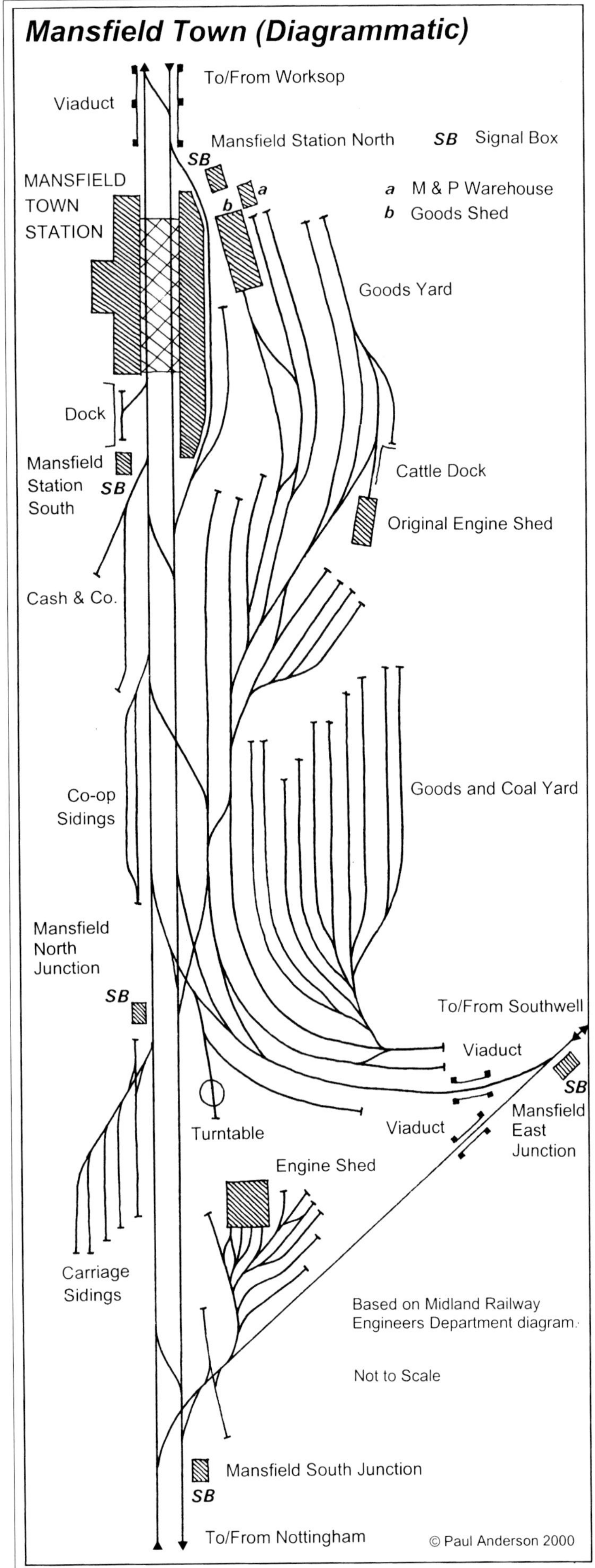

elling only as far as Mansfield Woodhouse, no doubt to get a view of their town from the new viaduct. The villagers of Shirebrook, Langwith and Creswell also turned out in force to witness the occasion – little did they realise how the line would change these communities. Initially, the timetable consisted of three Midland services each way between Mansfield, Worksop and Retford, together with three MS&L trains from Mansfield to Sheffield and back. The engine of the inaugural working from Sheffield was decorated with flags, flowers and evergreens – clearly the MS&L was determined to celebrate its running powers in style! Midland and MS&L goods traffic began in September and November 1875 respectively.

A journey from Mansfield to Worksop began in spectacular fashion with the lofty transect of Church Street and Market Street by means of the fifteen arch viaduct which reached a maximum height of about seventy feet. The line then curved its way through Crow Hill before running along an embankment as far as Mansfield Woodhouse. Another viaduct, approached by cuttings, spanned Pleasley Vale. A further cutting near Shirebrook was followed by the substantial excavation through more limestone at Langwith. Beyond Creswell the railway plunged into Whitwell tunnel (544 yards) before a gradual descent through spacious countryside to the Ryton Valley and Shireoaks West and East Junctions, much of it on embankments. Generally, the route was on a falling gradient from around 400ft. at Mansfield to just below 150ft. on the approach to the MS&L main line, although there were slight rises at Shirebrook, Langwith and Whitwell. The steepest gradient on the 13¾ mile line was a modest drop of 1 in 110 through Whitwell tunnel.

Stations on the Worksop line enjoyed a quality of architecture unsurpassed previously or subsequently on Mansfield's railways. The new building at Mansfield itself was a particularly good example of a medium size station, especially for the 1870s. Although single storey, it stood on a hill and managed to look quite prominent when viewed from nearly every direction. The main building stood on the down (northbound) side and was unusually deep from the platform face to the road elevation. In essence, it consisted of a large rectangular block parallel to the tracks and a somewhat taller centrally-placed entrance building projecting well into the driveway. Pale grey limestone was used throughout for the walls and the very low pitched hipped roofs had hardly any eaves at all.

Unusually for the Midland at this period, the overall feeling harked back to 'Railway Italianate' styling of the 1840s, details of the building accentuating this impression. The tall chimneys were distinctly classical, each of them having a prominent cornice supported by ten small brackets. Large quoins (corner stones) finished off each angle of the walls. All windows were square-headed and had exaggerated dripstones featuring scroll brackets, while the impressive entrance doorway and the rear arcade leading to the platform were round-headed. There was a more subdued version of this building on the up side. Even more remarkable for the Midland during the 1870s was the provision of an iron and glass pitched roof across the platforms and tracks. On 4th September 1892 a third platform face was added on the east side, beyond the train shed. Contemporary canopies provided this with some shelter.

The other five stations up to Worksop had a degree of symmetry about them, both individually and as a group. They were designed by J. Crossley, the Midland's engineer. Mansfield Woodhouse, appropriately, was almost entirely built of timber. The twin pavilion style was well established by now, but in this case the roof above the recessed central section was set back by only a couple of inches. Horizontal planking, square beading above the windows, highly ornate brackets supporting the eaves, low pitched roofs and elegant stone chimneys gave the buildings considerable character. The charm of this 'model station' was not lost on the *Mansfield Advertiser* which enthused, *'The building is entirely of wood and is relieved with some very pretty ornamentation. A kind of entrance hall, one side of which is nearly all glass, leads to the ticket office. The ladies waiting room is a little gem, tastefully furnished and carpeted.'*

Shirebrook, Langwith and Elmton & Creswell (originally just Cresswell, but with the extra 's'!) displayed the 'Midland

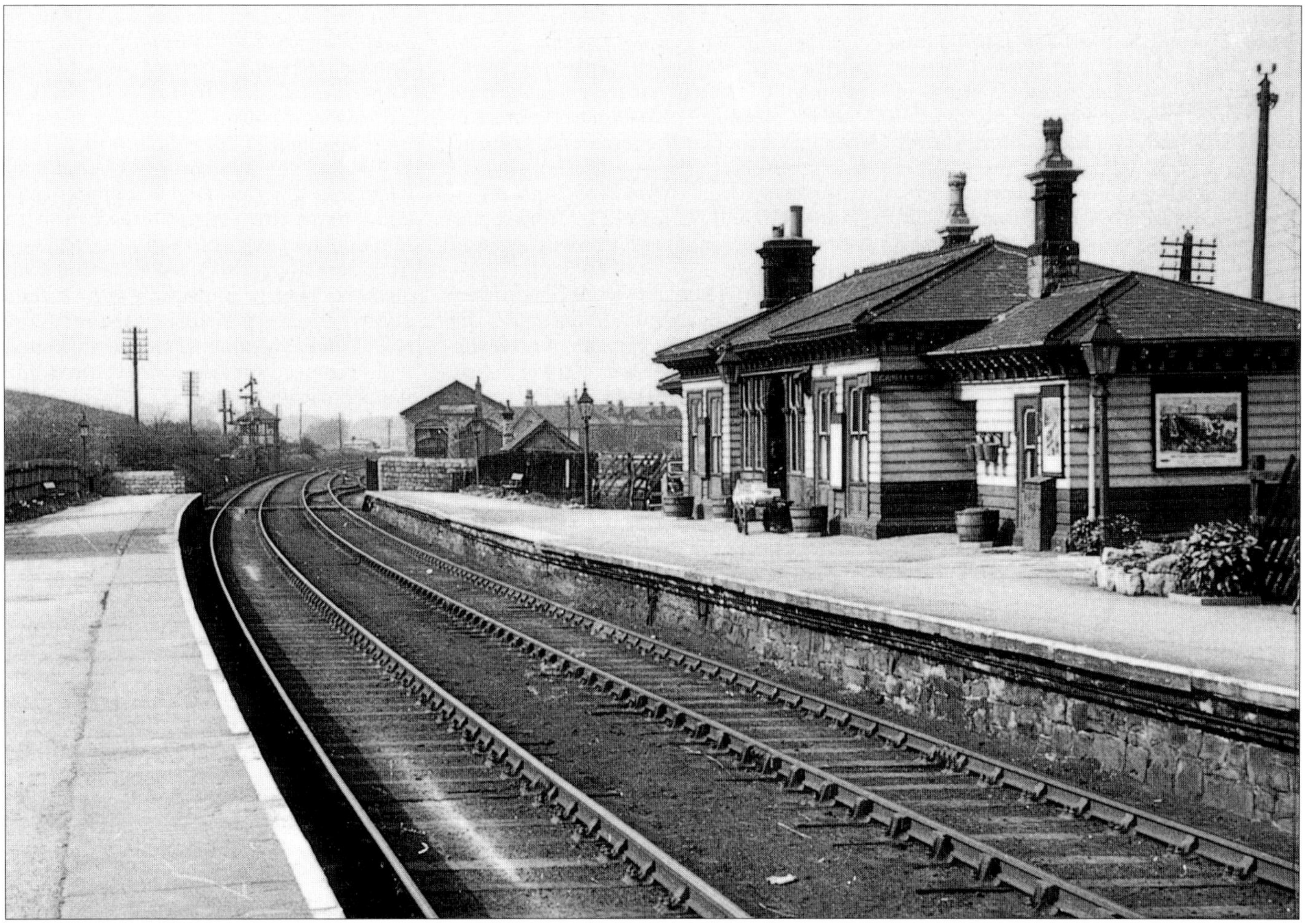

Mansfield Woodhouse station during May 1953. It incorporated 'some very pretty ornamentation' in the opinion of the *Mansfield Advertiser*, writing about the passenger facilities when they were brand new. The bracket signal in the distance controlled the divergence of the Pleasley line. Although the timber buildings are no more, the stone goods shed in the centre of this view has been incorporated in the present station. Photograph Robert Humm collection.

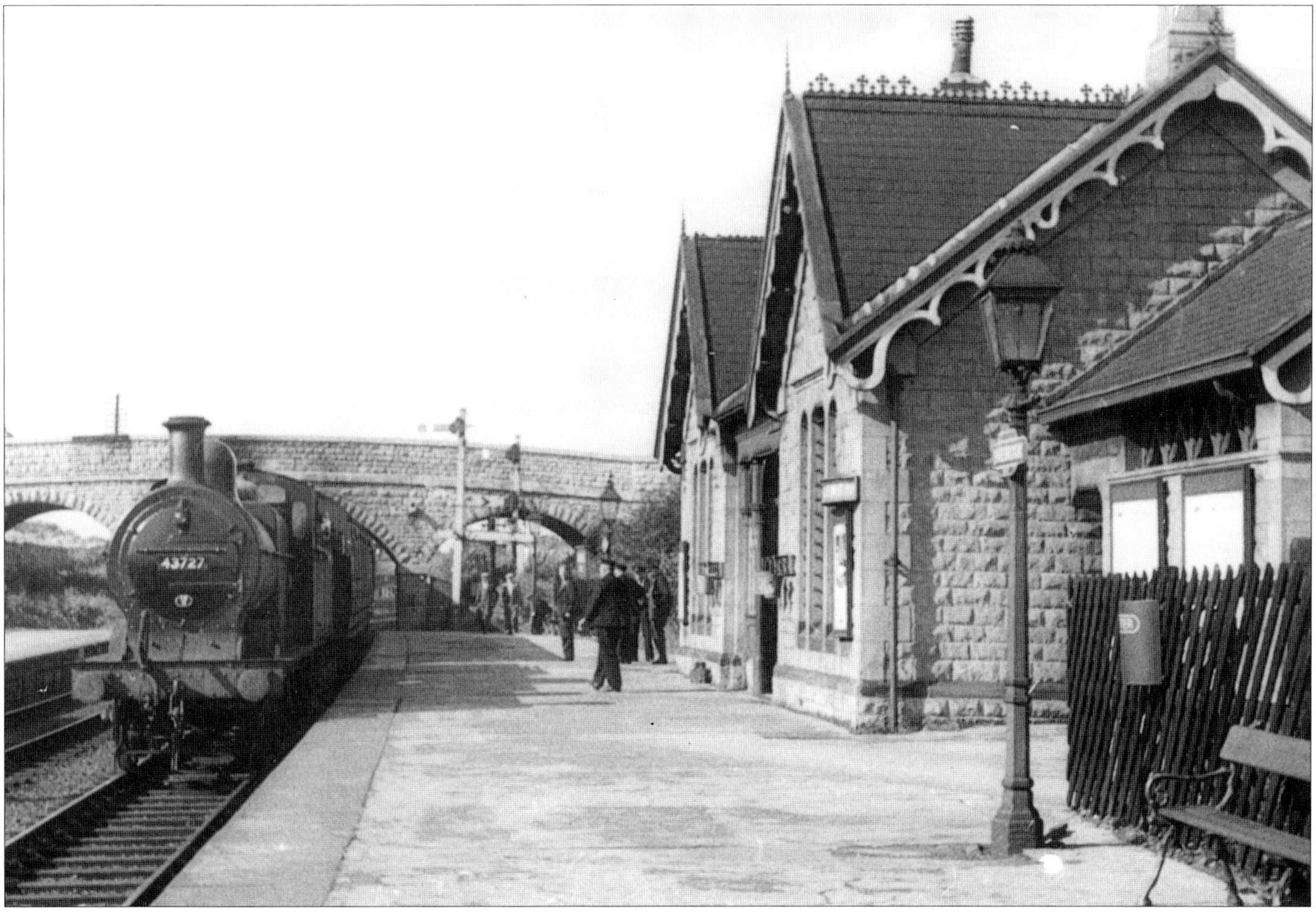

At Shirebrook the Midland used local limestone for the road overbridge and 'Derby gothic' station building. Mansfield 3F 0-6-0 No.43727 rolls into Shirebrook West with a Worksop-Nottingham Midland train on 2nd September 1953, a timeless scene which could almost be of Midland Railway vintage. Photograph H.C. Casserley.

Gothic' style so famously applied to the Settle & Carlisle stations. Local limestone was employed and the twin pavilions were very prominent by virtue of their steep roofs at right angles to the track. Flamboyant bargeboards, first seen on the Nottingham-Lincoln line, adorned each gable while lozenge windows, introduced by the Midland Counties, featured in the central screen. There were some delightful details, notably the spiky ridge tiles and the ornate finials at each apex, making these extremely attractive buildings. Whitwell, paid for by the Duke of Portland, reverted to the general outline of Mansfield Woodhouse, although rough-hewn stone was used in this case and the pavilions stood out more. Pairs of round-headed windows incorporated little columns with decorative capitals, a truly gothic feature straight out of a Victorian church. In marked contrast to all this splendid architecture, Langwith Colliery Platform (1895) and Shirebrook Colliery Platform (1911) were basic in the extreme and were only served by unadvertised miners' 'Paddy' trains,

Apart from holiday excursions and a summer-only Heysham-St Pancras express which ran prior to World War One and called only at Mansfield, passenger services between Nottingham and Worksop remained purely local in character. By 1890 fifteen trains a day headed north from Mansfield, although these included workings over the Teversall, Bolsover and Clowne lines which had been built through the coalfield. The MS&L (later Great Central) trains to Sheffield ceased in 1905, although a Midland (then LMS) service from Mansfield to Sheffield via the Lancashire, Derbyshire & East Coast Railway route through Clowne (Chapter 7) lasted from 1904 to 1939. Eventually most trains ran through from Nottingham to Worksop, although right at the end there were still short workings from Nottingham to Mansfield and Mansfield to Worksop. A survey of passenger services will be found in Chapter 6.

However, it was goods traffic – mainly coal – that increasingly dominated the line from the 1880s. Instead of attempting a detailed description, it is worth listing the various sidings and depots on the central section between Kirkby in Ashfield and Elmton & Creswell. The sheer quantity and variety of facilities along this 12½ mile stretch speak for themselves. This was the situation in 1912; passenger stations are shown in capital letters and each of these had an adjoining goods yard as well:
KIRKBY IN ASHFIELD; Kirkby Gasworks; Kirkby Sidings (Empties}; Butterley Co. Brick Yard Siding; Kirkby Colliery (Summit Pit); Kirkby Sidings (Loaded}; Butterley Co. Sand Sidings; SUTTON JUNCTION; Adlington's Flour Mill Siding; Meggitt's Bone Works Siding; Boot's Siding; Bleak Hills Siding; King's Mills (Caudwells) Siding; Sanderson & Robinson's Siding; Tomlinson's Quarry and Brickworks Siding; Witham's Timber Yard Siding; Cash's Siding; MANSFIELD; Sherwood Colliery & Sidings; MANSFIELD WOODHOUSE; Shirebrook Colliery & Sidings; Warsop Main Colliery Branch; Shirebrook Gasworks; SHIREBROOK; Burkitt's Siding; LANGWITH; Langwith Colliery & Sidings; Sheepbridge Co. Sidings; Norwood Sidings; Creswell Colliery & Sidings; ELMTON & CRESWELL.

Engine sheds at Mansfield and Kirkby in Ashfield dealt with most Midland traffic in the district. A small single-road shed near the original terminus at Mansfield was established when the line from Nottingham opened, but this soon became woefully inadequate as new lines and collieries opened. A standard four-road brick building with twin pitched roofs replaced the old facilities in 1882. It stood within the triangle formed by the Mansfield-Nottingham line and the north and south facing spurs of the Southwell route. For many years there was an impressive complement of twenty or so Johnson 0-4-4Ts for working passenger trains throughout the coalfield. Ex-London Tilbury & Southend 4-4-2Ts had replaced the residue of them by 1945, with these in turn finally displaced by Stanier 2-6-2Ts in 1956. A variety of 2F, 3F and later 4F 0-6-0s hauled coal and goods traffic, although a couple of Stanier 8F 2-8-0s arrived in 1945, the allocation swelling to a dozen by 1955. Mansfield shed closed in April 1960, men and locomotives transferring to Kirkby in Ashfield. Nevertheless, the building survives in private ownership.

Kirkby in Ashfield shed, just north of the station, was a straight three-road structure opened in 1903 to house up to fifteen engines. Before long, however, it was home to over three dozen 0-6-0s employed almost exclusively on coal traffic. Several Stanier 8F 2-8-0s went there

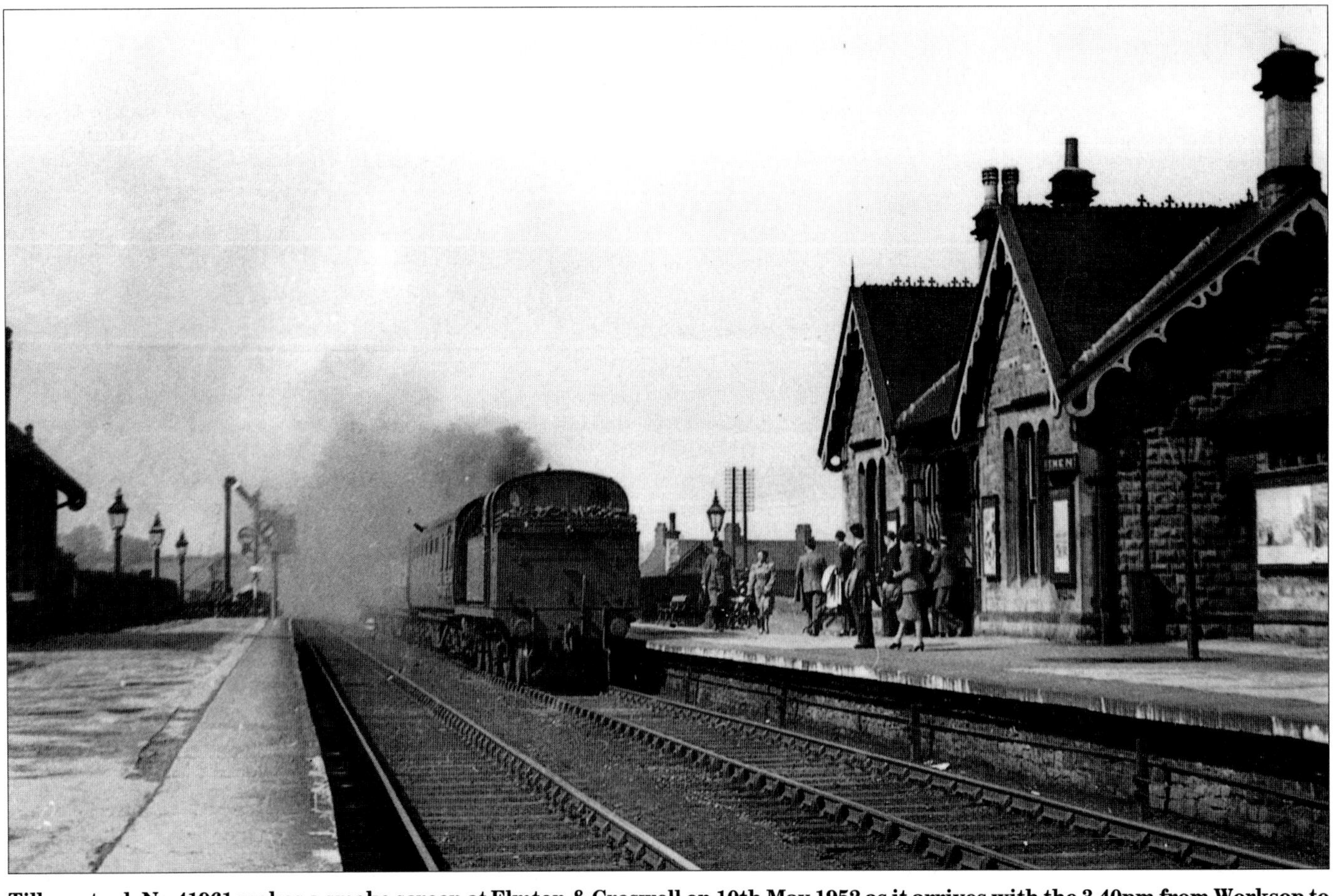

Tilbury tank No.41961 makes a smoke screen at Elmton & Creswell on 10th May 1952 as it arrives with the 3.40pm from Worksop to Nottingham Midland. Bright afternoon sunshine highlights the bargeboards and other ornate features of the attractive station building. Photograph H.B. Priestley.

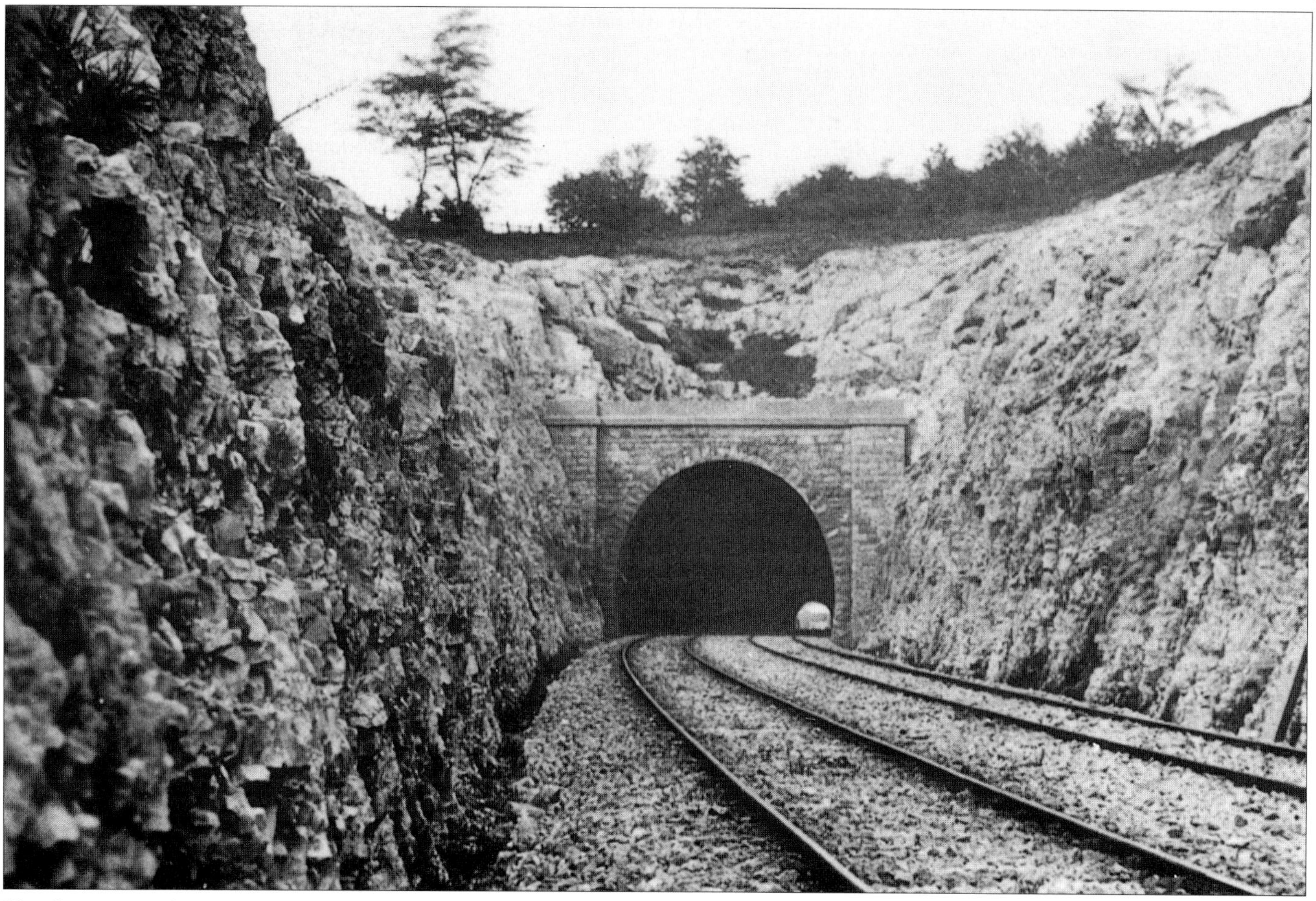

Massive excavations through tough Magnesian Limestone were a feature of the Mansfield-Worksop line. This is the south end of Whitwell Tunnel back in 1875 when the line was new. Photograph Mansfield Public Library.

Whitwell station was paid for by the Duke of Portland who resided at nearby Welbeck Abbey, the principal seat in the Dukeries. It was a stone version of Mansfield Woodhouse and incorporated subtle ornamentation, notably the little gothic columns separating the paired windows. This is the building on a rainy 28th July 1971, prior to being carefully dismantled and re-erected at Butterley by the Midland Railway Trust. Photograph Paul Anderson.

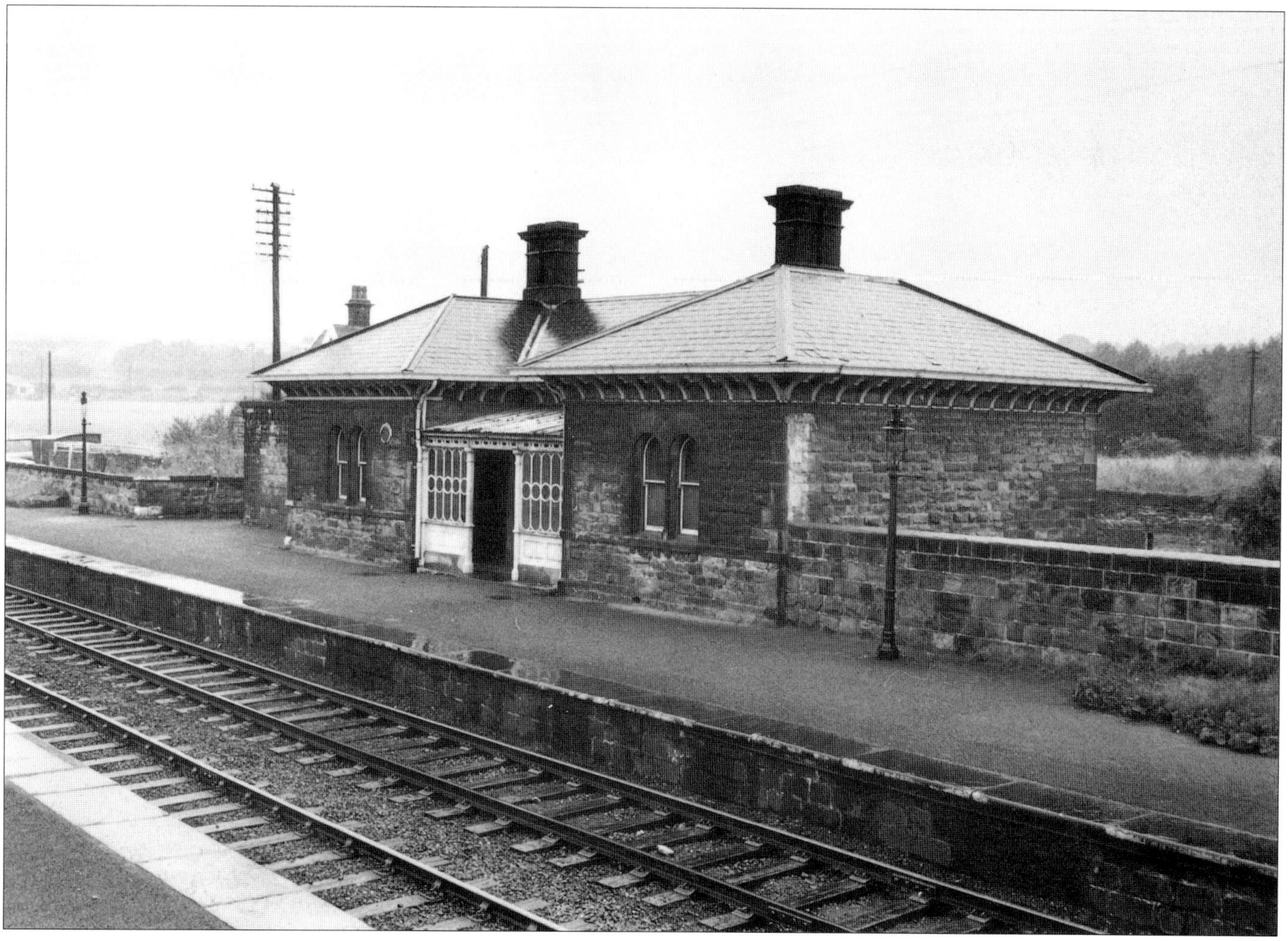

new during the 1930s and by 1945 no less than forty of these engines were allocated to Kirkby, Even so, twenty 0-6-0s were still required. In 1958 a large mechanical coaling plant was installed, followed by a two-road extension to the shed building. The facilities were still barely adequate for such a large stud of locos, and the situation worsened temporarily when Mansfield closed. Three 9F 2-10-0s arrived in 1964, but the shed finished with steam in October 1966. Diesels were housed in the extension for a few years, but after these moved to Shirebrook the buildings were demolished.

16D MANSFIELD Allocations 1950
Ex-Midland Johnson/Fowler 2P 4-4-0
40424, 40454
Ex-Midland Johnson 1F 0-6-0T
41885
Ex-London, Tilbury & Southend Whitelegg 3P 4-4-2T
41940, 41943, 41947, 41958, 41961, 41962
Ex-Midland Johnson 3F 0-6-0
43239, 43522, 43529, 43634, 43727
Ex-Midland Fowler 4F 0-6-0
43874, 43983, 43997, 44004
Ex-LMS Fowler 4F 0-6-0
44394, 44415, 44416
Ex-LMS Stanier 8F 2-8-0
48088, 48119, 48156, 48621, 48643, 48701
Note: No. 41885 was Mansfield Yard Pilot. The 2P 4-4-0s and 3P 4-4-2Ts were for passenger work, although the 3F and 4F 0-6-0s had occasional passenger turns.

16C MANSFIELD Allocation 1959
Ex-LMS Fowler 3MT 2-6-2T
40004
Ex-LMS Stanier 3MT 2-6-2T
40079, 40096, 40146, 40168, 40175, 40184
Ex-Midland Johnson 1F 0-6-0T
41712, 41844
Ex-LMS Fowler 4F 0-6-0
44252, 44415, 44416, 44441
Ex-LMS Ivatt 2MT 2-6-0
46501
Ex-LMS Stanier 8F 2-8-0
48001, 48024, 48088, 48119, 48156, 48272, 48277, 48282, 48405, 48442, 48447, 48541, 48621, 48643, 48701
Note: Nos.41712 and 41844 were Mansfield Yard Pilots. The 3MT 2-6-2Ts were for normal passenger work. No.46501 mainly worked the unadvertised train to Chilwell Ordnance Depot. The 4F 0-6-0s still had occasional passenger turns.

16C KIRKBY Allocations 1950
Ex-Midland Johnson 3F 0-6-0
43468, 43494, 43596, 43773
Ex-Midland Fowler 4F 0-6-0
43895, 43903, 43907, 44021
Ex-LMS Fowler 4F 0-6-0
44082, 44140, 44202, 44205, 44206, 44268, 44463, 44470, 44547, 44552, 44589
Ex-LMS Stanier 8F 2-8-0
48000, 48004, 48009, 48029, 48073, 48081, 48092, 48096, 48097, 48098, 48100, 48101, 48108, 48114, 48137, 48138, 48139, 48193, 48214, 48215, 48223, 48224, 48225, 48267, 48268, 48270, 48272, 48282, 48379, 48382, 48383, 48392, 48393, 48403, 48405, 48408, 48409, 48413, 48442, 48530, 48552
Ex-Midland Johnson 2F 0-6-0
58137
Note: No.58137 was for banking coal trains from the Pye Bridge line up to Kirkby in Ashfield.

16B KIRKBY Allocations 1959
Ex-Midland Johnson 3F 0-6-0
43287
Ex-Midland Fowler 4F 0-6-0
43903, 43907, 43923, 43933, 44005, 44023
Ex-LMS Fowler 4F 0-6-0
44118, 44190, 44202, 44268, 44418, 44470
Ex-LMS Stanier 8F 2-8-0
48003, 48004, 48006, 48008, 48009, 48029, 48073, 48081, 48092, 48096, 48097, 48098, 48100, 48102, 48114, 48137, 48193, 48214, 48215, 48223, 48224, 48225, 48267, 48334, 48379, 48383, 48392, 48393, 48395, 48413, 48528, 48552, 48673, 48770
Note that the codes for Mansfield and Kirkby sheds changed between the 1950 and 1959 listings.

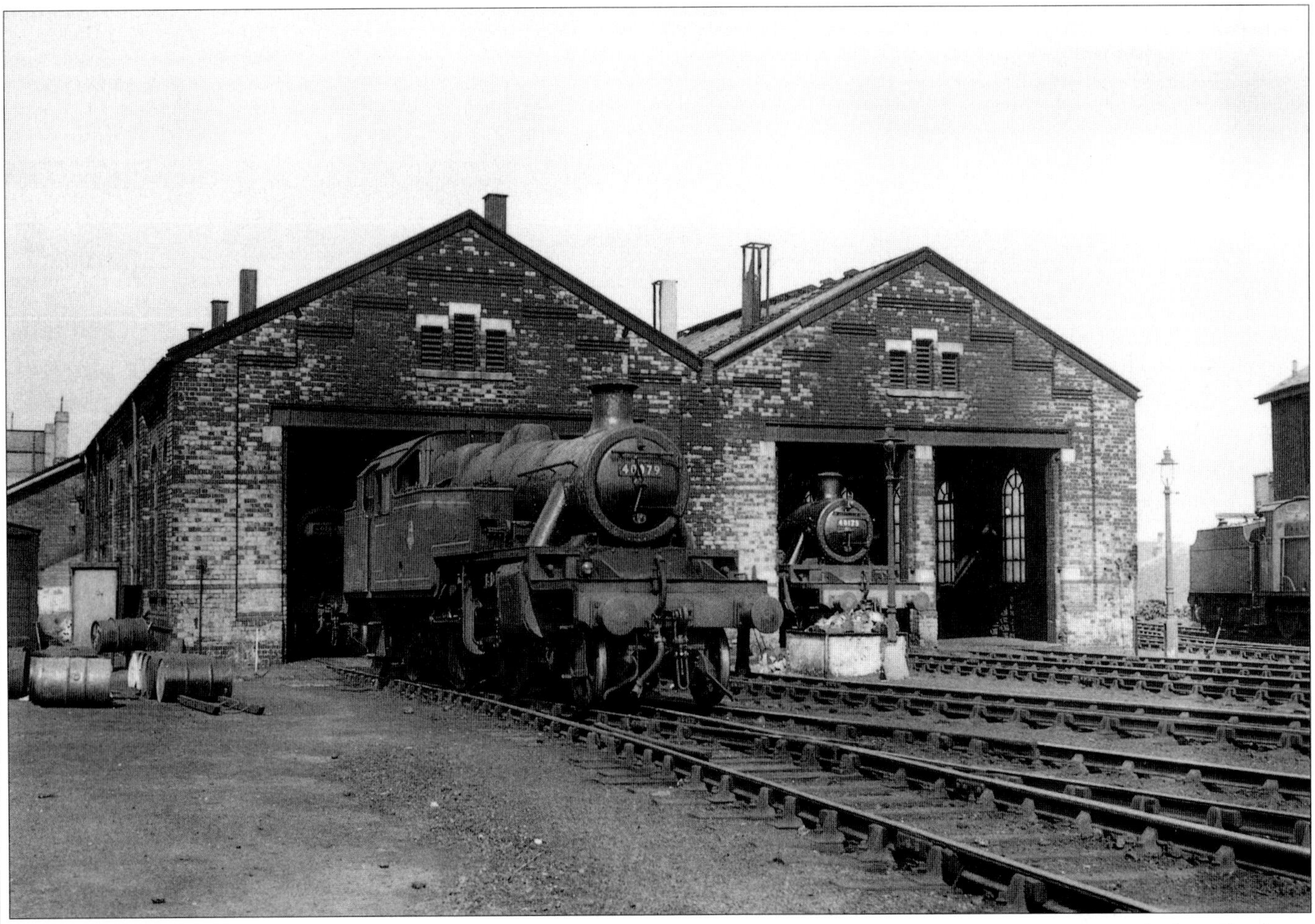

Mansfield shed on 5th May 1957 with three of its smart Stanier 3MT 2-6-2Ts at rest. Nos.40184, 40079 and 40175 had earlier been transferred from Hellifield, Kentish Town and Saltley respectively, to replace ageing Tilbury tanks on Nottingham-Worksop passenger trains. A 4F 0-6-0 languishes on the far right. Although long closed as a motive power depot, the structure remains intact and is still used for industrial purposes. Photograph Jack Cupit.

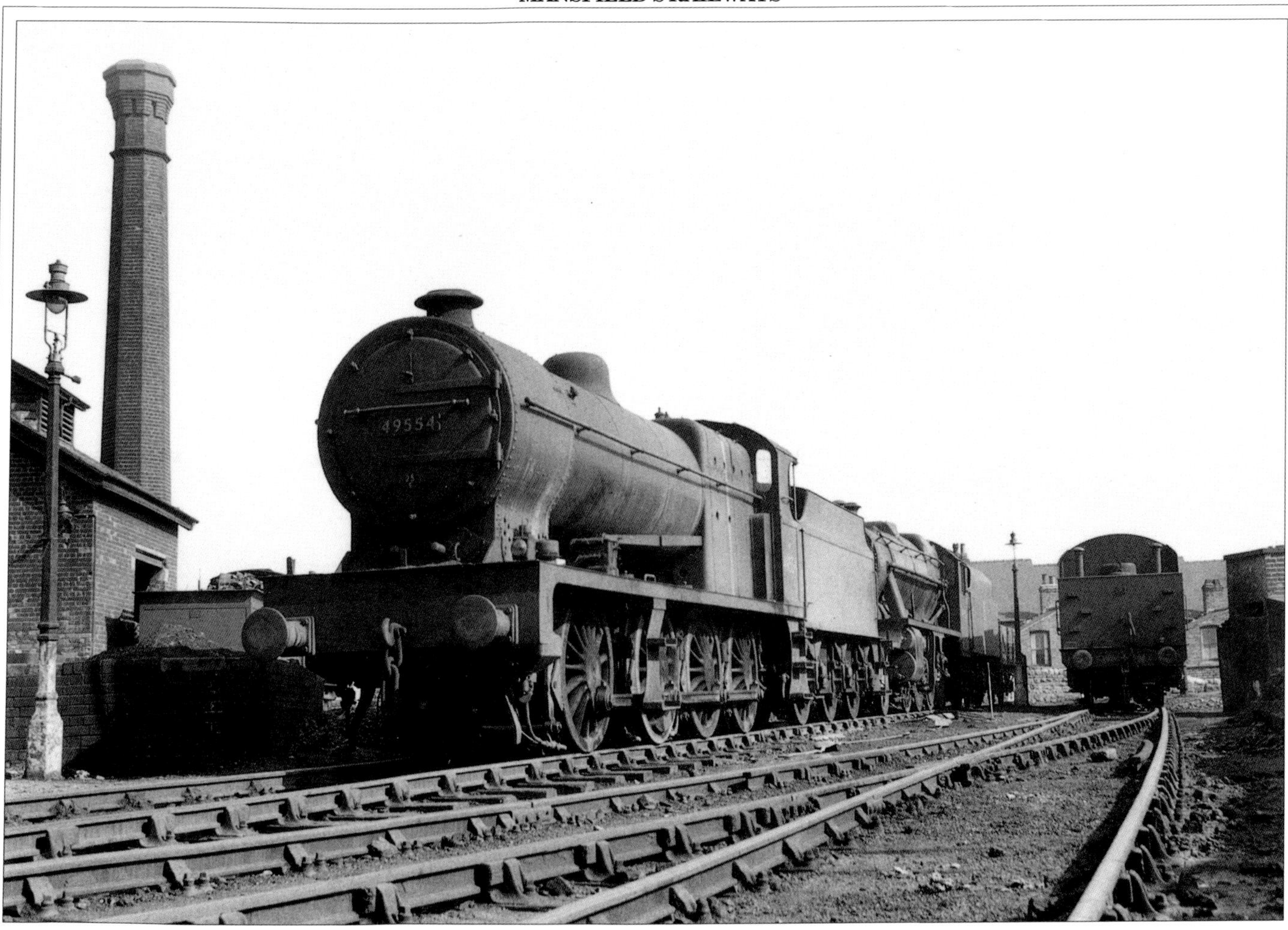

Mansfield shed often had a stranger in the camp, but rarely as exotic as this one! Spending a quiet Sunday away from home, ex-LMS Fowler 7F 0-8-0 No.49554 of Sowerby Bridge shed near Halifax keeps two domestic 8Fs company on 31st March 1954. Quite why it made its way to Mansfield is unknown. The terraces of Bradder Street in the background housed many railwaymen. Photograph Jack Cupit.

A panoramic view of Kirkby in Ashfield shed on 7th April 1963 with a fraction of the large allocation of 8F 2-8-0s simmering in the yard. On the extreme right in front of the ash plant is Black 5 4-6-0 No.44982 of Blackpool shed. Could the engine have come in on a return excursion, deputising for one from the East Midlands which had failed away from home? The Victorian houses in the background were down wind of both Kirkby shed and Summit Colliery, thus receiving liberal doses of drifting smoke. Now the pollution has gone – but so have the jobs. Photograph Jack Cupit.

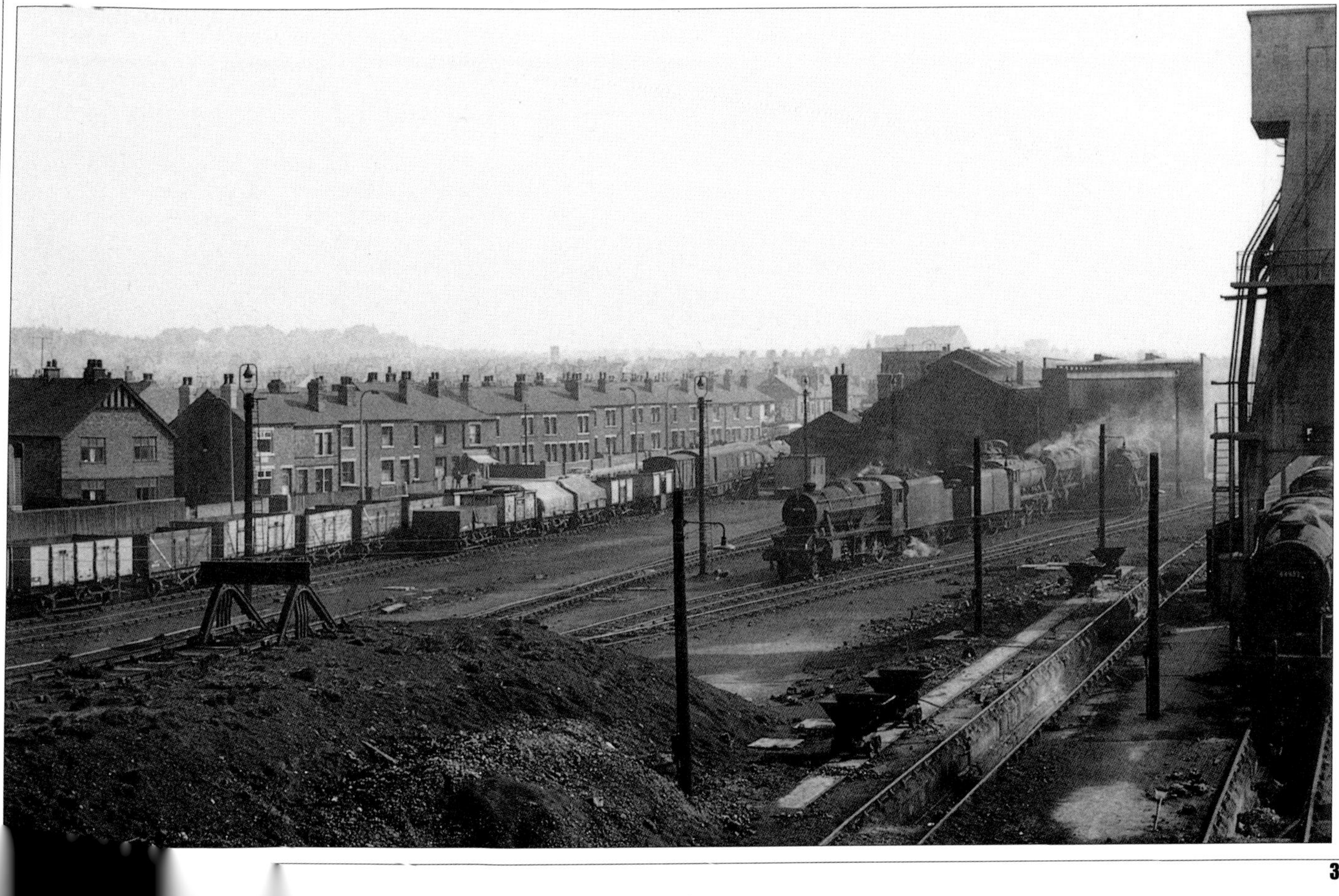

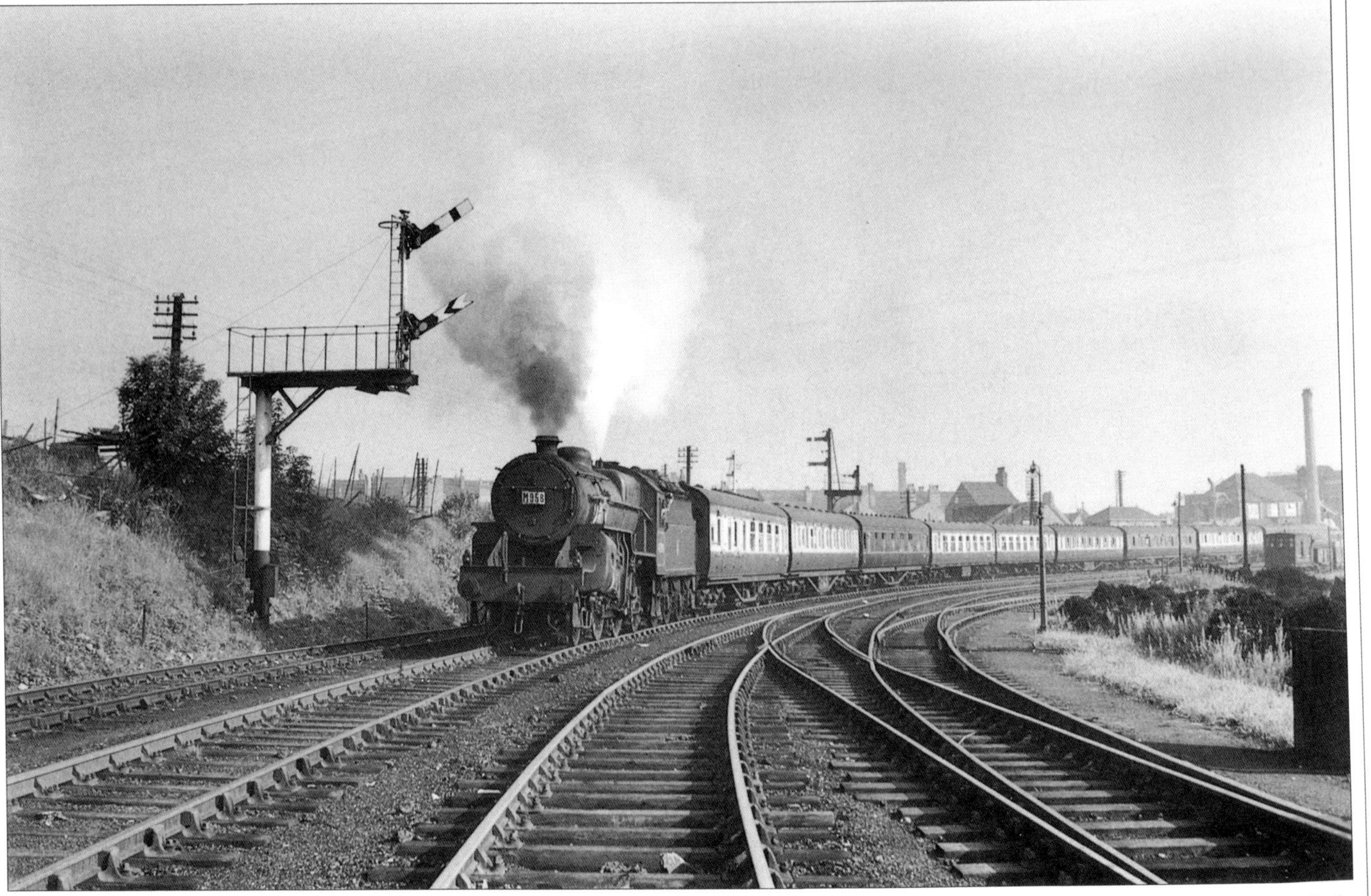

On 31st July 1957, Sheffield Crab No.42797 leaves Mansfield with an excursion from Teversall Manor to Cleethorpes. The train is taking the spur from North Junction to East Junction, the signal box controlling the former being visible above the sixth and seventh coaches. This curve is single track – all the other lines are sidings. After the regular passenger service was replaced by an LMS bus in 1929, the spur was normally only used by local goods trains, together with the occasional race special to Rolleston Junction. It closed in December 1966 because of the condition of the Maun viaduct. Photograph Jack Cupit.

The east to south curve was by far the busier connection with the Southwell line, mainly because of loaded coal trains heading for Kirkby Sidings and empties returning to the collieries. On 2nd December 1950, 8F No.48156 approaches Mansfield South Junction signal box with an up mineral working. Mansfield shed, the home of this engine, is prominent on the left. Just behind the camera, a path known as Cinderella Walk crossed the tracks by kissing gates, providing unofficial access to the shed. Photograph Jack Cupit.

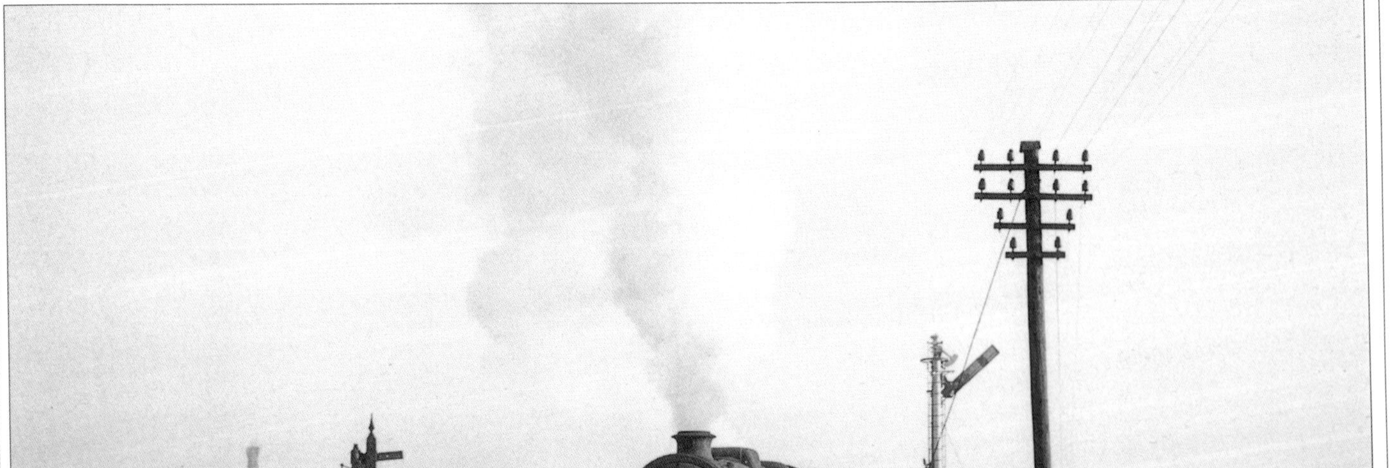

Chapter 5

MANSFIELD and SOUTHWELL

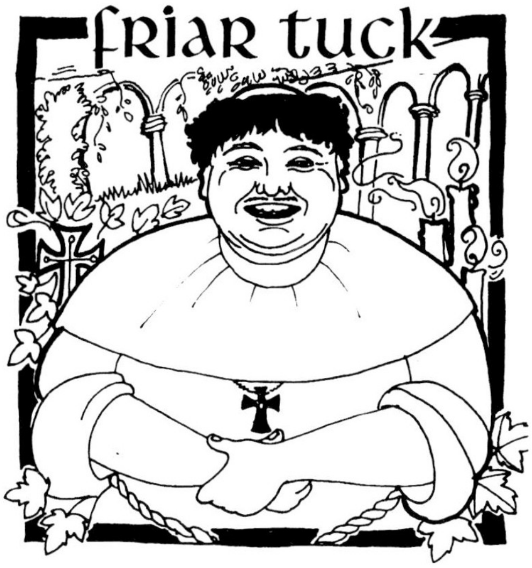

The railway which headed south eastwards from Mansfield past Rainworth, Farnsfield and Kirklington to Southwell could truly be called the line of the Forest, for this area was the heart of Sherwood. Blidworth, just south of Rainworth, was said to be the home of Maid Marian as well as the burial place of Will Scarlet, while the monumental fight between Robin Hood and Friar Tuck supposedly took place at nearby Fountain Dale. In a more prosaic vein, the name of Farnsfield was derived from 'fern', as in the forest undergrowth. Although the Midland's Mansfield to Southwell branch was single track and had an endearing charm all of its own, it was never meant to be a local link. If anything, it was seen as part of a strategic route connecting east and west Nottinghamshire, though the promise of lucrative coal traffic and the threat of Great Northern invasion was also very much behind its conception.

Southwell is a noble town and was a place of some significance over a thousand years ago. Since 1130 it has been famous for the splendid Minster with its twin west towers, later capped by tall spires. Framework knitting became firmly established during the 1700s and a couple of silk mills were operating by 1840, but essentially Southwell remained a major ecclesiastical centre and a market town for farming villages in the Greet Valley and surrounding hills. On 16th July 1846, just under three weeks before the Nottingham-Lincoln extension opened, an Act of Parliament was obtained for a 2½ mile branch from Rolleston Junction to Southwell. The line was very easy to build and opened on 1st July 1847. Although the town was considered important enough to warrant a railway, the service it received was abysmal at first. Trains were withdrawn at the beginning of August 1849, reinstated during April 1852, taken off again in March 1853 and finally brought back permanently on 1st September 1860. At one time, a horse-drawn carriage ambling along no doubt rusty track just once a week was deemed sufficient to meet demand in Southwell.

When this solitary weekly train ran, it was almost certainly in connection with market day at Newark, a bustling town on the River Trent six miles east of Southwell. Newark had been an important coaching stop on the Great North Road prior to the Railway Age, but remained prosperous because of its highly productive agricultural hinterland. Furthermore, there was a long tradition of mutually beneficial trade with the industrial Erewash Valley. When the Great Northern 'Towns Line' opened in 1852, Newark gained a new lease of life as a result of its strategic position on the main East Coast route. The town also became a natural starting point for a line westwards, should the Great Northern wish to launch an attack on the Erewash coalfield.

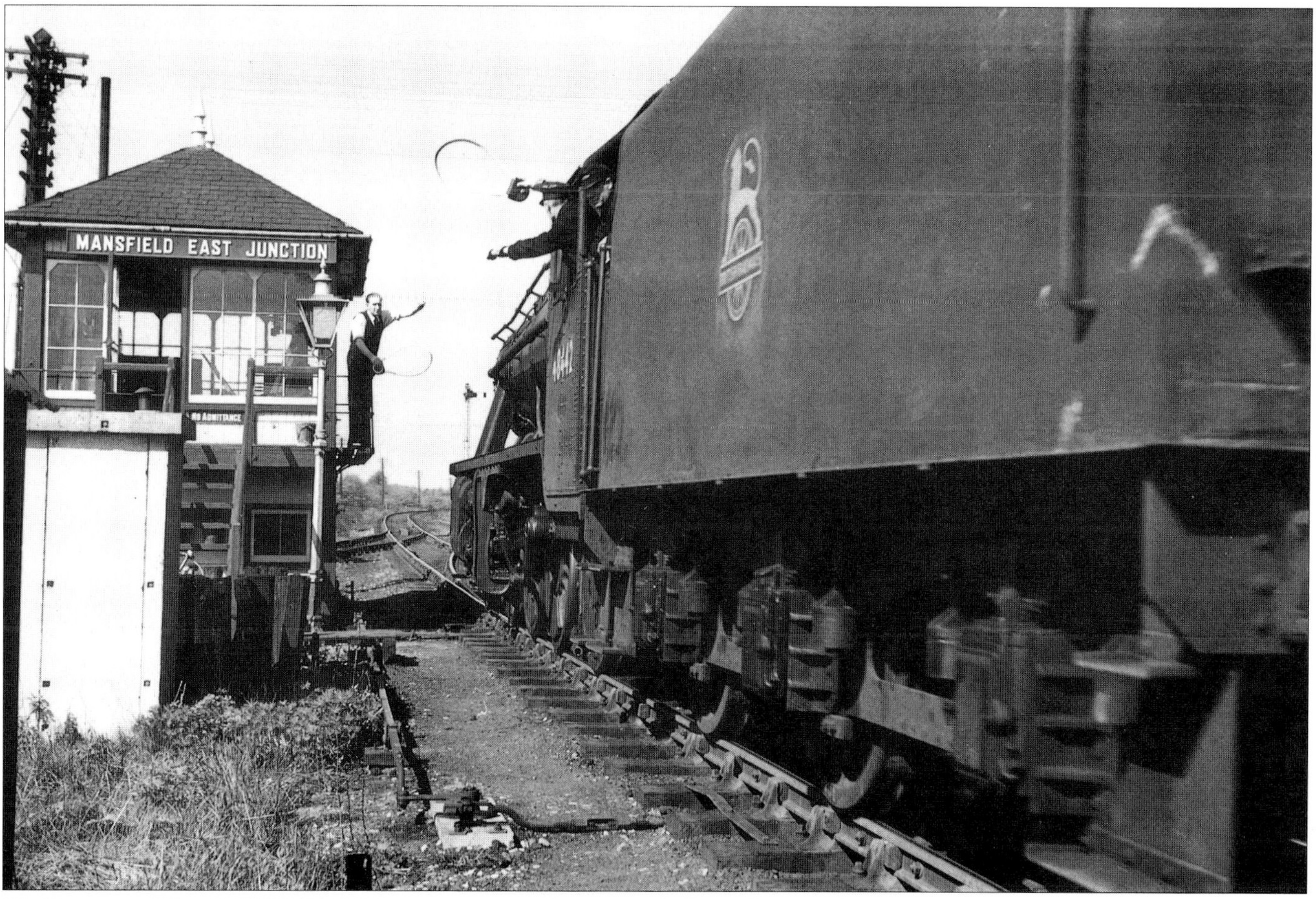

The fireman of Mansfield 8F No.48442 prepares to exchange single line tokens at Mansfield East Junction on 12th May 1956. This loaded coal train will take the line straight ahead towards Mansfield South Junction. Note the trap points beyond the signal box and the north curve bearing right immediately in front of the engine. Photograph Jack Cupit.

The Midland was fully aware of the vulnerability of its eastern flank and there was talk of a Mansfield-Southwell line while plans were being formulated for the Worksop extension. On the plus side, coal reserves were known to exist below the sandstone of Sherwood Forest and any objections from the Great Northern were bound to be dismissed as that company had no existing interests in either Southwell or Mansfield. However, the Midland's directors decided against the project as it was most unlikely that any deep coal would be mined in the foreseeable future and the potential income from agricultural traffic hardly justified the cost of building the line. Furthermore, coal rates between Mansfield and Newark would have to be reduced because of the shorter distance.

The Board had not reckoned with John Barrow of Southwell, a wealthy gentleman with influence in high places, who threatened to build the railway himself. Somewhat taken aback by his stance, the directors changed their minds and embraced the idea of keeping the Great Northern at bay while safeguarding an area rich in coal reserves. A major stumbling block remained, one that was worlds apart from the territorial ambitions of rival railway companies. Although the actual forest was still quite extensive at the time, large tracts had been cleared for farmland. For example, during the mid-1700s Parliament sanctioned the enclosure and clearance of a large area of woodland around Blidworth for agricultural purposes. Local people were proud and very conservative, as portrayed in James Prior Kirk's novel *Forest Folk*, so the industrialisation associated with railways was seen as an anathema. So, rather than stress the potential coal traffic, the Midland emphasised the advantages of the line to the rural economy. Farmers and foresters were largely quiescent and John Barrow was smiling, so Parliament duly sanctioned the railway as part of the Mansfield Lines Act of 5th July 1865.

In view of its heavy expenditure on the Bedford to St. Pancras project, the company sought an extension of time for the Mansfield-Southwell line. When the contractor finally got the go ahead, work progressed rapidly on this single track railway through relatively easy terrain and it opened for all traffic on 3rd April 1871. The distance from Southwell to the junction with the Mansfield-Nottingham line was 12¼ miles.

Once the line had climbed out of the Maun Valley, it was generally downhill all the way to Southwell and Rolleston Junction, along Bunter Sandstone as far as Farnsfield, and then on Keuper Sandstone into the Vale of Trent. Earthworks became lighter as the railway progressed eastwards, so much so that the last 3½ miles through Southwell to Rolleston Junction were laid directly on the ground surface. There were no level crossings on the Mansfield-Southwell section. Overbridges usually consisted of brick or masonry arches and the track was carried on a girder deck where underbridges were required. The only passing loop on the twelve miles of single track from Mansfield East Junction to Southwell was at Farnsfield, a telling indication of the amount of traffic expected at first.

At its western end the line began with two spurs, from Mansfield North Junction and Mansfield South Junction respectively, merging at Mansfield East Junction. Because of the angle of approach, the north facing spur was sharply curved, whilst its south facing counterpart was virtually straight. Each spur crossed the deep valley of the River Maun on its own substantial masonry viaduct. Beyond Mansfield East Junction, the railway climbed from around 400ft. above sea level to over 450ft., affording a fine view of Mansfield on the opposite side of the Maun Valley. A succession of cuttings took the line past stretches of heath, patches of woodland and several large sand quarries as far as Rainworth. Blidworth & Rainworth station occupied a morsel of level ground between a long embankment over the Rainworth Water Valley and the deep cutting through Python Hill.

At Rainworth the line was down to 350ft. and the descent continued past Allamoor Farm to Farnsfield, just above the 200ft. contour. Ahead lay the Keuper Sandstone escarpment, reaching 473ft. at Loath Hill off to the right and 358ft. above Whip Ridding Farm and Pudding Poke Wood away to the left. Fortunately, Ice Age glaciers had carved a gap through the ridge, so the railway managed to reach Kirklington and the upper Greet Valley without the need for tunnelling or adverse gradients. This remote corner of Nottinghamshire had a folklore all of its own and one of the most endearing stories concerns the vicar of Kirklington during the early 1800s. His favourite pastime was shooting ducks in marshland bordering the River Greet. The top of his wooden pulpit made an ideal hide, although it was always back in church for the Sunday service! A gentle descent to 100ft. at Southwell was followed by the lowly passage to Rolleston

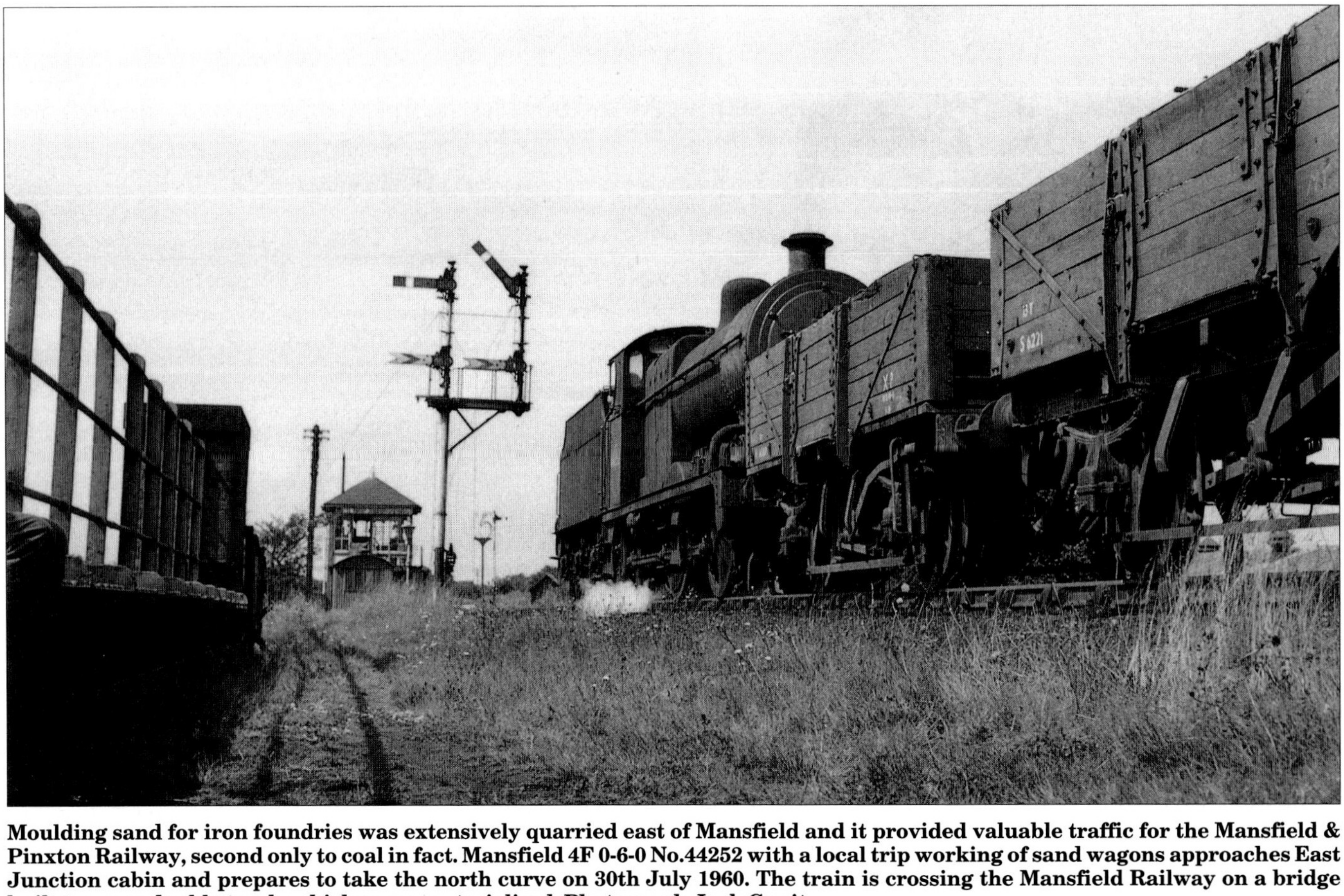

Moulding sand for iron foundries was extensively quarried east of Mansfield and it provided valuable traffic for the Mansfield & Pinxton Railway, second only to coal in fact. Mansfield 4F 0-6-0 No.44252 with a local trip working of sand wagons approaches East Junction cabin and prepares to take the north curve on 30th July 1960. The train is crossing the Mansfield Railway on a bridge built to carry double track, which never materialised. Photograph Jack Cupit.

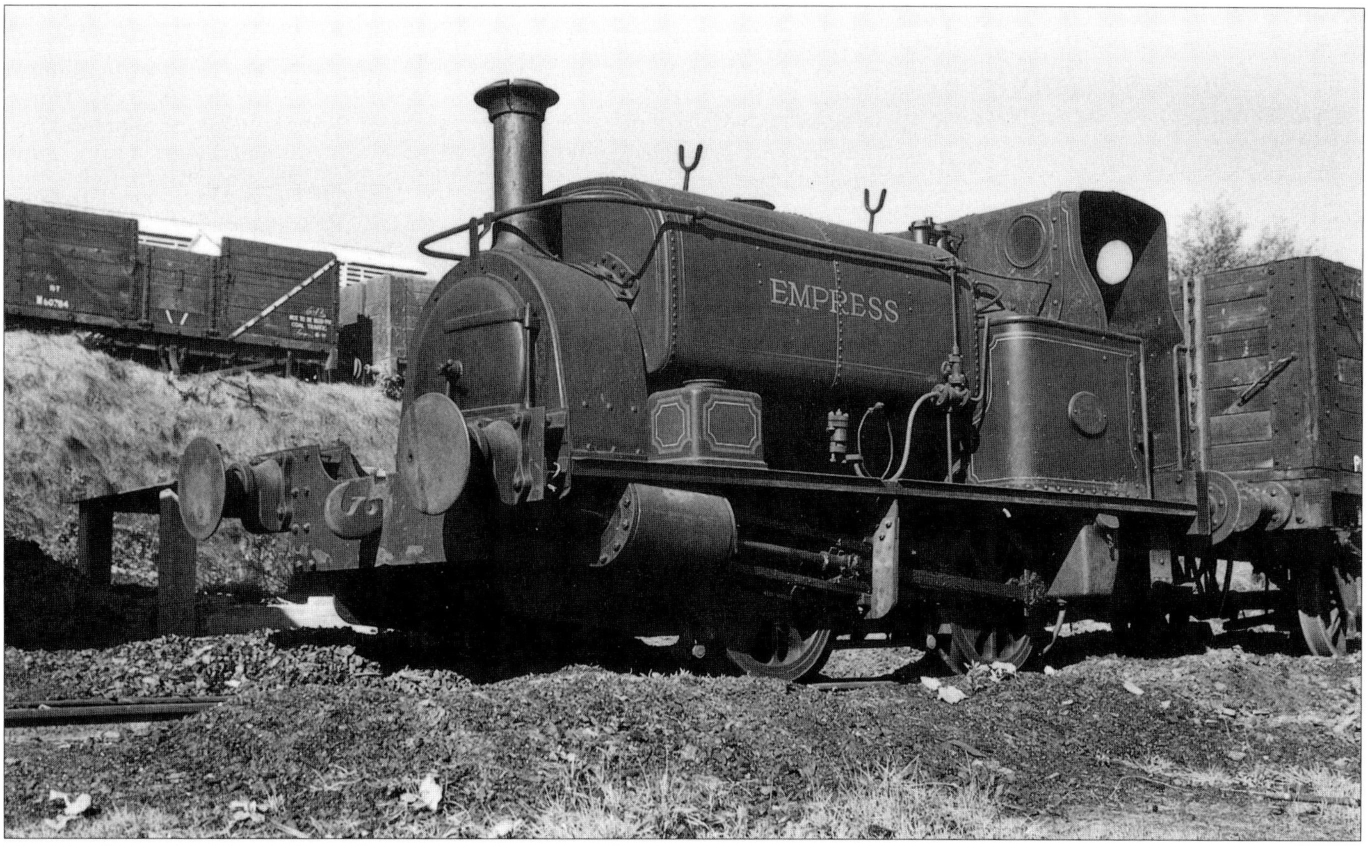

Mansfield Standard Sand Co. had an ancient Manning Wardle 0-4-0ST for working traffic between one of its quarries and the exchange sidings alongside the Southwell line. The industrial branch climbed steeply away from the sand pit and EMPRESS had its work cut out battling up the ferocious gradient with two loaded wagons. This view of the venerable engine was taken on 28th April 1951. Photograph Jack Cupit.

Junction less than 50ft. above sea level.

The three intermediate stations between Mansfield and Southwell were Blidworth & Rainworth (Rainworth until November 1877, then Blidworth until April 1894), Farnsfield, and Kirklington (Kirklington & Edingley until April 1904). They were unlike any other Midland buildings in the Mansfield area and very different from the Derby Gothic twin pavilion style about to make an appearance on the Worksop extension. In fact they looked more like mid-Victorian town houses than railway stations. Domestic accommodation, consisting of a fairly tall gabled block at right angles to the track and a short extension parallel to the platform, did indeed dominate the assemblage. The steeply pitched roofs incorporated attic rooms. Facilities purely for passenger use were almost apologetic, merely further extensions which were somewhat longer but much lower. A prominent dormer window above a porch

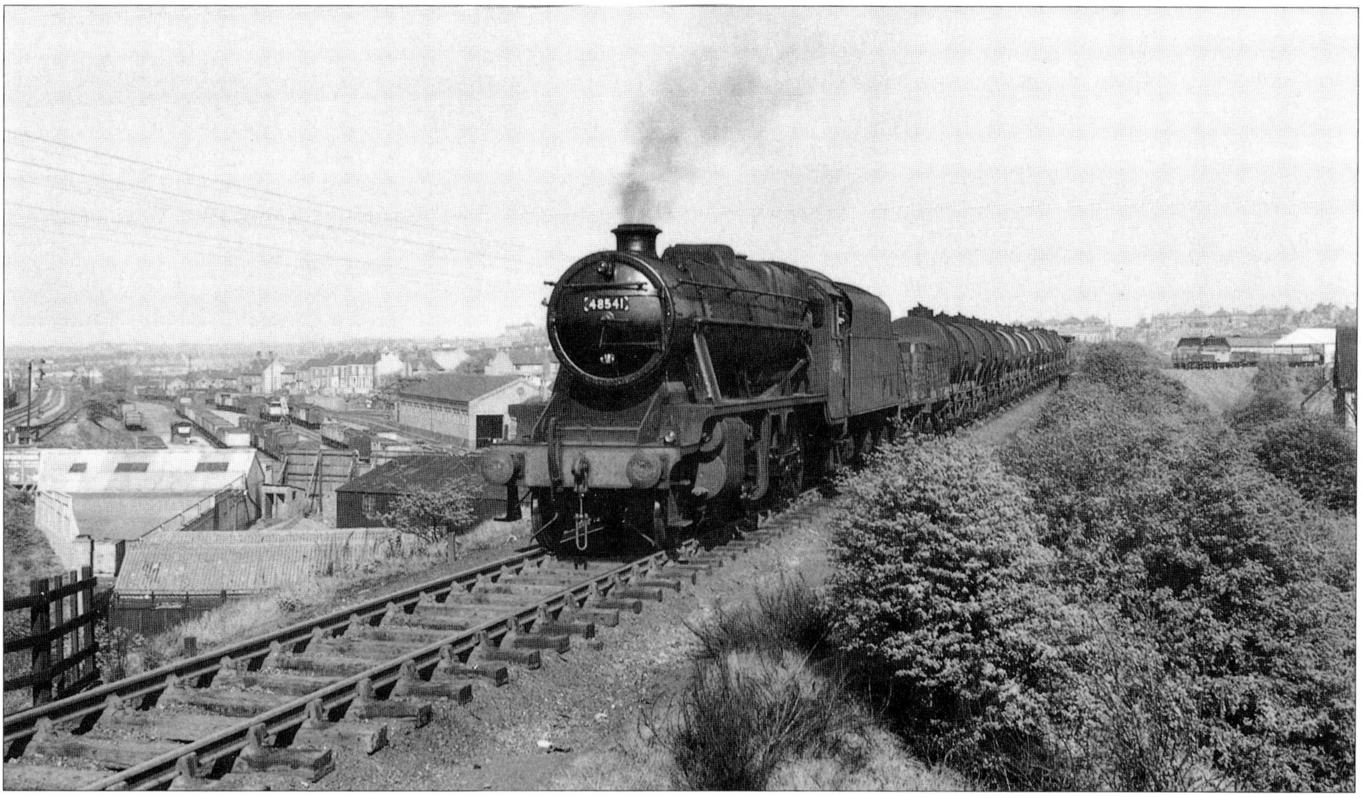

Nottinghamshire once had its own oilfield based on Eakring, where the 'nodding donkey' pumps were more evocative of Texas than Sherwood Forest. On 23rd April 1957, Mansfield 8F No.48541 approaches East Junction with a train of crude bound from Eakring loading sidings on the Mid-Notts Joint line to a refinery near Edinburgh. The extensive Mansfield Railway goods yard can be seen on the left, while one of the Standard Sand Co.'s branches is visible in the right background. Photograph Jack Cupit.

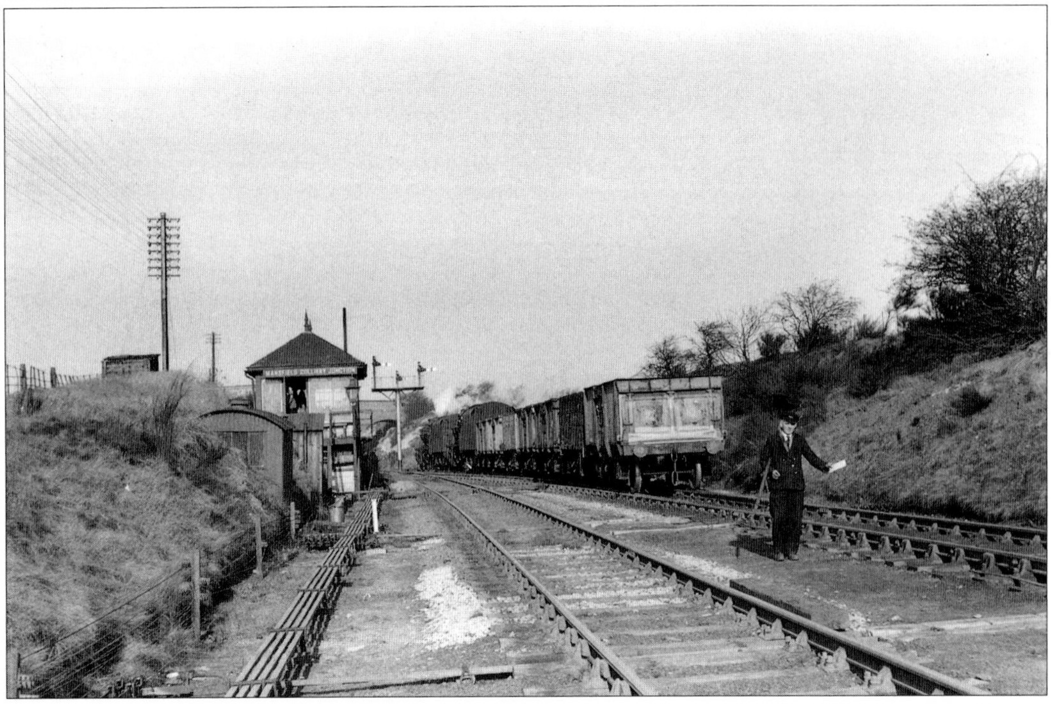

A pair of Kirkby 8Fs, Nos.48100 and 48528, shunting a trip working at Mansfield Colliery Junction on 28th January 1959. The signals, from left to right, control the Southwell line, a small yard of three sidings where coal wagons were sorted and yet more sand traffic was received and the branch to Mansfield (Crown Farm) Colliery. An unusual feature of this location were the wire-operated points at the bottom of the yard – the wires and pulleys are on the left. Photograph Jack Cupit.

faced the approach road, while a lean-to veranda with a gently sloping roof and glass screen provided shelter on the platform side. Red brick was the main building material for all three stations, although there was a touch of indulgent stonework in the form of Tudor lintels for the doorways and, strangely, the tiniest of the windows.

Southwell station was a real concoction. The original station house, which had a complex arrangement of very steep gables with exotic bargeboards and clusters of tall cylindrical chimneys, was similar to some of its near contemporaries on Hudson's Nottingham-Lincoln line. In almost bizarre contrast, crude wooden shelters were provided for waiting passengers. When the Mansfield line was built they were transferred to Beeston and replaced by yellow brick buildings with red brick relief and lozenge pattern windows. Neither of these were very pretty, and they had no affinity with the ancient town of Southwell, but the little goods office nearby was a gem, despite employing the same materials.

The passenger service over the Mansfield-Southwell line was always fairly meagre, usually two trains each way plus a couple of additional workings on Thursday, the market day in Mansfield. In 1907, for example, there were departures from Mansfield at 9.30am, 10.25am (Thursday only), 3.53pm, 6.17pm (Thursday only), and 8.45pm (Saturday only). Arrivals in Mansfield on Thursdays were at 9.10am, 11.44am, 6.12pm and 7.50pm. The 3.53pm from Mansfield reached Southwell at 4.20pm, a reasonable average of 28mph considering the three intermediate stops. Trains in the opposite direction were allowed another seven minutes because of the rising gradient.

Nevertheless, in its early years the line gained a reputation for acute lethargy. A long lasting legend in the railway folklore of the Mansfield area was that a passenger could alight at one of the intermediate stations, stroll to the village pub, down a pint, walk back to the station and join the same train. But it was more than a legend – it was actually true! According to the November 1876 timetable, the 12.00noon (Thursdays excepted) from Newark to Mansfield left Kirklington at 12.43pm and was booked to depart from Farnsfield at 1.30pm. Timings for the 8.35am from Newark were 8.58am from Kirklington and 9.03am from Farnsfield, so passengers on the midday train had up to 42 minutes to walk the half mile to the *Red Lion* and back! Furthermore, the remaining 7½ miles to Mansfield took 40 minutes, an average speed of just over 11mph, which was below the minimum required by the 1844 Cheap Trains Act for a 'Parliamentary' service!

In 1884 the diocese of Southwell was created and the ancient Minster raised to cathedral status. It seems that in response to representations from the Bishop of Southwell, one Mansfield train became a through working to Buxton via Ambergate, the Derbyshire spa town being at the furthest extremity of the new diocese.

Rainworth, Farnsfield and Kirklington goods yards were busy from the outset, dispatching grain, vegetables and livestock while receiving coal, machinery and all manner of sundries necessary for rural life. Without doubt, the railway proved a boon to local farmers, as promised by the Midland. Five sand quarries between Mansfield and Rainworth were served by Mansfield

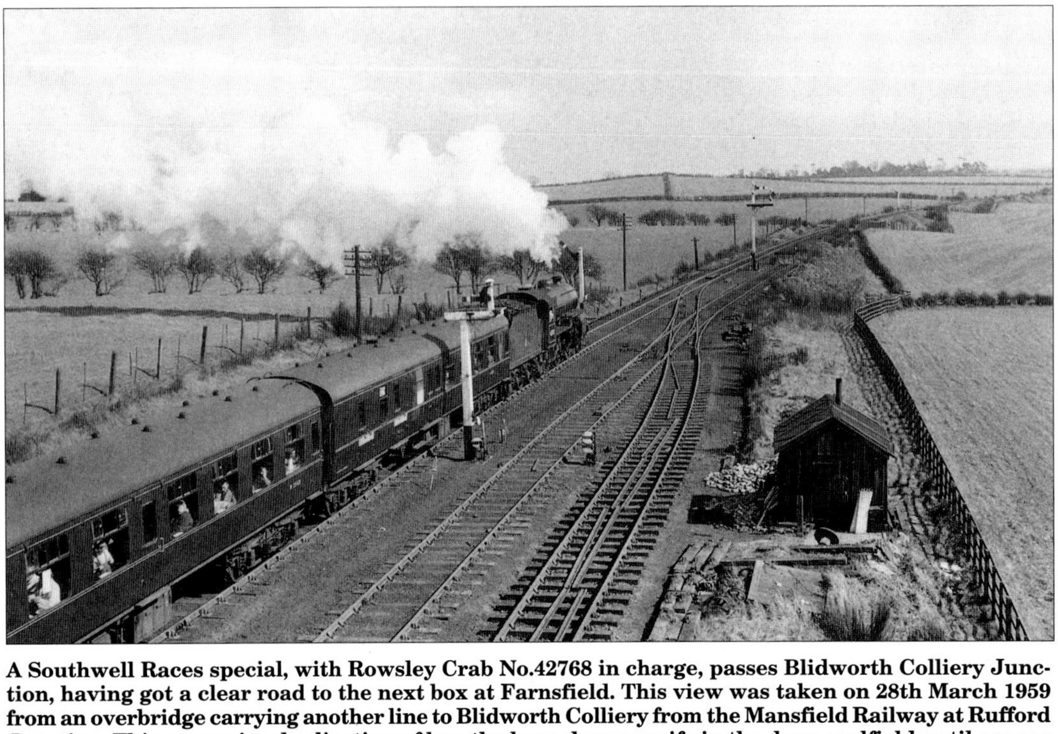

A Southwell Races special, with Rowsley Crab No.42768 in charge, passes Blidworth Colliery Junction, having got a clear road to the next box at Farnsfield. This view was taken on 28th March 1959 from an overbridge carrying another line to Blidworth Colliery from the Mansfield Railway at Rufford Junction. This expensive duplication of lengthy branches was rife in the deep coalfield until a more rational approach was adopted in the form of the LMS/LNER Mid-Notts Joint project. Photograph Jack Cupit.

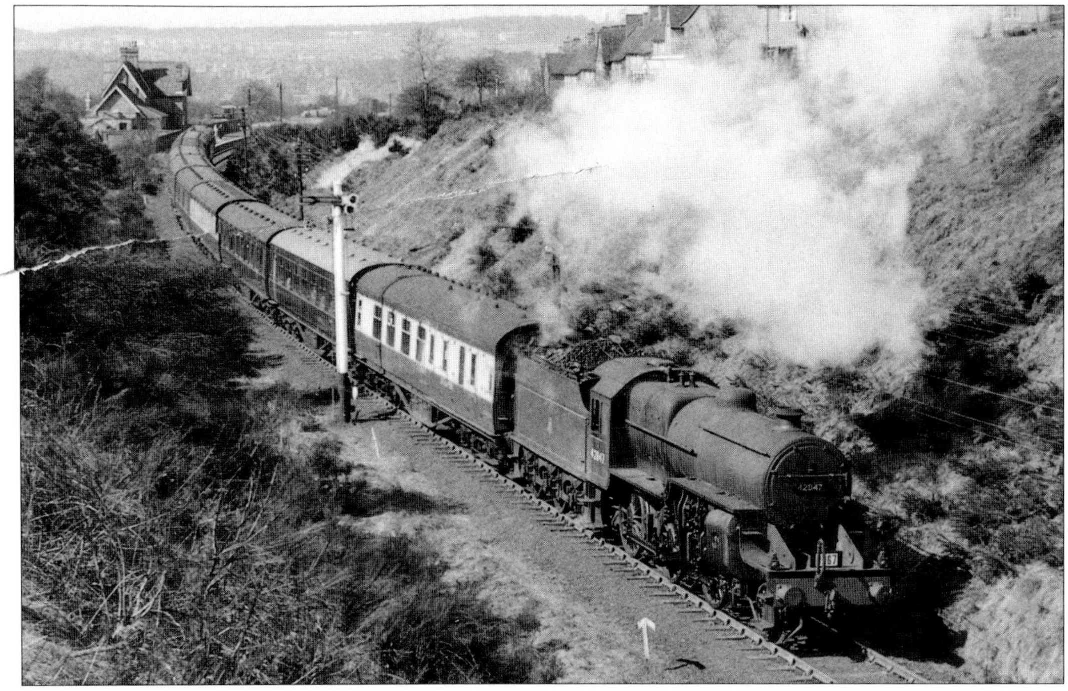

Derby Crab No.42847 heads a Hucknall-Rolleston Junction race excursion past Blidworth & Rainworth station on 28th March 1959. Among the heavy earthworks on the western section of the Southwell line was this cutting through Python Hill. A ridge of sandstone forming Ratcher Hill in the distance heralded more hard work for westbound trains approaching Mansfield. The Midland distant signal belonged to Rufford Colliery Junction. Photograph Jack Cupit.

Sand Co. Sidings, Berry Hill Sand Siding, Standard Sand Co. (and Tar Works) Siding and Sill's Sand Siding respectively. Newark Corporation Waterworks had rail facilities between Farnsfield and Kirklington. Eventually, however, the long anticipated deep mines which had been such a factor in building the line were sunk, the coal traffic then vastly outweighing any other business.

Mansfield Colliery began production in 1905 and the output was well over 4,400 tons a day by 1910. Rufford Colliery opened in 1913, a modern conveyor system allowing a record 1,147 tons to be removed from just one face twenty years later. Blidworth Colliery was sunk in 1923-24, followed by Bilsthorpe in 1927-28. While the latter was under construction, the number of coal mines in Britain reached its peak of no less than 2,569 separate shafts. The Midland and its successor, the LMS, did not have a monopoly of this latest wealth of 'black gold', for the Mansfield Railway and LMS/LNER Mid-Notts Joint Line also provided outlets, as explained in Chapter 9.

By the late 1920s, buses had enticed most passengers away from the Mansfield-Southwell trains, so regular services ceased as early as 12th August 1929. Specials continued, notably excursions for meetings at Southwell Racecourse near Rolleston Junction station. The shuttle between Rolleston Junction and Southwell expired on 15th June 1959, by which time ex-Great Central A5 4-6-2Ts had replaced the venerable Midland 0-4-4Ts which had been a familiar sight on the line for so long. Goods facilities at Farnsfield, Kirklington and Southwell were withdrawn on 27th April, 25th May and 7th December 1964 respectively, the line between Farnsfield and Southwell then closing completely. Private traffic to a mill at Southwell survived for a while, workings being via Rolleston Junction. Blidworth & Rainworth yard closed on 1st February 1965 and coal trains from Farnsfield ceased shortly afterwards, although coal continued to make its way via Mansfield South Junction until September 1983. Meanwhile, former railway property found other employment. The station houses at Farnsfield and Kirklington were modernised as desirable dwellings, the goods shed at Farnsfield was used to store pantomime scenery, and the trackbed between Farnsfield and Southwell was converted into a footpath known as the Southwell Trail.

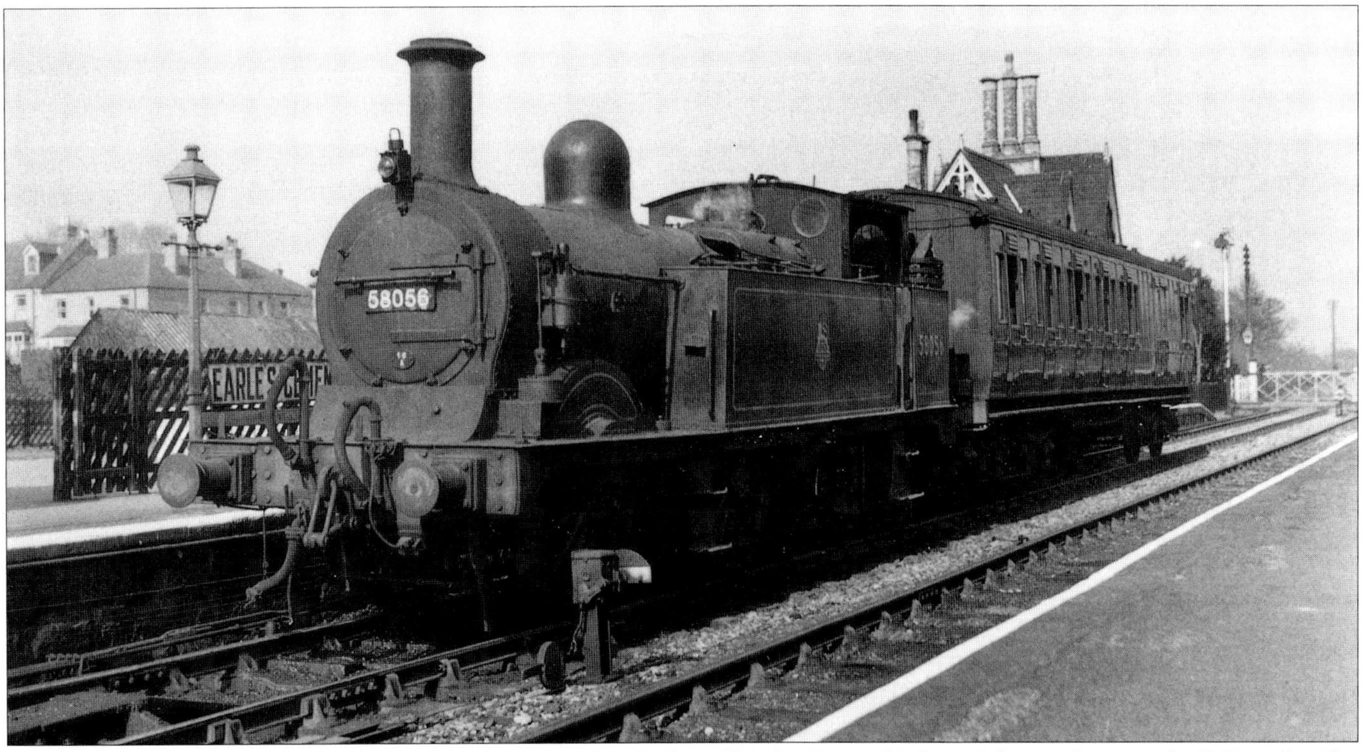

Southwell is remembered for its Minster, the Saracen's Head where Charles I spent his last night as a free man in 1646, and as the birthplace of Bramley apples. Half a century ago, it was even more famous among railway enthusiasts as the haunt of 'The Paddy', a single carriage push-pull outfit which provided connections with Nottingham-Lincoln services at Rolleston Junction. Johnson 1P 0-4-4T No.58056, based at Nottingham, waits with a vintage Midland coach on 19th April 1952. Note the extravagant gothic station house. If Barchester ever had a station, this could well be it! Photograph Jack Cupit.

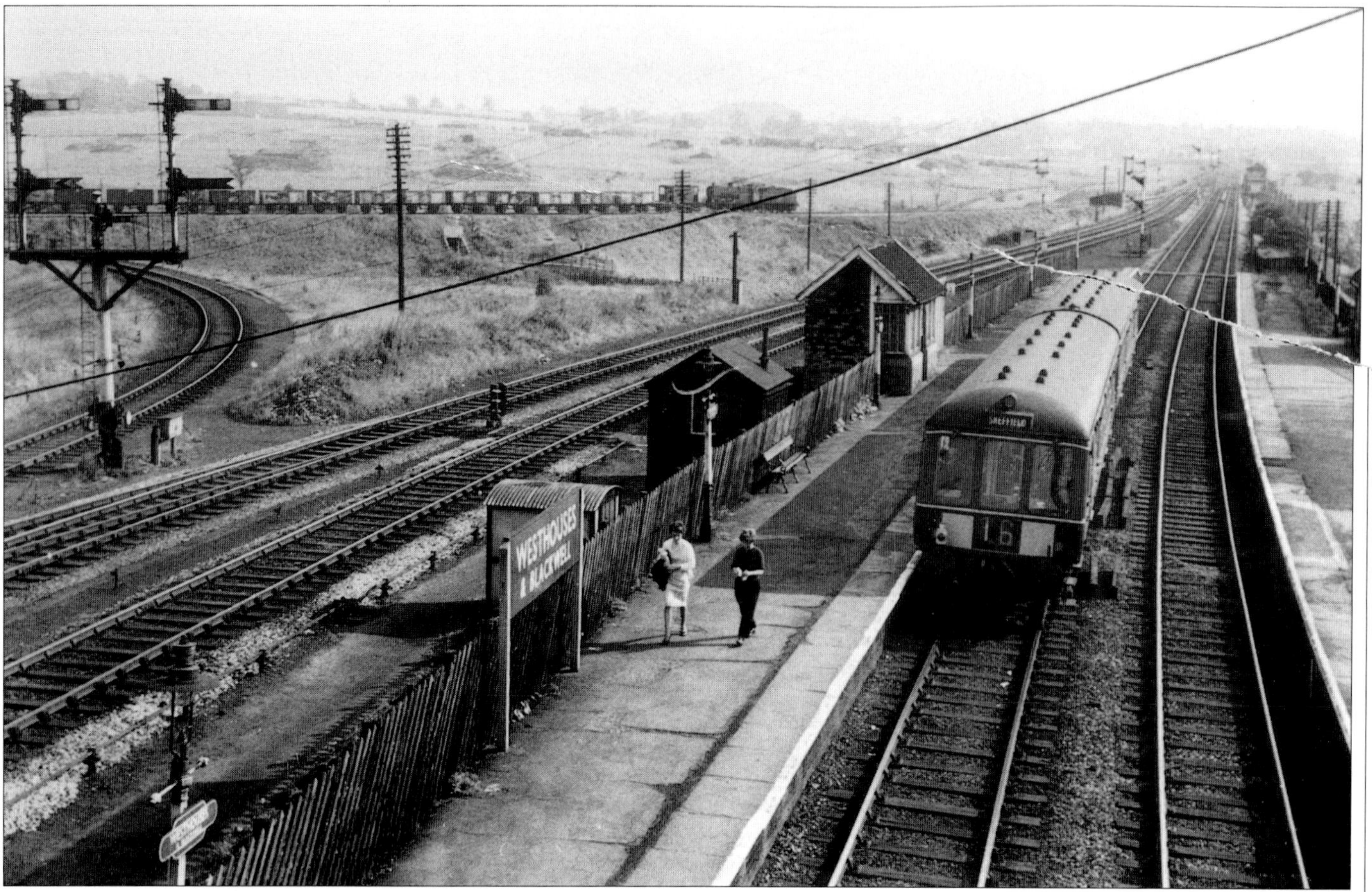

The Midland Railway's western approach to the coalfield was from Tibshelf South Junction on the Erewash Valley Extension, just behind this viewpoint. A Sheffield-Nottingham local, formed by a Derby Twin railcar with E50004 nearest the camera, pauses at Westhouses & Blackwell on 13th August 1965, less than eighteen months before stopping trains were withdrawn and the station closed. In the left background a 4F 0-6-0 with coal empties stands on the southern spur of the Blackwell branch which served New Hucknall Colliery and Westhouses shed. Photograph H.B. Priestley.

With the railway on an embankment, a conventional twin pavilion building was not possible at Tibshelf & Newton. Instead, a single block featuring a short extension, a porch and an angled corner occupied this awkward site at ground level, small waiting rooms being provided on the platforms. The Great Central main line spanned the road just behind the camera and gave Tibshelf more convenient facilities in the middle of the village. This is the long closed Tibshelf & Newton station on 25th August 1971, owned by West Street Motors which enticed customers with the sign 'Railway Sleeper Logs 3 shillings a bag'. Photograph Paul Anderson.

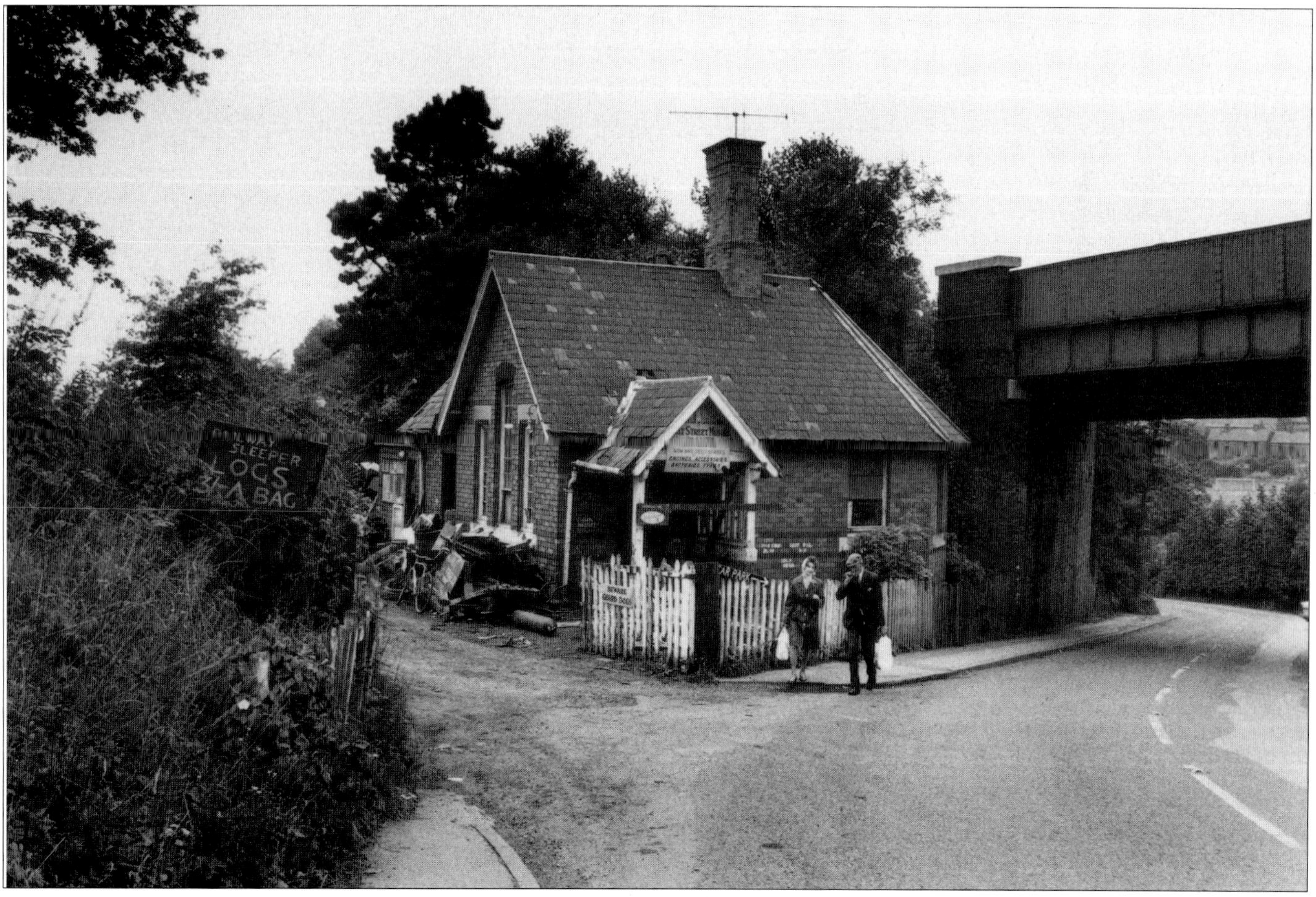

Chapter 6

CONSOLIDATING THE COALFIELD

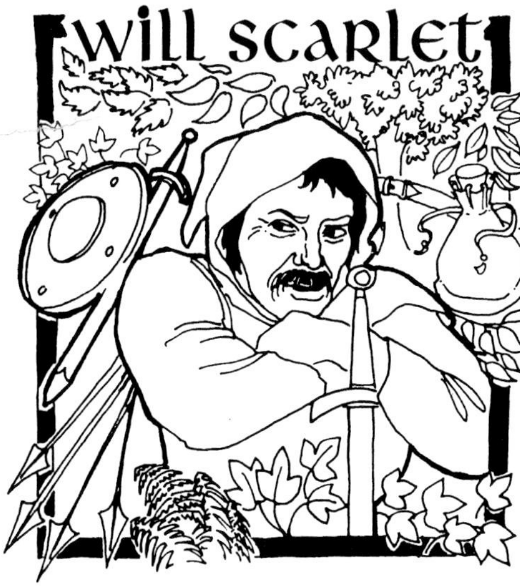

Between the Nottingham-Worksop line in the east and the Erewash Extension/North Midland route to the west, a network of largely single-track railways grew up to serve the developing coalfield. The area concerned is that bounded by Staveley, Creswell, Sutton in Ashfield and Alfreton, many of the small communities within it once relying on Mansfield and Chesterfield for other than basic needs. At first glance, this compact 26 mile system appears to consist of through routes from Barrow Hill to Elmton & Creswell and Westhouses & Blackwell to Mansfield Woodhouse, together with a connection from Staveley to Pleasley and a short appendage from Sutton Junction to the centre of Sutton in Ashfield. In reality, the actual genesis was very complex, involving no less than eight separate schemes over thirty-three years.

The territorial ambitions of both the Great Northern and Manchester, Sheffield & Lincolnshire influenced every Midland move in the coalfield. Naturally, the established company wanted a monopoly of traffic at each mine in the area and some stretches of line anticipated the sinking of new collieries. It was a fascinating network, traversing exposed coal measures in the west and Magnesian Limestone in the east. As the limestone began with a pronounced escarpment, the lines were forced to climb steeply in three places. By and large, passenger services were an afterthought, although they were introduced fairly rapidly once a decision had been made. For two or three decades, stations such as Glapwell, Pleasley and Teversall played an important role in their respective communities, but patronage declined swiftly once buses had made their debut.

Midland plans for securing its future in north-east Derbyshire can be traced back to the late 1850s when rumours of expansion first emanated from the Great Northern boardroom. A branch to Staveley from the Mansfield-Worksop line proposed in 1859 was considered, but the idea faded away when the main scheme was abandoned. Staveley was a natural goal. Iron had been produced there since the 1600s, the Chesterfield Canal had stimulated trade and wagonways had been laid from Inkersall, Commonspot and Glasshouse to carry coal, coke and sand. Richard Barrow purchased the furnaces in 1840, enlarged the works and built a mineral line to the nearby North Midland Railway. Further expansion led to the creation of the Staveley Iron & Coal Co. during the early 1860s, by which time the large Seymour and Hartington Collieries had opened to supply the complex.

Further south, there had been coal pits at Teversall since the 1600s and these had always enjoyed modest prosperity because of the demand for fuel in Mansfield. By 1860 there were plans to sink deep mines in the area, thus arousing the Midland's interest. This time there was no hesitation, and on 7th June

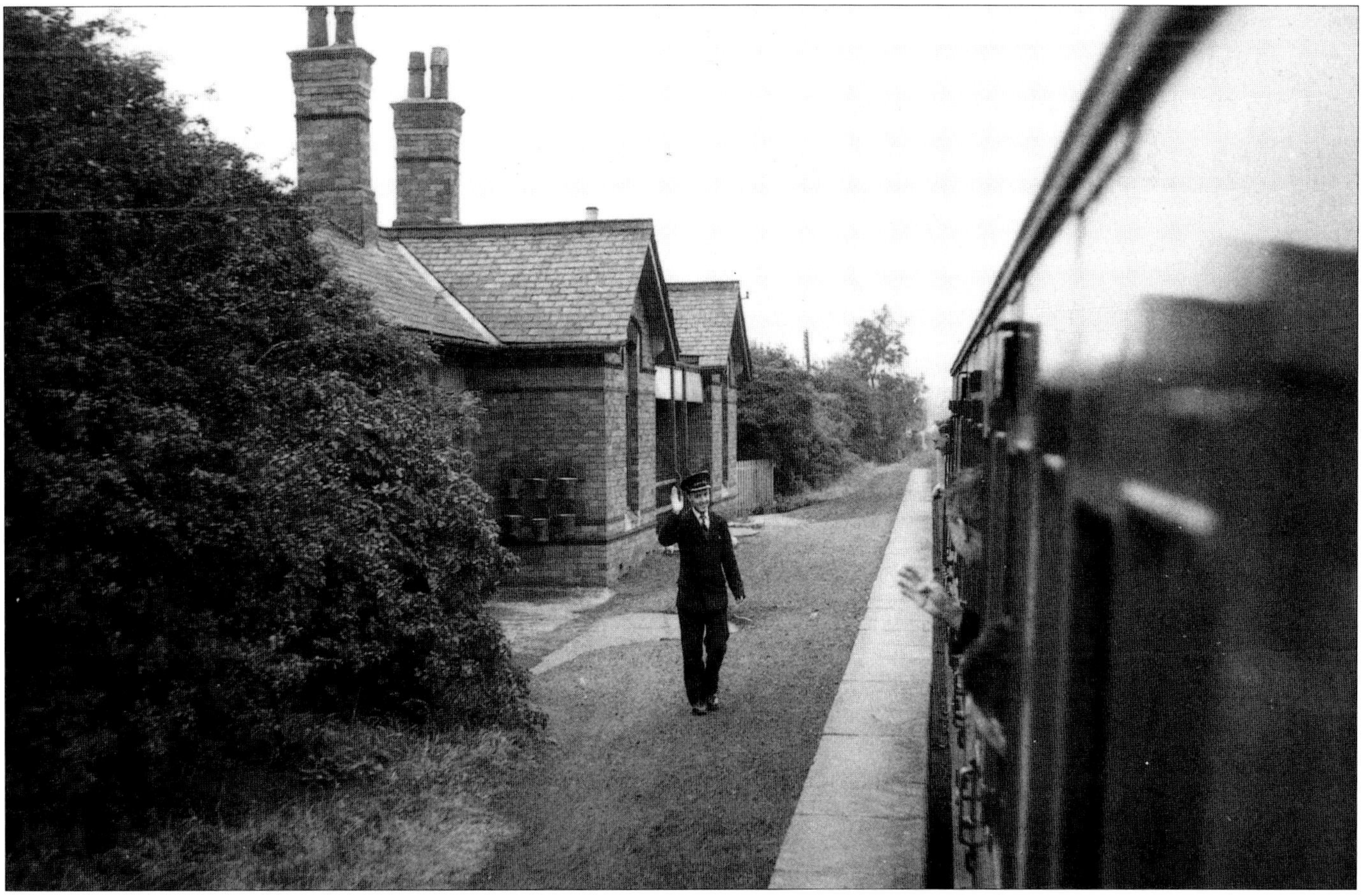

Teversall's station master bids farewell to a departing railtour on 19th September 1959, nearly thirty years after regular services ceased, but five years before excursions finished. Goods facilities were withdrawn on 7th October 1963. This station was renamed Teversall Manor in July 1950 to avoid confusion with the obscure Great Northern terminus at a lower level off to the right. Photograph courtesy Robert Humm.

1861 Parliament sanctioned the Tibshelf & Teversall branch from West House (later Westhouses & Blackwell station) on the Erewash Valley Extension. The latter began to carry goods traffic in November 1861. Shortly afterwards the Midland turned its attention to Staveley again, and on 21st July 1863 the company acquired an Act for its Doe Lea Valley line, from the North Midland route near Staveley to the growing town of Bolsover. This bout of enterprise ended with the comprehensive Mansfield Lines Act of 8th July 1865 (see Chapters 3, 4 and 5) which included a link between Seymour Junction on the Doe Lea Valley and Creswell on the Worksop Extension.

Goods and mineral traffic over the Tibshelf & Teversall and Doe Lea Valley branches commenced on 1st May 1866. The former was 4¼ miles long and climbed from 350ft. above sea level at Westhouses to over 550ft. at Whiteborough, largely at 1 in 60. Deep cuttings were required at Tibshelf and Whiteborough. From the summit, a gentle descent along the upper Meden Valley brought the line down to 500ft. at Teversall (the spelling Teversal is relatively recent). A short extension served Teversall Colliery (1868) and a mineral line rose to the dizzy height of 600ft. to reach Tibshelf No.2 Colliery (1870). The 4¾ mile Doe Lea Valley route was a much tamer affair. After skirting Staveley Works, the branch rose almost imperceptibly to 250ft. at Bolsover, requiring hardly any earthworks in the process. Eventually, this relatively short stretch of track served no less than six collieries: Hartington, Speedwell, Ireland, Seymour, Markham and Bolsover.

From 1868 to 1871 the British economy was in deep depression, hampering the development of the coalfield and railway system alike. Almost inevitably a boom followed and locally this gave rise to a bout of 'Coal Fever' during 1872-73. Numerous collieries subsequently opened, including Sutton (1873), Silverhill (1875) and Pleasley (1877). The Midland had to respond quickly, especially as a Great Northern invasion looked increasingly likely. On 28th July 1873 an Act was obtained for the Doe Lea Extension from Bolsover to Glapwell, the Teversall & Pleasley line, and the Skegby branch to Sutton Colliery. Furthermore, plans were also formulated for a route through to Mansfield, Parliamentary approval for the Pleasley Extension to Mansfield Woodhouse duly coming on 30th June 1874.

It will be noted that there has been no mention of the Seymour Junction-Creswell line for a while. This was actually completed in January 1872 but remained largely dormant apart from mineral traffic coming out of Barlborough Colliery (1873) at the mid-way point near Clown (the spelling Clowne was not adopted until 1951). The 5¾ mile line opened in its entirety on 1st June 1875, at the same time as the Mansfield-Worksop route. From about 200ft. at Seymour Junction, the single track climbed to 450ft. at Clown, over 2½ miles of the ascent being at 1 in 66, while the descent to 270ft at Creswell included two miles at 1 in 72. Three substantial cuttings through Magnesian Limestone and an embankment nearly 70ft. high were among the numerous earthworks.

The 1½ mile Skegby branch opened on 1st February 1877, followed by the 2¼ mile Teversall & Pleasley extension on 2nd April 1877. In this area the limestone escarpment is barely noticeable, mainly because the coalfield hills reach a similar altitude. The line from Westhouses had thus already done all the necessary climbing and the track beyond Teversall began to fall away along the flanks of the Meden Valley. A long cutting through the hillside above Newbound Farm was followed by a sharp descent at 1 in 60 which took the rails down to 450ft. at Pleasley. Unfortunately, these modest developments marked the end of new construction for a while, the Great Victorian Depression of 1875-85 being the culprit. Capital was in short supply, so in June 1878 Parliament granted the Midland more time to build its Doe Lea and Pleasley Extensions.

Construction work on the Pleasley Extension to Mansfield Woodhouse commenced during April 1880 and mineral traffic began to use the 2¾ miles of new track from 1st March 1882. Physically, this was a fairly ambitious section of line. From Pleasley it dropped at 1 in 60 to a five-arch viaduct across the River Meden, then clung to the steep, tree-lined southern slope of Pleasley Vale where the stream runs in a gorge dominated by Hollins Cotton Mill. There was a pressing need to drop from 400ft. in the Vale to 350ft. at Mansfield Woodhouse, so a rock cutting was gouged out of the hillside to permit a descent at 1 in 66. In the same year, 1882, the Midland formulated plans to link the Doe Lea Valley line with the Westhouses-Mansfield Woodhouse route, and an Act for the Doe Lea & Teversall Junction Railway was

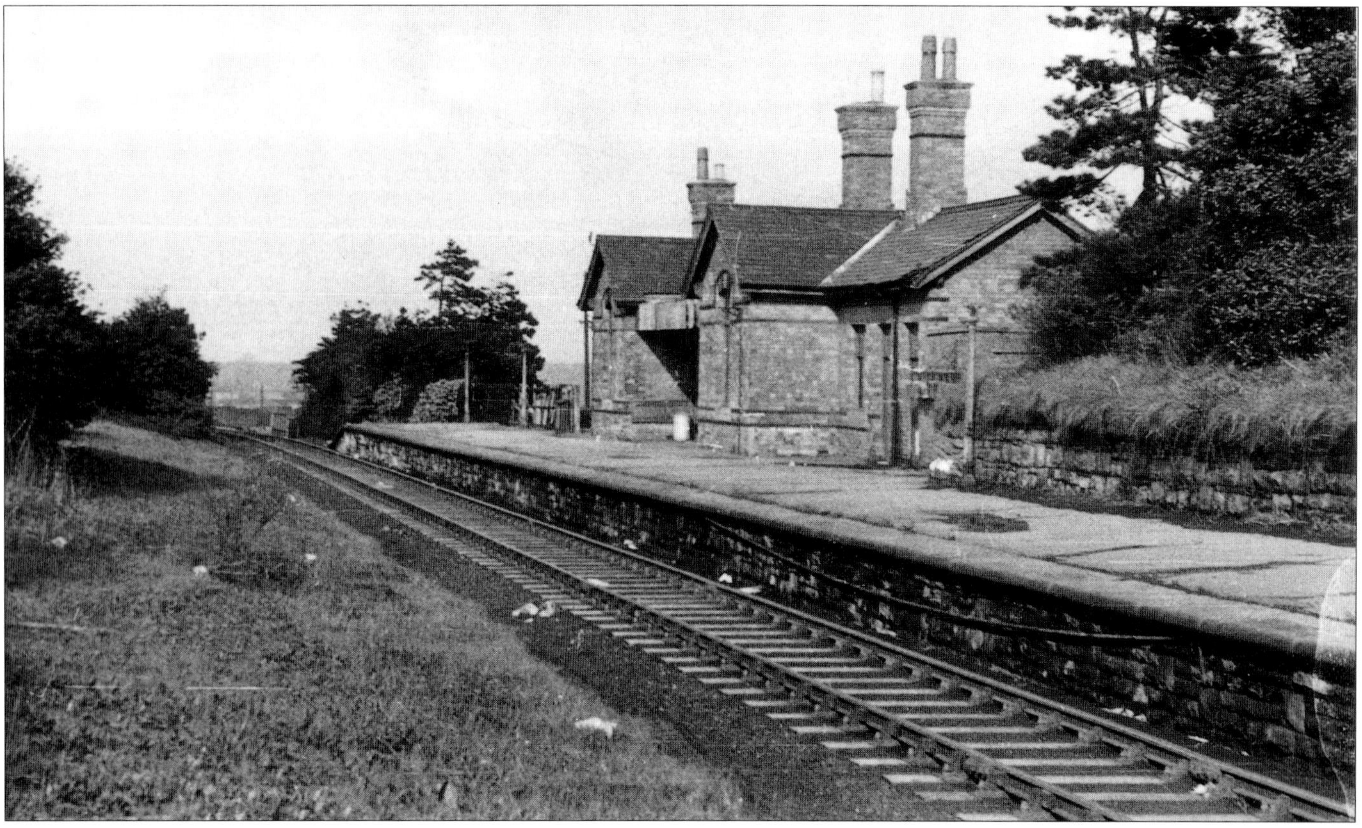

Pleasley station, which lost its regular passenger services in July 1930, was still maintained in reasonable condition for dealing with excursions and goods traffic when this view looking towards Pleasley Vale was taken on a pleasant evening in May 1950. The design was a simplified version of the ornate Kimberley style and dated from 1886. Goods facilities were withdrawn in September 1952 and special passenger trains ceased during 1964, by which time the station was known as Pleasley West, to distinguish it from the former Great Northern facilities a couple of hundred yards away to the left. Photograph Douglas Thompson.

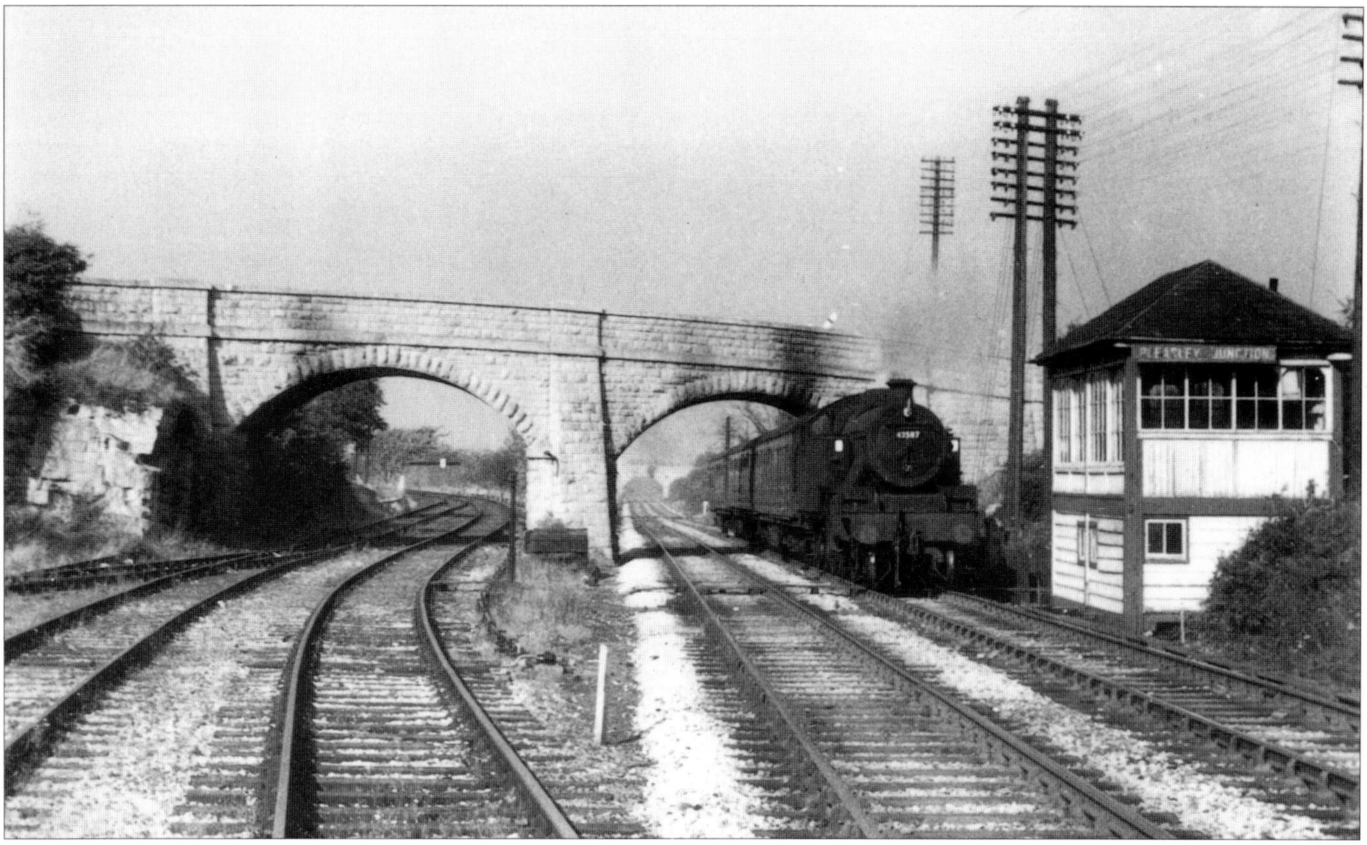

Pleasley Junction, half a mile north of Mansfield Woodhouse, marked the eastern end of the coalfield branches from Staveley and Westhouses via Pleasley Vale. On 12th October 1963, Stanier 2-6-4T No.42587 based at Kirkby shed heads the 1.30pm Saturdays only Worksop-Mansfield up the 1 in 242 past Pleasley Junction box. The line from Pleasley Vale comes in through the other arch of the elegant stone bridge carrying a bridle road from Shirebrook to Mansfield Woodhouse. Photograph H.B. Priestley.

duly passed on 16th July 1883. Glapwell Colliery began to draw coal in 1882, but the 2¾ mile Doe Lea Extension from Bolsover to Glapwell did not open until 1st September 1886 – no less than thirteen years and one month after it was sanctioned by Parliament! The first mile or so of track from Bolsover to the Sutton Scarsdale-Palterton Road was virtually level, although it was dominated by the limestone escarpment and Bolsover Castle. Beyond here, the gradient steepened to 1 in 100, then 1 in 80 and finally 1 in 66 on the approach to Glapwell. After another lengthy gestation period, the 2¾ mile Doe Lea & Teversall Junction opened on 1st November 1890 and proved the most steeply graded section of track in the Mansfield area, a couple of private industrial lines excepted. South of Glapwell, the rails turned towards the limestone escarpment, entering a kind of amphitheatre overlooked by Griff Wood before plunging into the 929yd Rowthorn

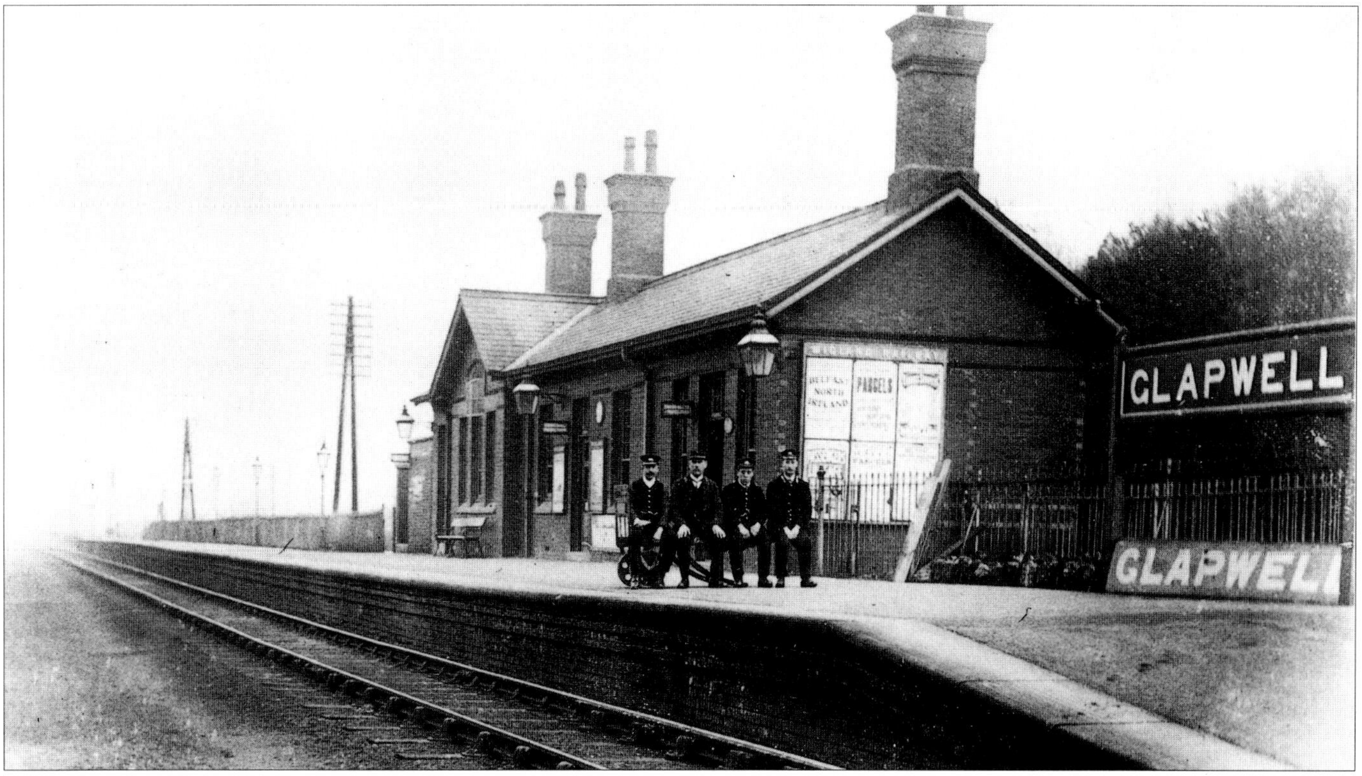

Glapwell station, around the turn of the century, with the staff posing in serious mood. Three of them sport the almost mandatory moustache. The single-pavilion building, dating from 1892, is in fine condition, complete with a poster for Belfast *North* Ireland and a new sign replacing the original one which has been propped up against the iron railings. These were an unusual feature as the Midland favoured diagonal slatted fencing. In the early 1970s the building was used as a meeting room for the Full Revival Gospel Mission! Photograph D.F. Tee, courtesy Robert Humm.

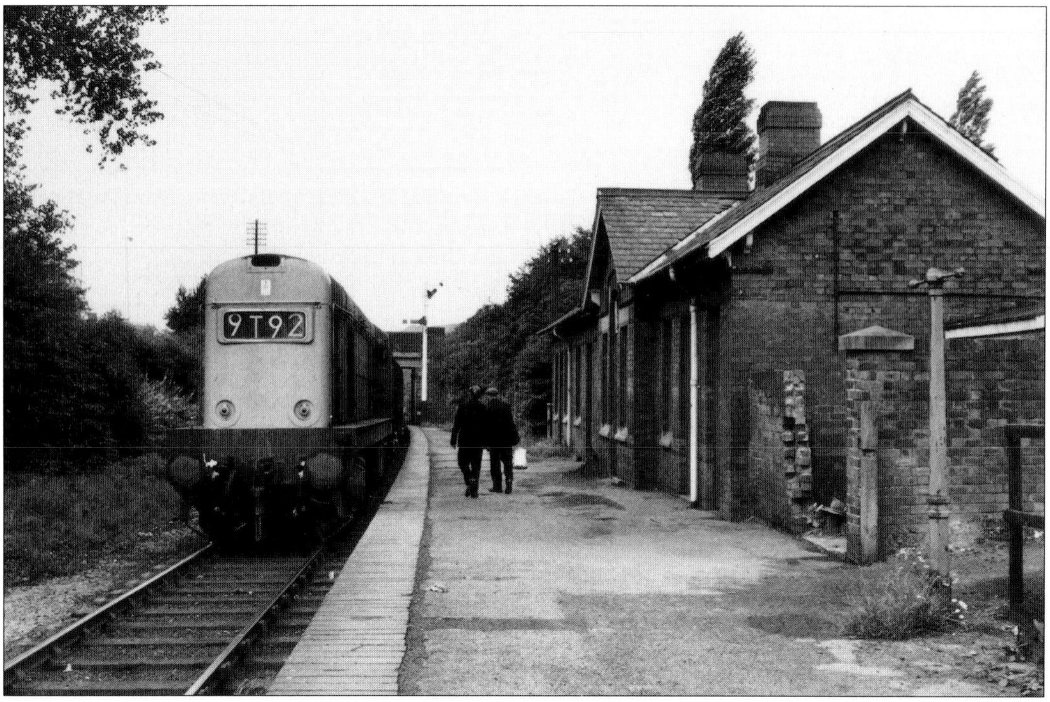

Bolsover's Doe Lea Valley station was renamed Bolsover Castle in September 1950 to distinguish it from the equally inconvenient facilities at Carr Vale on former Lancashire, Derbyshire & East Coast metals. An English Electric Type 1 picks up a couple of railway workers as it pauses with coal empties for Glapwell Colliery on 8th September 1971. Special passenger trains continued until the early 1970s but the building was demolished in March 1981. Photograph Paul Anderson.

Tunnel. From Glapwell to the southern end of the tunnel there was a relentless climb at 1 in 50, the gradient only easing where the track emerged at 500ft. in a valley overlooked by the wooded grounds of Hardwick Hall. The great Elizabethan mansion itself, built by the infamous Bess of Hardwick, was hidden from the railway. A modest descent, followed by a slight rise, brought the branch to Pleasley Colliery West Junction on the Westhouses-Mansfield Woodhouse line. Besides the tunnel, heavy earthworks were necessary and during construction a cutting slip and embankment collapse caused considerable delay.

One characteristic distinguished the Glapwell-Pleasley line from earlier coalfield branches: it had a passenger service from the outset. Much earlier, there were plans for stations at Newton Road (Tibshelf) and Fackley (Teversall) when the Tibshelf & Teversall opened in 1866, but these did not materialise. Miners' trains between Staveley and Seymour began in 1876 and were extended to Glapwell in 1886, by which time they served five pits. However, by the 1880s farming villages such as Pleasley had expanded to become predominantly mining communities and rows of colliery cottages had created entirely new settlements, such as Doe Lea. No doubt encouraged by Mansfield councillors, the Midland looked at the possibility of introducing passenger services over the route from Westhouses in 1882, while three years later persistent lobbying by Chesterfield Town Council led to a decision to provide similar facilities on the Clown and Doe Lea Valley lines. There was more to the process than building stations and putting trains on. In fact, a fair amount of money had to be spent bringing the track and signalling up to passenger standards for government approval.

Four services each way between Mansfield and Alfreton via Mansfield Woodhouse and Westhouses & Blackwell commenced on 1st May 1886. Weekday departures from Mansfield were at 7.15am, 9.37am, 1.15pm and 6.40pm, the overall journey time being just under forty minutes. Intermediate stations were provided at Pleasley, Teversall, Woodend and Tibshelf & Newton. During January 1893, Woodend was renamed Whiteborough after a nearby farm, which later rejoiced in the enigmatic name City of Whiteborough! Next came the Mansfield-Chesterfield trains via Elmton & Creswell and Staveley, which began on 1st November 1888. They left Mansfield at 6.55am, 11.10am and 3.40pm on weekdays and took just under an hour. Stations were provided at Clown, Netherthorpe and Staveley; the last of these was situated on the main line and replaced the original North Midland facilities nearby. In June 1900, Netherthorpe was renamed Staveley Town and Staveley became Barrow Hill & Staveley Works. Finally, Doe Lea Valley services from Mansfield to Staveley via Pleasley and Netherthorpe started on 1st November 1890, trains leaving Mansfield at 7.40am, 1.30pm and 5.00pm. The journey took forty minutes and there were connections for Chesterfield at Staveley. New stations opened at Rowthorn & Hardwick, Palterton & Sutton and Bolsover, with Glapwell joining them on 1st September 1892, after representations by local residents.

The final Midland venture in the Mansfield area was a short branch to Sutton in Ashfield from

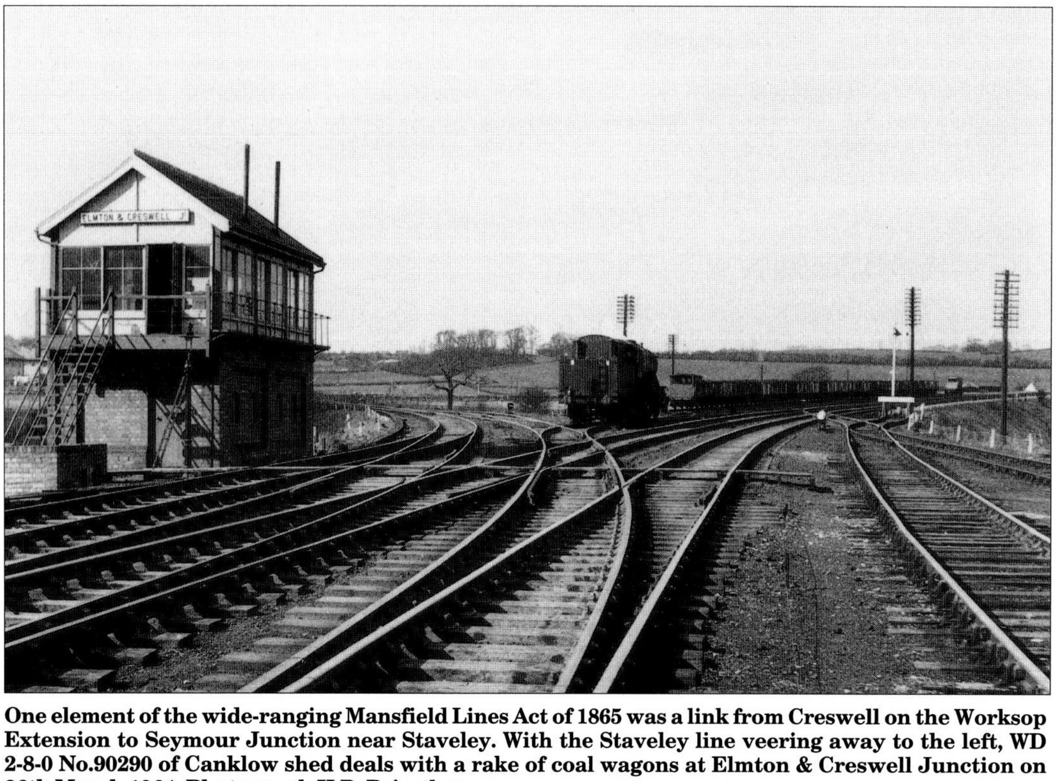

One element of the wide-ranging Mansfield Lines Act of 1865 was a link from Creswell on the Worksop Extension to Seymour Junction near Staveley. With the Staveley line veering away to the left, WD 2-8-0 No.90290 of Canklow shed deals with a rake of coal wagons at Elmton & Creswell Junction on 26th March 1964. Photograph H.B. Priestley.

the Nottingham-Mansfield line. Goods and industrial sidings apart, this was about the only section of railway in the whole district not directly associated with coal mining. The original Sutton station (later Sutton Junction) was a mile from the place it purported to serve and the town council hoped in vain for something more convenient. However, the situation changed in 1889 when the Great Northern revealed plans to build its Leen Valley Extension through the middle of Sutton. Fearful of traffic loss, the Midland immediately sprang into action and on 25th July 1890 obtained an Act for the branch from Sutton Junction to Sutton in Ashfield. The line began to carry goods traffic on 20th November 1892 and the inauguration of passenger services on 3rd May 1893 was marked by an extravagant civic ceremony, the like of which had not been seen locally since the Mansfield & Pinxton opened.

Exactly three quarters of a mile long and double track throughout, the Sutton branch fell towards the junction, mainly at 1 in 66. Earthworks were minimal and there was just one overbridge. In its way this modest railway was as much a symbolic barrier against intruders as Hudson's Nottingham-Lincoln line, but eventually Great Northern and Great Central coal trains passed beneath it on their own tracks. Initially, the terminus had a fairly generous service of fourteen arrivals from Sutton Junction, five of them through workings from Mansfield, and fourteen departures, four of which continued to Mansfield. The shuttle soon became something of a local institution and was affectionately known as the 'Penny Emma'.

Most of the thirteen stations built in 1886-1893 for the coalfield lines reflected another distinctive phase of the Midland's architectural history. John Crossley retired in 1878 and was succeeded by Charles Trubshaw. This young engineer introduced his own ideas, although he retained the twin pavilion concept for most new buildings on the system. Fancy bargeboards and gothic touches were consigned to history; roofs usually had a much lower pitch, and chimneys became very tall and dominant. The use of local stone was abandoned in favour of red brick with terracotta decoration, the current fashion. Kimberley, built in 1882 on the Basford-Bennerley Junction route, was an early example and a rather exotic one. Various 'Arts & Crafts' motifs such as sunflowers adorned the building, which still survives and should be cherished.

On the Westhouses-Mansfield line, subdued versions of the new twin-pavilion style appeared at Pleasley and Teversall. They had plain rather than ribbed brickwork on the chimneys and the terracotta motifs were absent. When a similar building was constructed at Sutton Junction a few years later, the floral decorations reappeared and two of the four chimneys (one of them belonging to a small waiting room on the up platform) reverted to ribbed brickwork! Simpler structures, consisting of a single pavilion flanked by one long and one short wing, were erected at Clown, Bolsover and Glapwell. Although economy was clearly a consideration, the usual large chimneys and narrow terracotta mouldings under the eaves added character in true Midland tradition.

At Tibshelf & Newton the track was on an embankment and at Staveley Town it was in a cutting, so compact booking offices with steeply-pitched roofs were provided at street level. Two local stations dating from this era did not conform to the general trend. Barrow Hill was a huge and very dour twin-pavilion affair with recessed gothic arches in the gable end brickwork – a curious stylistic throwback to the 1870s. In marked contrast, the terminus at Sutton in Ashfield was sedate, elegant, and the last Midland Railway building in the area constructed of local limestone. Dignified chimneys reminiscent of Mansfield station peeped above a generous canopy carried on flat girders supported by simple columns.

Midland passenger trains around Mansfield reached their peak between 1893 and 1914. During these two glorious decades, engines and crews from Mansfield shed worked fifteen or more different services over nearly 200 miles of line, though not all at the same time. Around twenty Johnson 0-4-4Ts were available for such duties, excellent machines belonging to a massive class of 206 engines which were familiar on passenger trains throughout the Midland system. Their turns included the three minute run from Sutton to Sutton Junction and the 1¼ hour stint from Mansfield to Sheffield. They simmered at Ambergate as Manchester expresses headed into the limestone hills and rested at Retford as Great Northern flyers stormed towards Kings Cross. Yet the little tanks were really at home on the single track branches, where they virtually became part of the landscape.

On a damp and chilly autumn morning, a Mansfield-Chesterfield train emerged from patchy mist hanging in the cuttings at Clown and ambled down to Staveley where a yellow smog shrouded the pit heaps and colliery chimneys. In deepest winter, the trees were heavy with snow as a Mansfield-Alfreton train climbed through Pleasley Vale and left a trail of white smoke drifting idly against

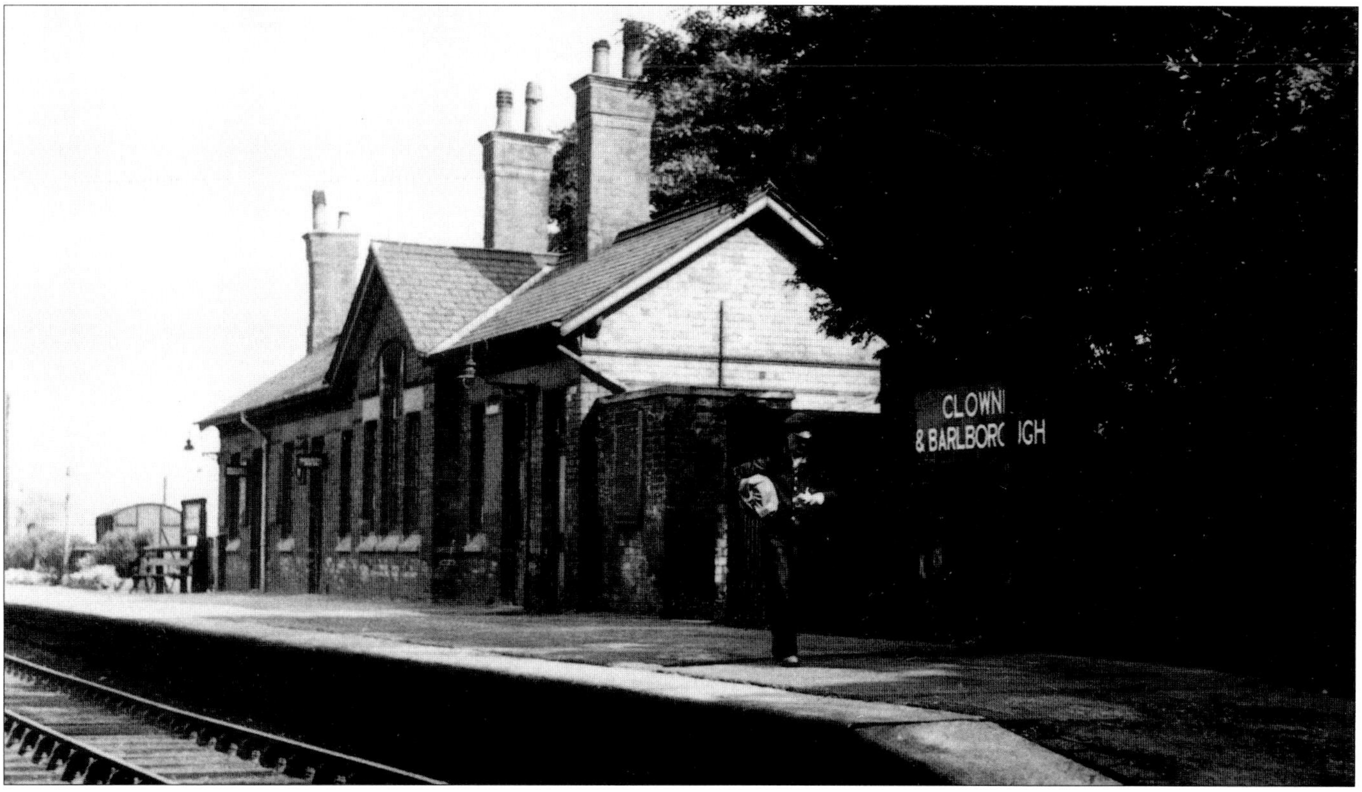

Clown became Clown & Barlborough in July 1938 and Clowne & Barlborough in June 1951, the brand new nameboard in this July 1951 view reflecting the final change. Regular passenger services ceased in 1954, goods facilities were withdrawn in July 1960, and the summer Saturdays Radford-Blackpool finished in 1962. Photograph Douglas Thompson.

the clear blue sky. Low afternoon sunlight warmed the noble stone of Hardwick Hall and hedgerows showed the first signs of spring as a Barrow Hill-Mansfield train tackled the climb from Glapwell to Rowthorn Tunnel. In high summer, a shimmering haze blurred the hills above Farnsfield as a Mansfield-Newark train clattered into the distance, leaving the upper Greet Valley to the sounds of the skylark, woodpecker, bumble bee and grasshopper once more.

It all seemed so permanent, yet there was an ominous sign when advertised services from Sutton Junction to Sutton in Ashfield were withdrawn on 1st January 1917 as a wartime economy measure, less than a quarter of a century after they were introduced. The shuttle was reinstated by the LMS on 9th July 1923, but ceased again from 4th May to 20th September 1926 as a result of the General Strike. Whiteborough lost both passenger and goods facilities on 4th October 1926. Although the inconvenient location of the station did not help, this closure was significant as the first in the Mansfield area resulting from road competition. Enterprising individuals using surplus army lorries from World War I were making an impact on goods transport in rural areas and buses were in the ascendancy as well. W.T. Underwood started to run services from Clown to Staveley, Worksop and Mansfield in 1920. The company changed its name to East Midland Motor Services in 1927 and was purchased jointly by the LMS and LNER a year later. Mansfield District Traction operated the railway replacement service to Southwell in conjunction with LMS.

Meanwhile, the LMS was losing interest in its passenger trains through the coalfield. By 1930, the 6.58am from Mansfield to Alfreton was the only westbound working of the day on the Teversall and Tibshelf line and a return journey over the route was impracticable. The Doe Lea Valley still had three trains each way, but they were losing money. Therefore, on 28th July 1930, the Mansfield-Alfreton and Mansfield-Barrow Hill passenger trains ceased, the expensive section between Glapwell and Pleasley closing to all traffic less than forty years after it opened. Rowthorn Tunnel found employment as a mushroom farm and was later used for storing ammunition. Collieries were closing as well, Seymour in 1918, Barlborough in 1928 and Tibshelf in 1939, for example. Goods facilities were withdrawn from Palterton & Sutton in December 1939. Advertised passenger services on the Sutton in Ashfield branch, twelve into the terminus and fifteen out, ceased on 26th September 1949. One return workmen's train continued until 1st October 1951, when goods traffic finished and the branch closed completely. Passenger trains stopped calling at Staveley Town from 5th August 1952, by which time the Elmton & Creswell-Chesterfield service was down to one working each way, Mondays to Fridays only. These were withdrawn on 5th July 1954. Pleasley West goods (the suffix was added in 1950) closed on 1st September 1952, followed by facilities at Tibshelf & Newton on 6th May 1957. Goods traffic at Bolsover Castle and Teversall (still spelt with double 'l') Manor ceased on 1st November 1962 and 7th October 1963 respectively, the suffixes again dating from 1950.

Excursions and seasonal trains used some of the closed passenger stations, but

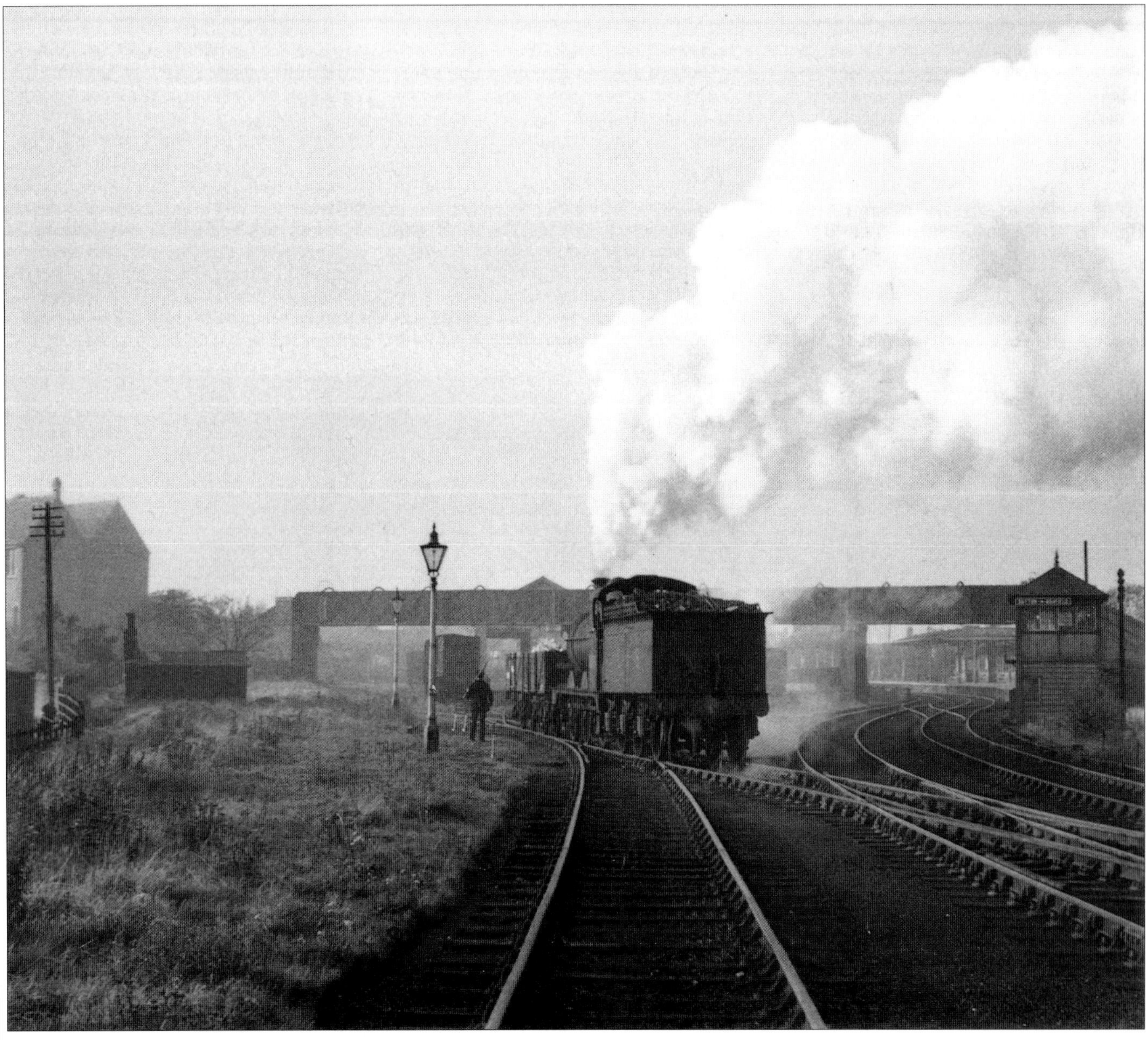

Having arrived with the daily pick-up goods, an ex-Midland 3F 0-6-0 shunts wagons at Sutton in Ashfield's spacious terminus on 25th October 1948. The ample goods shed is to the left of the train, behind the long footbridge, whilst the passenger station can be glimpsed on the right. Photograph Jack Cupit.

they began to fade away as well. The summer Saturdays Radford-Blackpool North, which ran via Clowne, finished on 11th August 1962 and the end of specials from Teversal and Pleasley resulted in the closure of the line from Mansfield Woodhouse to Hollins Mill sidings, on 3rd March 1964. A further retrenchment came on 4th January 1965 with the end of the Hollins Mill-Pleasley Colliery section. After a respite, the coalfield lines continued to retreat the way they had come. Glapwell to Bolsover closed officially in October 1978, although the last train from Glapwell Colliery had been about a year earlier and Pleasley to Teversal finished in July 1981. The last charter from Bolsover Castle, a class 47 diesel with nine coaches bound for London Liverpool Street, ran on 15th November 1980 and the branch was cut back to Seymour Junction in January 1988. With the subsequent closure of Teversal and Silverhill Collieries, the Midland's coalfield lines were no more, apart from the route through Clowne which was in situ but derelict at the time of writing.

Departures from Mansfield, November 1876

At this time, the through station, Southwell branch and Worksop extension were all new. The timetable contained this note: 'Passengers are only booked to Newstead when they have business at the Abbey ... or have permission from Mr Webb to alight, or are connected with the New Colliery at Newstead'.

SO Saturdays Only; SX Saturdays Excepted

6.15am	*Newark*
6.20am	*Nottingham (via Pye Bridge)*
7.10am	*Worksop and Retford*
7.10am	*Nottingham (via Pye Bridge)*
8.10am	*Nottingham (via Hucknall)*
8.55am	*Pye Bridge*
9.35am	*Newark*
9.55am	*Pye Bridge and Ambergate*
10.10am	*Nottingham (via Pye Bridge)*
10.20am	*Nottingham (via Hucknall)*
10.35am	*Sheffield (MS&L)*
11.25am	*Nottingham (via Hucknall)*
11.45am	*Worksop and Retford*
11.50am	*Pye Bridge and Ambergate SO*
1.00pm	*Nottingham (via Pye Bridge)*
1.30pm	*Pye Bridge SO*
1.50am	*Pinxton & Selston SX*
2.10pm	*Nottingham (via Hucknall)*
3.10pm	*Sheffield (MS & L)*
3.40pm	*Newark*
3.50pm	*Pye Bridge*
4.00pm	*Nottingham (via Hucknall)*
5.15pm	*Pye Bridge and Ambergate*
5.20pm	*Worksop and Retford*
5.55pm	*Pye Bridge*
7.05pm	*Nottingham (via Hucknall)*
8.15pm	*Sheffield (MS & L)*
9.00pm	*Pye Bridge*

Pye Bridge trains connected with Erewash Valley services between Chesterfield and Nottingham. They did not serve Kirkby in Ashfield as the deviation line was yet to be built and the original Mansfield & Pinxton alignment was followed.

Departures from Mansfield, July 1914

Immediately before World War I, the Midland system around Mansfield had been at its maximum for over twenty years. Passenger services had reached their zenith and it was possible to reach every town and most large villages in the area by train.

MSO	*Mondays & Saturdays Only*
WSO	*Wednesdays & Sat Only*
ThO	*Thursdays Only*
ThSO	*Thursdays & Saturdays Only*

5.40am	*Nottingham (via Hucknall)*
6.03am	*Nottingham (via Pye Bridge)*
6.35am	*Pye Bridge and Ambergate (via Butterley)*
6.45am	*Chesterfield (via Clown) and Worksop (train divides at Elmton & Creswell)*
6.50am	*Pye Bridge*
6.58am	*Alfreton (via Teversall)*
7.10am	*Worksop and Retford*
7.15am	*Sutton Junction*
7.30am	*Barrow Hill & Staveley Works (via Bolsover)*
7.30am	*Nottingham (express via Hucknall)*
7.53am	*Pye Bridge*
8.00am	*Nottingham (via Hucknall)*
8.25am	*Chesterfield (via Clown) MSO*
8.35am	*Nottingham (via Hucknall)*
8.40am	*Pye Bridge*
9.30am	*Southwell and Newark*
9.32am	*Nottingham (express via Hucknall)*
9.38am	*Alfreton (via Teversall)*
9.40am	*Pye Bridge, Ripley and Heanor*
9.45am	*Sutton in Ashfield and Nottingham (via Hucknall)*
10.23am	*Worksop*
10.25am	*Newark ThO*
10.29am	*Sheffield Midland (via Clown LD & EC)*
10.32am	*Nottingham (express via Hucknall)*
10.50am	*Sutton in Ashfield and Nottingham (via Hucknall)*
11.35am	*Pye Bridge and Ambergate (via Butterley)*
12.00am	*Nottingham (express via Hucknall)*
12.20pm	*Worksop*
12.50pm	*Nottingham (via Hucknall) SO*
12.52pm	*Sheffield Midland (via Clown LD & EC) SO*
1.05pm	*Pye Bridge and Ambergate (via Butterley) SO*
1.05pm	*Barrow Hill & Staveley Works (via Bolsover) SX*
1.10pm	*Alfreton (via Teversall) SX*
1.17pm	*Chesterfield (via Clown)*
1.18pm	*Nottingham (via Hucknall)*
1.35pm	*Pye Bridge*
1.45pm	*Barrow Hill & Staveley Works (via Bolsover) SO*
2.00pm	*Sheffield Midland (via Clown LD & EC)*
2.03pm	*Nottingham (express via Hucknall)*
2.05pm	*Alfreton (via Teversall) SO*
2.15pm	*Worksop*
2.25pm	*Nottingham (via Hucknall)*
2.42pm	*Elmton & Creswell SO*
3.30pm	*Nottingham (express via Hucknall)*
3.38pm	*Sutton in Ashfield and Pye Bridge*
3.53pm	*Southwell and Newark*
4.00pm	*Nottingham (via Hucknall)*
4.06pm	*Chesterfield (via Clown) and Worksop (train divides at Elmton & Creswell)*
4.15pm	*Sheffield Midland (via Clown LD & EC)*
4.18pm	*Nottingham and London St Pancras (Isle of Man Boat Express) SO*
4.50pm	*Pye Bridge*
4.53pm	*Barrow Hill & Staveley Works (via Bolsover) SO*
5.04pm	*Barrow Hill & Staveley Works (via Bolsover) SX*
5.10pm	*Nottingham (express via Hucknall)*
5.15pm	*Alfreton (via Teversall) SX*
5.55pm	*Elmton & Creswell SO*
6.10pm	*Nottingham (via Hucknall) SX*
6.17pm	*Southwell and Newark ThO*
6.20pm	*Nottingham (via Hucknall)*
6.30pm	*Pye Bridge and Ambergate*
6.32pm	*Worksop*
6.50pm	*Sheffield Midland (via Clown LD & EC)*
7.05pm	*Barrow Hill & Staveley Works (via Bolsover) SO*
7.30pm	*Nottingham (via Hucknall) SO*
7.35pm	*Sutton in Ashfield and Pye Bridge*
8.10pm	*Alfreton (via Teversall) SO*
8.13pm	*Nottingham (via Hucknall)*
8.15pm	*Worksop (and Chesterfield via Clown SO)*
8.45pm	*Southwell and Newark SO*
9.25pm	*Nottingham (via Hucknall) SO*
9.35pm	*Pye Bridge ThSO*
10.14pm	*Sutton in Ashfield and Nottingham (via Hucknall)*
10.22pm	*Barrow Hill & Staveley Works (via Bolsover) SO*
10.37pm	*Worksop WSO*
11.15pm	*Nottingham (via Hucknall) SO*
1.17am	*Elmton & Creswell (Sunday morning, but effectively a late Saturday night train)*

The Nottingham 'expresses' called at Kirkby in Ashfield, Sutton Junction, Hucknall and Bulwell. Various connections with trains from Mansfield were advertised as follows: **Nottingham**-Derby, Leicester, London St Pancras, West Country, Manchester, Liverpool; **Worksop**-Sheffield Victoria, Retford; **Pye Bridge**-Nottingham, Ripley, Heanor, Chesterfield, Sheffield; **Ambergate**-Derby, Matlock, Buxton, Manchester, Liverpool; **Newark**-Lincoln (Midland); **Alfreton**-Chesterfield, Sheffield; Chesterfield-Sheffield; Barrow Hill-Chesterfield, The North; **Langwith Junction**-Chesterfield Market Place, Edwinstowe, Ollerton, Lincoln (GN). Services discontinued by this time included Mansfield-Retford and Mansfield-Ollerton. Unadvertised workmen's services such as Mansfield-Shirebrook Colliery Platform also ran.

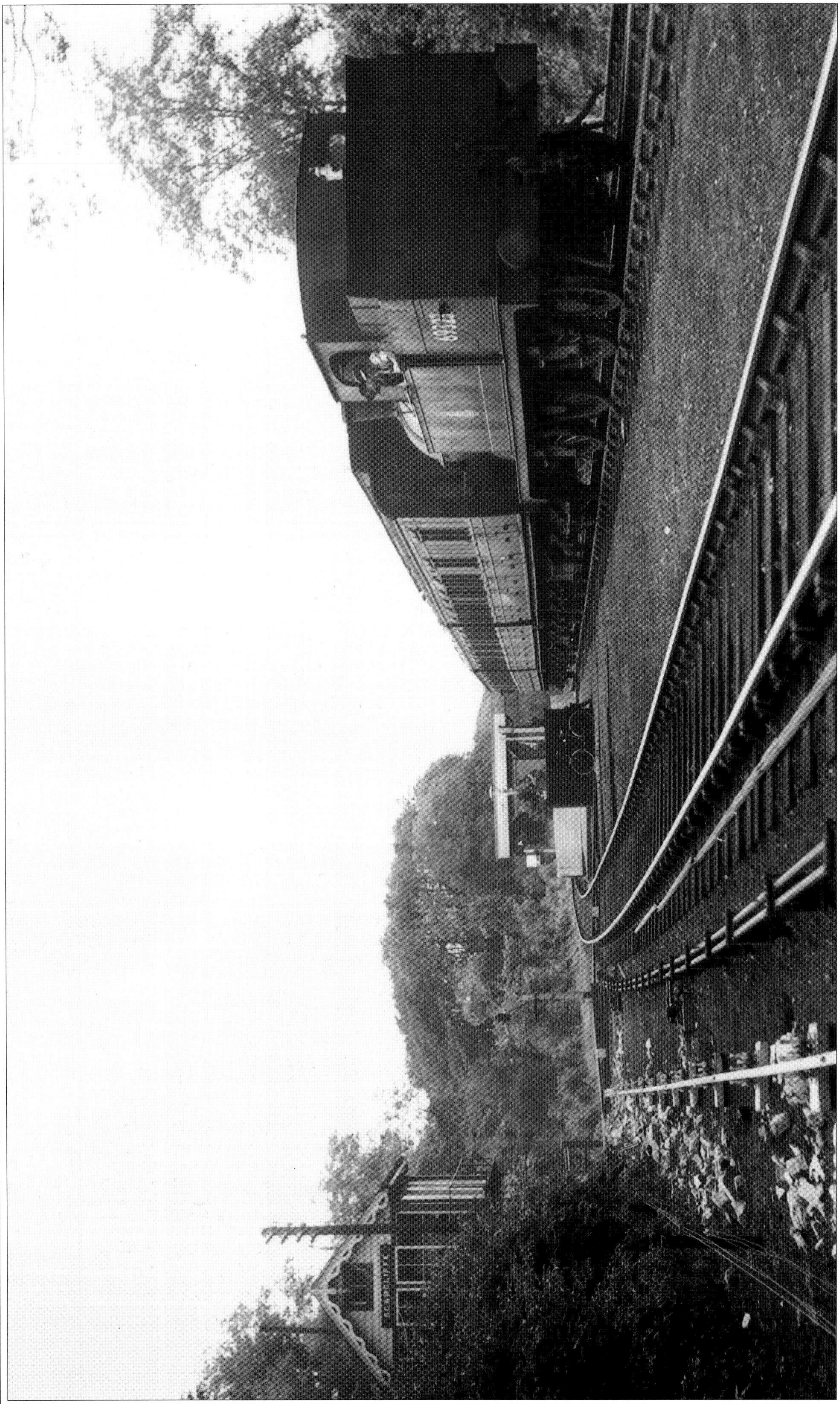

Ex-MS&L N5/2 0-6-2T No.69323 of Langwith shed leaves Scarcliffe with the 1.15pm from Chesterfield Market Place to Mansfield Central on 5th August 1950. Rising ground in the background marks the beginning of a very deep limestone cutting leading to Bolsover Tunnel, a monumental piece of engineering which was blighted with structural and drainage problems from the outset. It was finally abandoned towards the end of 1951, resulting in the withdrawal of passenger services west of Langwith Junction and the complete demise of this stretch of track through Scarcliffe. Photograph R.J. Buckley.

Chapter 7

COAST to COAST?

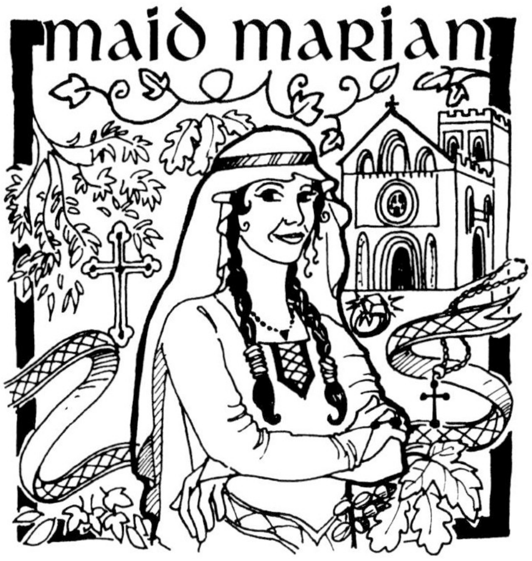

Despite a succession of threats from the outset, the Midland's monopoly at Mansfield and throughout the adjoining coalfield remained intact for almost half a century. Both the Great Northern main line to the east and the Manchester, Sheffield & Lincolnshire route to the north were at a comfortable distance, while the North Midland and Erewash Extension tracks of the Midland Railway effectively protected the western flank. However, the company was justifiably wary of developments to the south. There was a modest Great Northern presence at Nottingham from the mid-1850s and within thirty years the intruder's coal trains were serving pits in both the Erewash and Leen valleys. However, the first incursion into the burgeoning coalfield west of Mansfield came during the early 1890s when an MS&L branch from Beighton to Annesley opened, a precursor of the London Extension. The Great Northern gained access to more or less the same territory just before the turn of the century. Finally, a locally promoted railway emerged at Mansfield itself, tapping new collieries east of the town and providing alternative goods and passenger services to Nottingham and elsewhere.

These developments are examined in Chapters 8 and 9, but another line must be considered first. For various reasons, the Lancashire, Derbyshire & East Coast Railway was closely associated with the MS&L (and its successor the Great Central), the Great Northern, the Mansfield Railway, the far-off Great Eastern Railway and even the Midland. Although its conception was local, the proprietors were very ambitious, as the title of this chapter suggests. Unfortunately, early aspirations proved wildly over-optimistic and the company had to be content with developing mineral traffic north of Mansfield rather than serving Lancashire, the east Coast and, for that matter, all but a small part of Derbyshire. Furthermore, in the presence of powerful neighbours, its independent existence was always precarious, lasting just sixteen years.

This great coast to coast scheme was the brainchild of William Arkwright, who owned the Sutton Scarsdale estate south-west of Bolsover. During the mid-1880s he decided to exploit the rich coal reserves beneath his land, but had little confidence in either the Midland or MS&L as satisfactory outlets for the proposed collieries. A private mineral line seemed the best solution. Meanwhile, plans were afoot for other railways to tap the northern part of the Nottinghamshire/Derbyshire coalfield. In 1887 a prospectus was issued for the 'Chesterfield & Lincoln Direct', which would pass through the estate and had strong Midland backing. During the same year, landowners further east gained parliamentary approval for the Newark & Ollerton Railway as a means of trans-

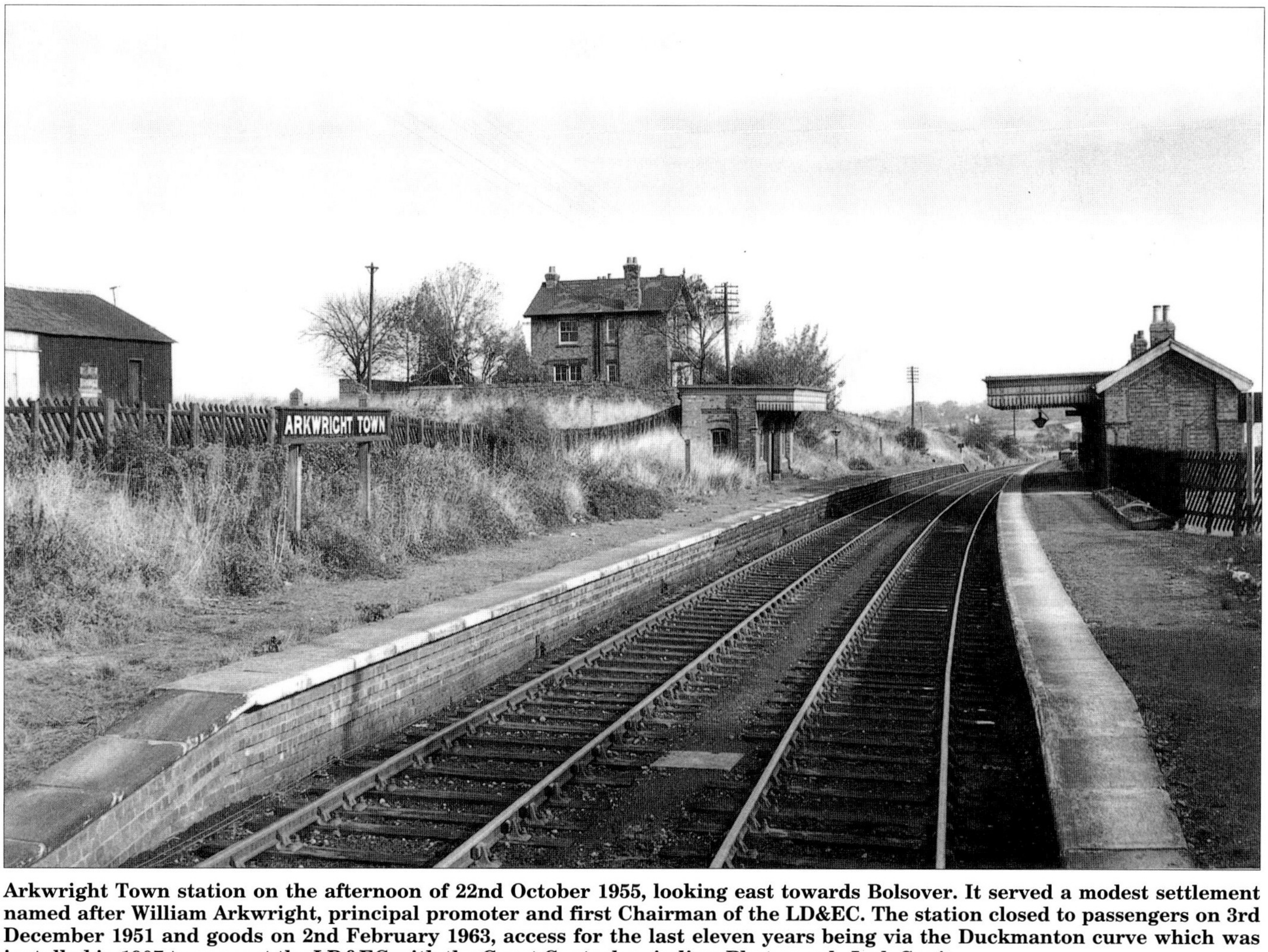

Arkwright Town station on the afternoon of 22nd October 1955, looking east towards Bolsover. It served a modest settlement named after William Arkwright, principal promoter and first Chairman of the LD&EC. The station closed to passengers on 3rd December 1951 and goods on 2nd February 1963, access for the last eleven years being via the Duckmanton curve which was installed in 1907 to connect the LD&EC with the Great Central main line. Photograph Jack Cupit.

porting their coal. Arkwright asked the Great Northern to adopt this line and extend it to Chesterfield, but the response was negative. There was no option but to go it alone.

Suddenly, the vision expanded drastically to incorporate docks on both the east and west coasts, with coal exports in mind. Arkwright solicited support from wealthy neighbours such as the Duke of Newcastle and they expressed wholehearted enthusiasm, as did the proprietors of the Macclesfield & Warrington and Lincoln & East Coast railways, which had already been authorised. Furthermore, powers for constructing docks at Sutton on Sea on the Lincolnshire coast had existed since 1884. The prospects looked excellent! Obviously there was going to be a lot of opposition from other railway companies, so detailed planning was done in secret. The proposals were made public in November 1890 and, not surprisingly, raised a few eyebrows.

A main line extending for no less than 130 miles from the Manchester Ship Canal at Warrington to North Sea docks at Sutton on Sea was to run via Macclesfield, Buxton, Baslow, Chesterfield, Ollerton, Lincoln and Stainfield. In addition, forty miles of branches were to be built, notably the line from Langwith to Beighton. Hefty engineering works included tunnels south of Bolsover and beneath Lincoln cathedral, a huge bridge across the Trent and, most fantastic of all, a 272ft high viaduct in Monsal Dale, which would have dwarfed the existing 72ft Midland structure. A director of that company commented, 'I shall believe it when I see it.' There were 37 petitions against the scheme. Landowners were easily pacified and the Cheshire Lines, London & North Western, Great Northern and Great Eastern railway companies soon withdrew their objections. This left the Midland and MS&L as the only serious adversaries, the latter being particularly antagonistic in view of the fact that the new railway would parallel its own main line throughout.

The Bill for the Lancashire, Derbyshire & East Coast was presented to Parliament in 1891 and on 5th August the company duly acquired its Act, which included authorisation to raise £5 million of capital. Edward Watkin of the MS&L was incensed, especially as his submission for the London Extension was thrown out at the same time. His outburst that the LD&EC was 'as mad a scheme as was ever presented to Parliament' proved prophetic, for the largest railway project ever sanctioned in Britain in a single Act had more than a touch of the 1840s Mania about it.

An extravagant ceremony at Chesterfield on 7th June 1892 accompanied the cutting of the first sod by Mrs Arkwright, who invited guests to travel with her over the entire line three years later. Unfortunately the company was soon in serious financial trouble, only £400,000 having been subscribed by the spring of 1894. As a result, the disillusioned directors had no choice but to go cap in hand to an established railway for help. Although the Great Eastern required four million tons of coal a year to satisfy its customers, it did not have access to a single colliery. The line from March to Lincoln, owned jointly with the Great Northern, had been in operation for a decade and the LD&EC was an obvious extension into the coalfield. The Liverpool Street board accordingly came up with £1¼ million in return for running powers, although there were strict conditions. The cash was for the completion of the Chesterfield-Lincoln section alone, so the ambitious transect of Derbyshire was officially abandoned in July 1895. Just four years after it was authorised, the coast to coast dream was reduced to a humble local line, forced to hand over its coal traffic to the big boys at Lincoln.

By autumn 1896 the residual core of the LD&EC was virtually complete, apart from Bolsover tunnel and the adjacent rock cutting at Scarcliffe. Mineral traffic from Barlborough Colliery (near Clown on the Beighton branch) to Pyewipe Junction on the GN/GE Joint line west of Lincoln, commenced on 16th November 1896. A connection with the Midland at Clown, together with branches to Creswell, Langwith and Warsop Main collieries came into operation at the same time. Less than a fortnight later, the Great Eastern started to exercise its running powers in order to reach the 'black gold'. On 15th December 1896, a passenger service of three trains each way between Edwinstowe, Ollerton, Tuxford and Lincoln began. Goods traffic from Langwith Junction to Bolsover and Chesterfield commenced on 8th February 1897, along with a spur to Bolsover colliery.

The official opening of the LD&EC took place at Chesterfield on 8th March 1897 with the customary champagne and speeches, but it was a subdued affair compared with the euphoric occasion five years earlier when Mrs Arkwright broke the ground with her ceremonial spade. A

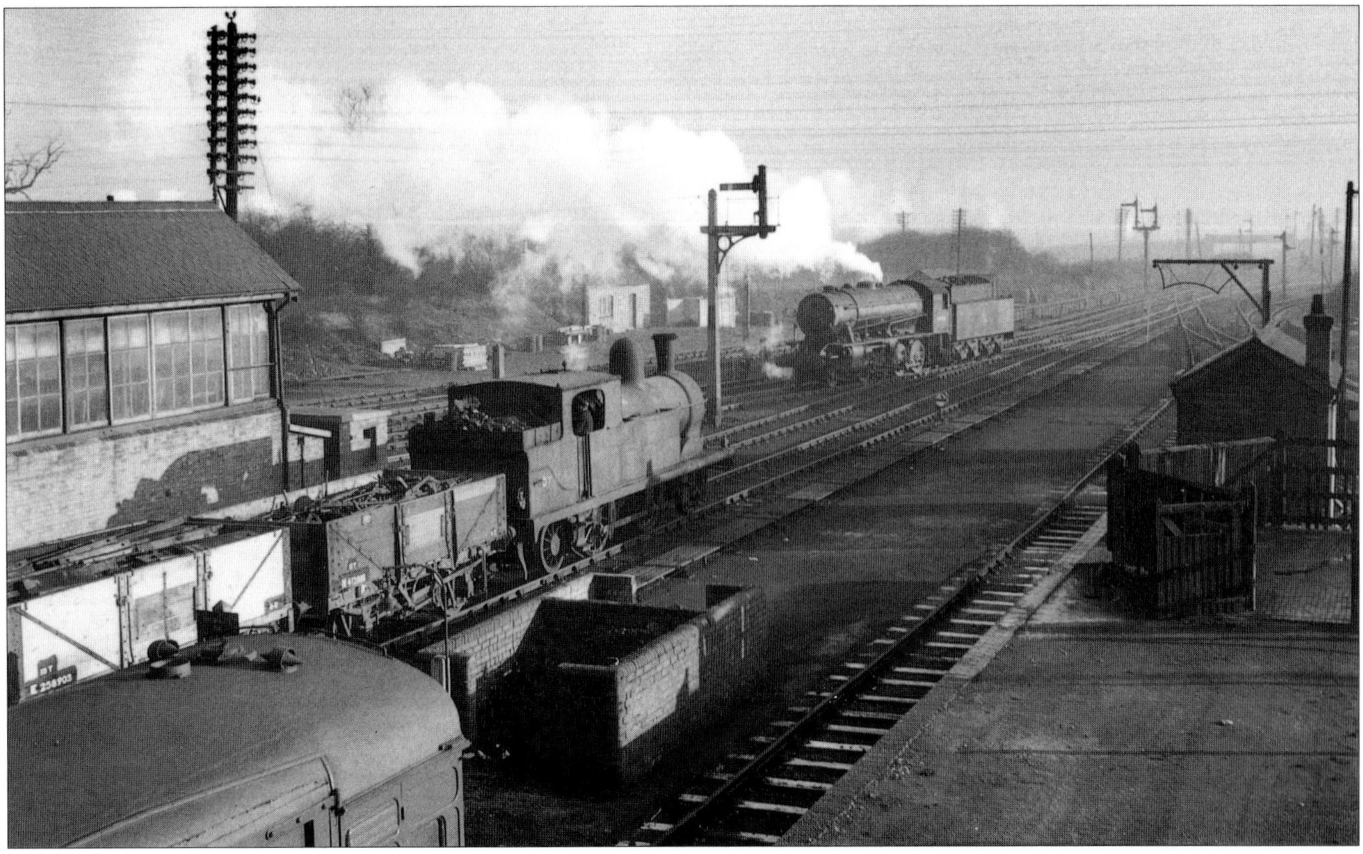

A complete railway landscape at Langwith Junction, in low sunlight on the cold afternoon of 2nd January 1954. Langwith N5/2 No.69284 bides its time with wagons of permanent way scrap, possibly from the redundant line towards Bolsover Tunnel, while a WD 2-8-0 ambles on to the main line. A forest of signals controls the divergence of the Great Northern Leen Valley Extension and access to various sidings. Photograph Jack Cupit.

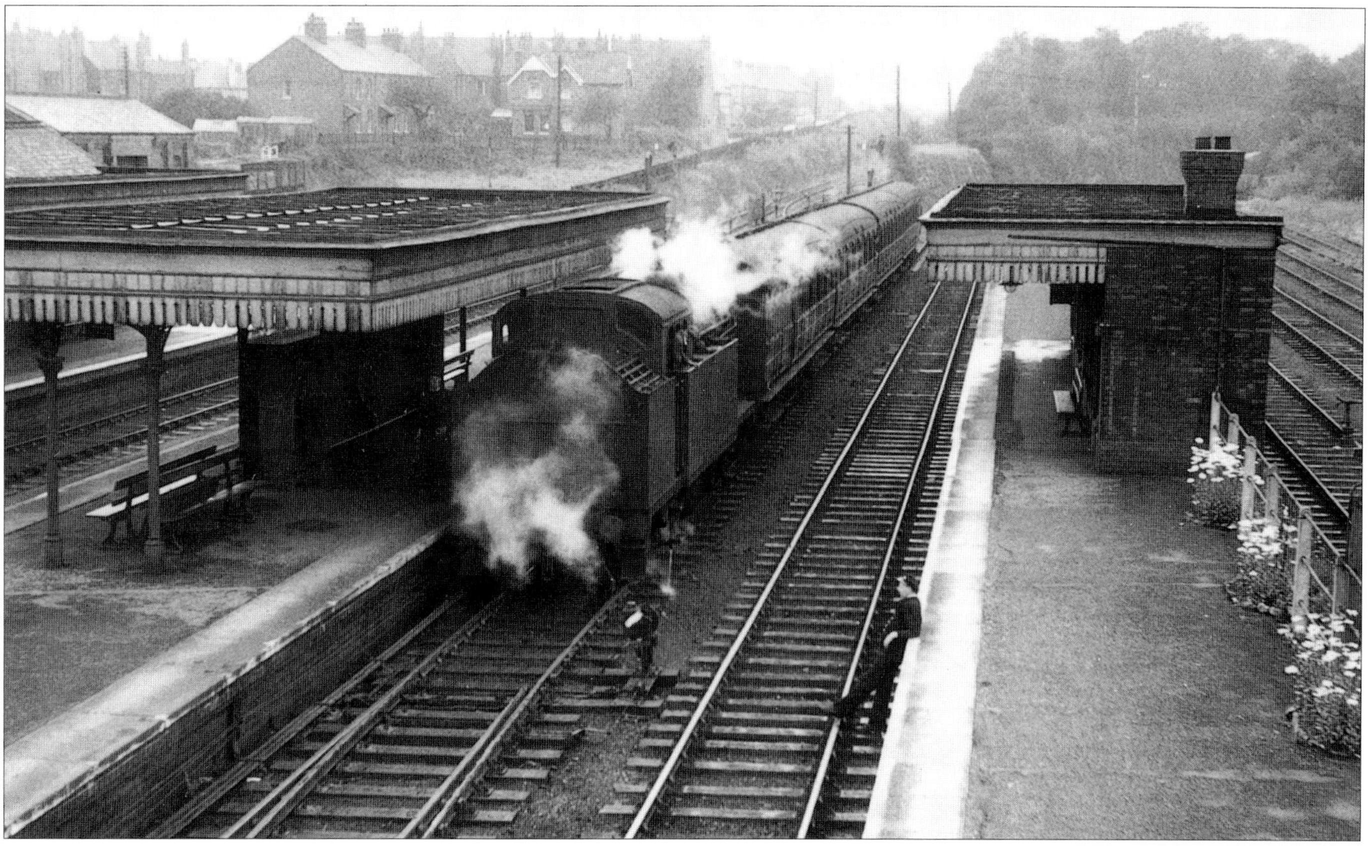

Ex-Great Central A5 4-6-2T No.69816 waits at Shirebrook North with the 1.35pm from Nottingham Victoria to Ollerton via Skegby on 10th August 1957. The return working from Ollerton met holiday trains from the East Coast routed via Mansfield and provided connections to Shirebrook, Pleasley and Skegby. The generous layout of erstwhile Langwith Junction is evident in this view – as is the docile nature of its activities, typified by the member of staff nonchalantly leaning against the platform. The former route to Chesterfield climbed away in the centre background, while the Sheffield line veered away to the right. Photograph R.J. Buckley.

special then ran to Edwinstowe, the guests aboard no doubt admiring the pristine interior of Bolsover tunnel which had been specially illuminated by torches. An advertised passenger service comprising four trains each way between Chesterfield and Lincoln, supplemented by return workings from Tuxford to Chesterfield and Bolsover to Chesterfield then commenced. There were also two trains each way between Langwith Junction and Clown. More mineral traffic was gained with the opening of a spur to Markham Colliery in June 1897, and additional passenger stations opened at Creswell & Welbeck on the Clown branch and Scarcliffe on the main line on 1st June 1897 and 3rd January 1898 respectively.

Although revenue from the conveyance of coal was virtually guaranteed, local passenger business was likely to be fairly sparse, so the LD&EC styled itself the 'Dukeries Route' from the outset in order to tempt those who were curious about the great houses and country estates bordering its line. The slogan was applied to everything from the lofty viaduct at Chesterfield to dog tickets, an early example of what is now called 'branding'. However, it would be a mistake to think that the company was just making the best of its truncated lot, for expansion had been an issue in the boardroom for several years and refused to go away. During the summer of 1896 the LD&EC gained Parliamentary approval for a branch from Edwinstowe to Mansfield, prompting the Midland to offer the interloper running powers to their passenger station via a connection at Langwith. Lack of money quashed the scheme, although the line from Edwinstowe was eventually built by the Mansfield Railway (Chapter 9). Another attempt to

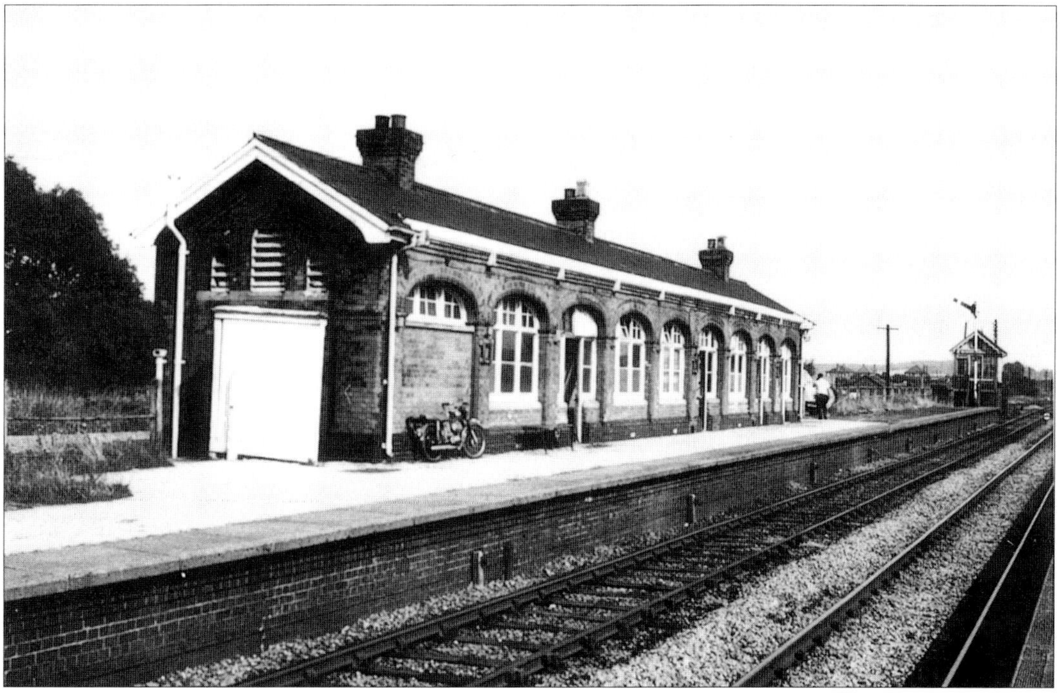

The distinctive architectural style adopted by the LD&EC is apparent in this view of well-maintained Warsop station, on 17th August 1971. Note the repetitive segmental arches and abundance of glazing, better displayed after the canopy was removed following withdrawal of passenger services in September 1955. The track is also maintained in good condition because of its intensive use for coal traffic. Besides the mandatory goods yard, Warsop had a rail-connected sand quarry, which during the early 1950s warranted the attention of a pilot engine for two hours each morning. Photograph Paul Anderson.

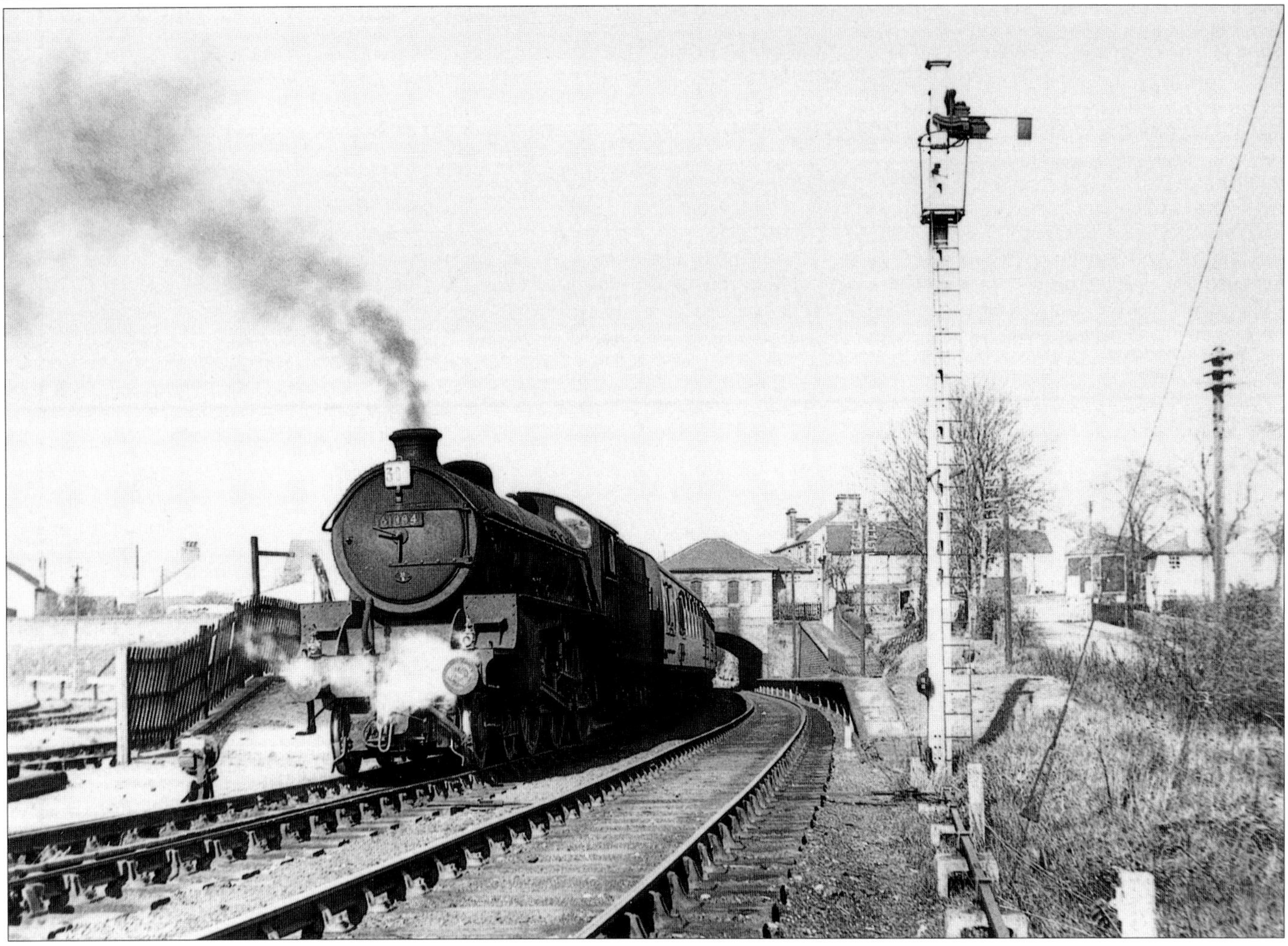

Such was the profusion of passenger services in the coalfield, that from 1904 it was possible to catch a Midland train to Mansfield from both stations in Clowne. This is the former LD&EC station, near the summit of the Sheffield branch, known locally as the 'Clog & Knocker'. Despite closure to regular passenger service in September 1939, the route was used (in conjunction with the Leen Valley Extension) for diversions off the Great Central main line. There were also excursions. On 17th April 1960, Canklow's B1 4-6-0 No.61004 ORYX waits at Clowne South with the 9.25am special to Skegness. The ex-Midland station is off to the right. Photograph R.J. Buckley.

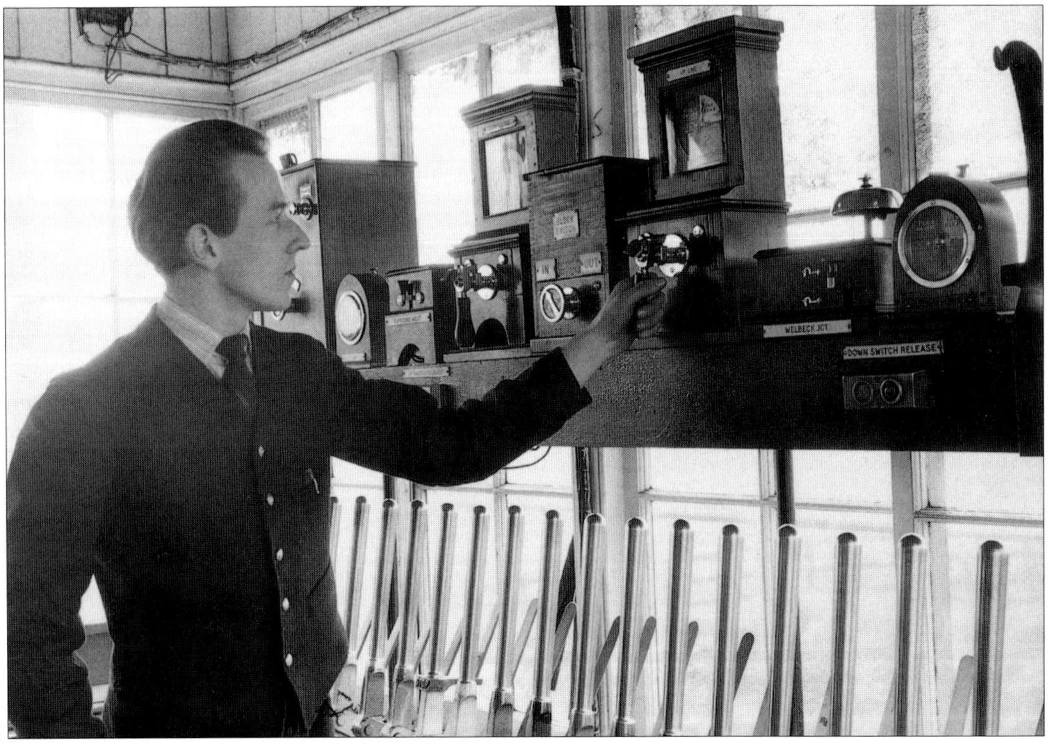

Clipstone Siding signal box opened in early LD&EC days to serve the Duke of Portland's nearby Cavendish Lodge Farm and later controlled access to a modest goods and cattle dock. As traffic grew, it was also a useful break in the long block section between Warsop and Edwinstowe. The Clipstone signalman, seen here on 18th March 1950, was a jazz trumpeter and practised between trains at the mercifully remote cabin! The photographer acquired an inkwell embossed with LD&EC from this box, in return for one of Woolworth's smartest glass versions costing 6d. Photograph Jack Cupit.

reach the proposed docks at Sutton on Sea was made in 1897 when plans for the Lincoln & East Coast Railway were resurrected, but this scheme was finally abandoned in 1902.

Nevertheless, by a series of connections the LD&EC became an integral part of the railway system north of Mansfield. The extension from Barlborough Colliery to Beighton on the MS&L (by now the Great Central) opened for mineral traffic on 21st September 1898, and the east-south curve to the Midland's Mansfield-Worksop line at Langwith was brought into operation on 9th January 1899, Midland passenger services from Mansfield to Edwinstowe and Ollerton commencing on 20th March. With the opening of the Sheffield District Railway through Tinsley and a link to the North Midland route at Beighton, Mansfield-Clown-Sheffield passenger trains with Midland engines and crews but LD&EC coaches commenced on 30th May 1900. These reversed at Warsop until the west-south curve at Langwith opened on 1st October 1904. By this time there were six services each way between Mansfield and Sheffield, but only two return workings covered the whole of the main line from Chesterfield to Lincoln.

Despite fund raising difficulties, no expense was spared in the creation of the LD&EC and a Board of Trade Inspector declared that it was one of the best constructed lines he had ever seen. As the route crossed the grain of the land, engineering work was heavy. Soon after leaving the terminus at Chesterfield, the railway ran on a high embankment then crossed the River Rother, North Midland line and MS&L Chesterfield loop on a viaduct 700ft long and 63ft high. This complex structure was composed of seven brick arches and four girder spans, some on the skew. A 1½ mile climb at 1 in 100, partly through cuttings up to 65ft deep, took the tracks to the 501yd Duckmanton Tunnel, and after a descent at 1 in 100 they passed through Arkwright Town station, 3¼ miles from Chesterfield. Sutton Scarsdale Hall was just over a mile from here, although the railway itself was dominated by Arkwright Colliery.

The Magnesian Limestone escarpment demanded a relentless three mile gradient of 1 in 120, which lifted the railway from 390ft to 520ft above sea level and proved the most difficult section to build. An embankment up to 80ft high, punctuated by an eight arch brick viaduct, 370ft long and 70ft above the Midland branch, crossed the Doe Lea Valley. Then came Bolsover station (6½ miles) which was no more convenient for the town than the Midland facilities. High above was the castle, a Jacobean edifice on the site of the original Norman stronghold. Shortly afterwards, the line plunged into Bolsover Tunnel, a 1 mile 864yd bore which was very wet and troublesome from the outset. Finally, a precipitous rock cutting led to Scarcliffe station (8¼ miles) and the summit of the LD&EC. A four mile descent at the now familiar in 1 in 100 initially followed the embryo River Poulter, which had been modified downstream to provide ornamental lakes in the ducal estates. Another rock cutting marked the approach to Langwith Junction station (10 miles) where the Clown line trailed in.

Near Warsop (12¼ miles) the River Meden marked the boundary of Sherwood Forest and the landscape became more agricultural, although several large collieries eventually opened within sight of the line. A short climb up the Bunter Sandstone outcrop at 1 in 150 brought the railway to Clipstone, which did not have a passenger station but boasted the ruins of a medieval hunting lodge called King John's Palace. Apart from a couple of adverse gradients of a minor nature, it was downhill all the way to Lincoln from here. Edwinstowe (16½ miles) was at the heart of the Robin Hood legend, for the outlaw reputedly wed Maid Marian here. Ollerton station (18¼ miles) had many noble visitors for nearby Rufford Abbey, including King Edward VII. After spanning the Great Northern main line at Dukeries Junction near Tuxford (25 miles), the LD&EC strode across the Trent flood plain by means of a superb viaduct comprising fifty-nine brick arches and four bowstring girder spans over the river itself. The railway joined the Great Northern/Great Eastern Joint line at Pyewipe Junction just west of Lincoln, thirty-eight miles from Chesterfield and 120ft above sea level.

Gradients on the Beighton branch were as daunting as those on the main line. From Langwith Junction the tracks fell for a mile to the River Poulter, then climbed from 380ft to 530ft in 4½ miles, the summit being at Clown. The descent to 230ft at Beighton Junction (12¼ miles) was an almost continuous 1 in 100, culminating in a stretch of 1 in 80. In the reverse direction the drivers and firemen of loaded mineral trains had their work cut out during the relentless ascent form the Rother Valley, which included 501yd Spinkhill Tunnel. Much of the line was in cuttings and over half of it closely parallel the Midland tracks through Langwith, Creswell and Clown.

LD&EC stations were distinctive and, in common with everything else on the line, solidly built. Red brick was employed and although no particular style was adopted there was a vague hint of the Jacobean revival that was coming into fashion. Most buildings featured an arcade on the platform face, the tops of the arches being segmental (made up of a curve of various radii rather than plain round or pointed gothic). Within each arch was a recess incorporating woodwork for the proliferation of windows and doorways. Overall, the structures were long and low, with shallow gabled roofs, stubby chimneys, plain bargeboards and flat or hipped gabled canopies. Warsop, a typical example, had nine bays to the arcade, but in view of its importance, Langwith stretched to no less than thirteen.

There were several deviations from the standard station type. Scarcliffe, being later, had an island platform with a

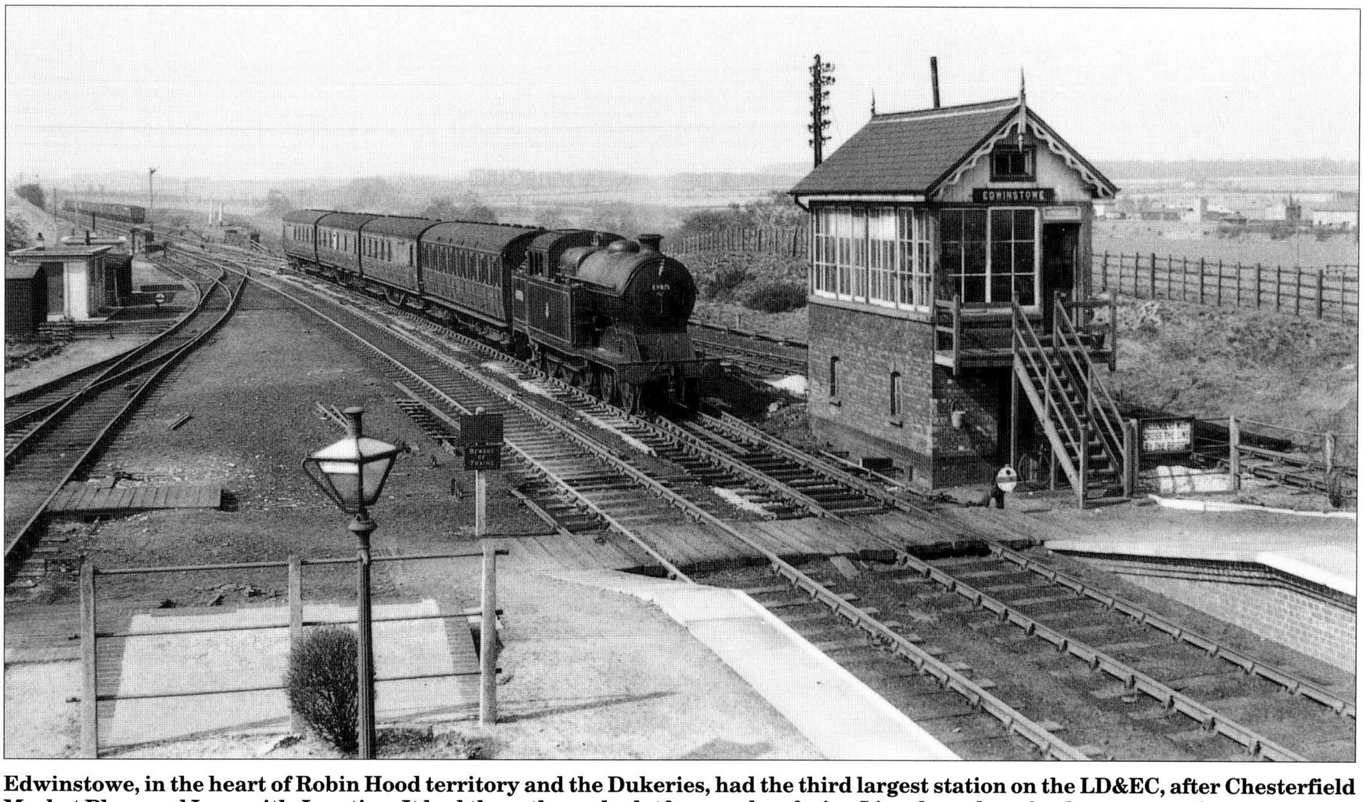

Edwinstowe, in the heart of Robin Hood territory and the Dukeries, had the third largest station on the LD&EC, after Chesterfield Market Place and Langwith Junction. It had three through platforms, a bay facing Lincoln and a refreshment room for many years. Colwick A5 No.69801 rolls in with a train from Nottingham Victoria and Mansfield Central on 10th April 1954. Apart from excursions, there was never a Sunday service at Edwinstowe, apparently a relic of the early influence of ducal landowners. Photograph Jack Cupit.

modest timber building, no doubt for economy. Clown incorporated a substantial booking office at road level, actually on the overbridge. Chesterfield Market Place had a large three storey building featuring a fair amount of stonework and stronger Jacobean touches. The terminus had four platforms, as did Langwith Junction. Edwinstowe was to be the main station for tourist traffic and had three through platforms plus a bay facing Lincoln. It also boasted a refreshment room, run by Mansfield Brewery, and the railway-built *Dukeries Hotel* which completely burned down in 1929.

Although the demand for passenger services, especially east of Langwith Junction, never lived up to expectations, mineral traffic flourished. In 1896 there were just four goods trains each way, but ten years later the number had risen to seventy-five and the LD&EC was ripe for picking off by one of the larger companies. The Midland seemed indifferent at first and the Great Eastern would still have running powers whoever owned the line. Rather more interest was shown by the Great Northern, but in the end the Great Central stepped in. The take-over was effective from 1st January 1907 and proved to be amicable, an ironic outcome in view of the wrath shown by the MS&L chairman when the railway was authorised. Junctions were installed between the two systems at Duckmanton near Arkwright Town and Beighton. Coal traffic from pits such as Bolsover (1891) and Warsop (1895) was further augmented by the opening of larger collieries at Welbeck (1915), Ollerton (1925) and Thoresby (1928).

The LD&EC established its locomotive, carriage and wagon workshops at Tuxford, and this was also the site of one of the two engine sheds. Another shed was provided at Langwith. Eventually a total of thirty-four tank engines was owned by the company, made up of six 0-4-4Ts for passenger work, eighteen 0-6-2Ts for mineral traffic, four small 0-6-0Ts for shunting and six hefty 0-6-4Ts for hauling heavy coal trains through to Grimsby Docks. By the end of 1906, all but twelve of these were based at Langwith. During Great Central, LNER and early BR years, Langwith was one of the principal sheds in the North Midlands coalfield.

After the Great Central took over in 1907, LD&EC locos were mainly redeployed, although a handful continued to serve the area over the next four decades. The GC drafted in several of its own designs to Langwith. On the goods side, Robinson 0-8-0s (LNER class Q4) became the mainstay of mineral traffic over the LD&EC for many years, although they were gradually replaced by O4 2-8-0s. These rugged machines were built for the heavy coal trains from Yorkshire and Nottinghamshire pits to Immingham Docks, Langwith having no less than forty-one of them by 1946. The last Langwith O4 departed in 1965 when the shed closed. The Q4s returned to the former LD&EC shed, albeit in rebuilt form as Q1 0-8-0Ts, and stayed for most of the 1950s. Class J11 0-6-0s were used for local mineral duties and also appeared on passenger trains.

On the passenger side, LD&EC 0-4-4Ts (LNER Class G3) continued to work from Langwith until the early 1920s when Class C14 4-4-2Ts displaced from Marylebone suburban services took over. Exiled Great Northern C12 4-4-2Ts also appeared on Chesterfield-Lincoln trains over the years and former Metropolitan Railway H2 4-4-4Ts put in an appearance during the 1940s. There was an astonishing development in 1942 when Langwith acquired two of Robinson's massive 4-6-0 passenger engines, CITY OF MANCHESTER and CITY OF CHESTER (LNER Class B2, then B19). They were intended for workers' specials to Ranskill Ordnance Factory near the GN main line north of Retford, but proved unsuitable and were sent back to Immingham after a month. Replacements were Class D11 'Directors' SOMME, MARNE and MONS, which also left when the pressing need for ammunition receded. Powerful ex-Great Central A5 4-6-2Ts displaced from London suburban duties worked most of the residual Shirebrook-Lincoln trains until they were withdrawn.

Langwith was the 'Crewe' of the system, with services to Chesterfield, Lincoln, Sheffield and Mansfield. During 1917, Edwinstowe acquired a direct service to Nottingham when passenger traffic over the Mansfield Railway commenced (chapter 9). The only development during the next two decades came on 2nd June 1924 when Langwith Junction station was renamed Shirebrook North. However, retrenchment began with the end of Mansfield-Sheffield passenger trains via Shirebrook North and Clown on 10th September 1939, only World War Two allowing the postponement of further withdrawals. By the late 1940s, mining subsidence had warped the Doe Lea viaduct and created yet more difficulties with Bolsover Tunnel, which was already subject to single track working. On 3rd December 1951 the Lincoln Central-Chesterfield Market Place service was cut back to Shirebrook North, and the line through Scarcliffe and Bolsover

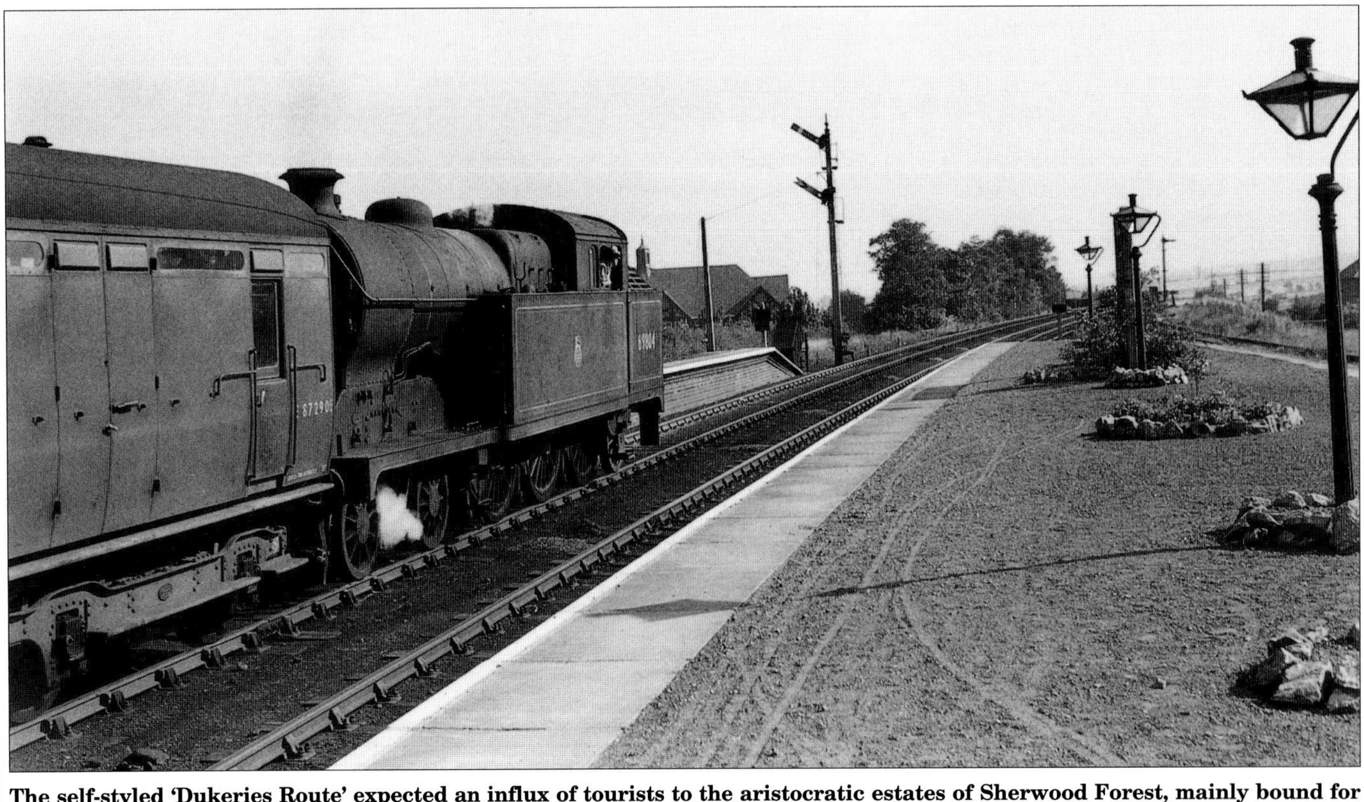

The self-styled 'Dukeries Route' expected an influx of tourists to the aristocratic estates of Sherwood Forest, mainly bound for Edwinstowe via the interchange station at Dukeries Junction on the Great Northern main line. Edwinstowe itself celebrated Queen Victoria's Jubilee by purchasing a water cart to settle dust from the tramping feet of expected sightseers and indeed, 34,000 people used the station during its first year. In quieter times, Langwith A5 No.69804 pauses at Edwinstowe with a Shirebrook North-Lincoln Central train amid exotic lamp posts and manicured flower beds on 17th September 1955. Photograph Jack Cupit.

Arkwright Town completely abanned. Access to Chesterfield goods yard a the connection at Duckmanton was aintained until 4th March 1957.

Meanwhile, Shirebrook-Lincoln trains ad finished, on 19th September 1955, llowed by the closure of Edwinstowe tation on 2nd January 1956 when servces to Nottingham Victoria via Mansfield Central were withdrawn. Seasonal holiday trains to Skegness and elsewhere continued to call at Shirebrook North, Edwinstowe and Ollerton until 5th September 1964 and erstwhile Langwith Junction retained its goods facilities until 4th January 1965. Most of the Beighton branch was closed on 9th January 1967, although the first two miles of track was retained for seven years to provide a link between former LD&EC and Midland metals via a connection at Whaley Thorns. Seaside specials also ran from Clowne until 1964. During the autumn of 1980, the track from Pyewipe Junction to High Marnham Power Station was closed, rendering the massive Trent viaduct redundant. Nevertheless, a few miles of the 'East to West' (a term frequently used during its promotion) survived into 2000, serving Thoresby, Welbeck and Clipstone collieries, doing the very job which brought it into being over a century ago.

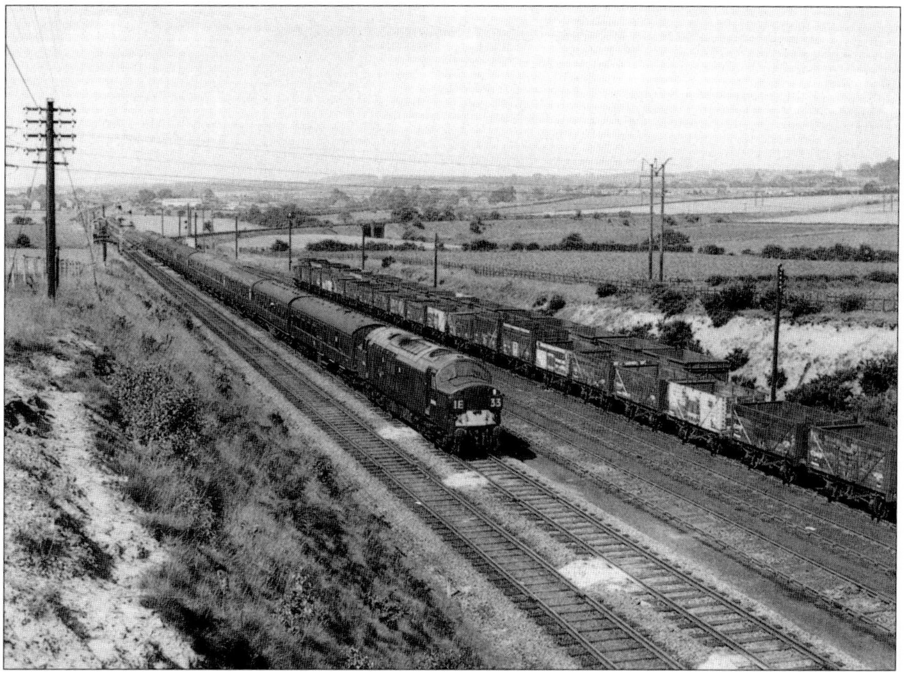

English Electric Type 3 No.D6745, based at Sheffield Darnall, passes Thoresby Colliery Junction with a Saturdays only Manchester-Skegness train on 27th July 1963. Edwinstowe nestles in the middle distance, while Birklands Wood (containing the famous Major Oak) forms the skyline. The branch to Thoresby mine veers off to the right, crossing the River Maun by a plate girder bridge. Photograph Jack Cupit.

40E LANGWITH Allocations 1950

Ex-GC and ROD O4 2-8-0

63577, 63585, 63597, 63615, 63625, 63632, 63644, 63648, 63656, 63658, 63665, 63666, 63677, 63679, 63683, 63703, 63707, 63709, 63715, 63717, 63724, 63741, 63750, 63757, 63758, 63759, 63765, 63776, 63800, 63807, 63809, 63833, 63837, 63840, 63842, 63870, 63884, 63900, 63902

Ex-GC J11 0-6-0

64281, 64289, 64297, 64310, 64321, 64358, 64378, 64379, 64389, 64414, 64418, 64426, 64427

Ex-MS&L N5 0-6-2T

69284, 69319, 69323, 69327

Ex-GC A5 4-6-2T

69812, 69815, 69818

Ex-LNER Q1 0-8-0T (rebuilt from Robinson Q4 0-8-0)

69928, 69929

41J LANGWITH Allocations 1959

Ex-GC and ROD O4 2-8-0

63577, 63597, 63607, 63622, 63632, 63634, 63635, 63636, 63643, 63664, 63665, 63679, 63683, 63691, 63703, 63707, 63715, 63717, 63722, 63732, 63739, 63758, 63765, 63776, 63800, 63829, 63833, 63840, 63842, 63853, 63861, 63870, 63893, 63902, 63912

Ex-GC J11 0-6-0

64314, 64316, 64317, 64324, 64332, 64333, 64346, 64352, 64354, 64362, 64364, 64379, 64427

Ex-Ministry of Supply J94 0-6-0ST

68026, 68080

Ex-GE J69 0-6-0T

68554

Ex-MS&L N5 0-6-2T

69286, 69299

Ex-Ministry of Supply WD 2-8-0

90043, 90051, 90088, 90162, 90259, 90275, 90287, 90302, 90411, 90431, 90438, 90449, 90492, 90545, 90554, 90577, 90594, 90657

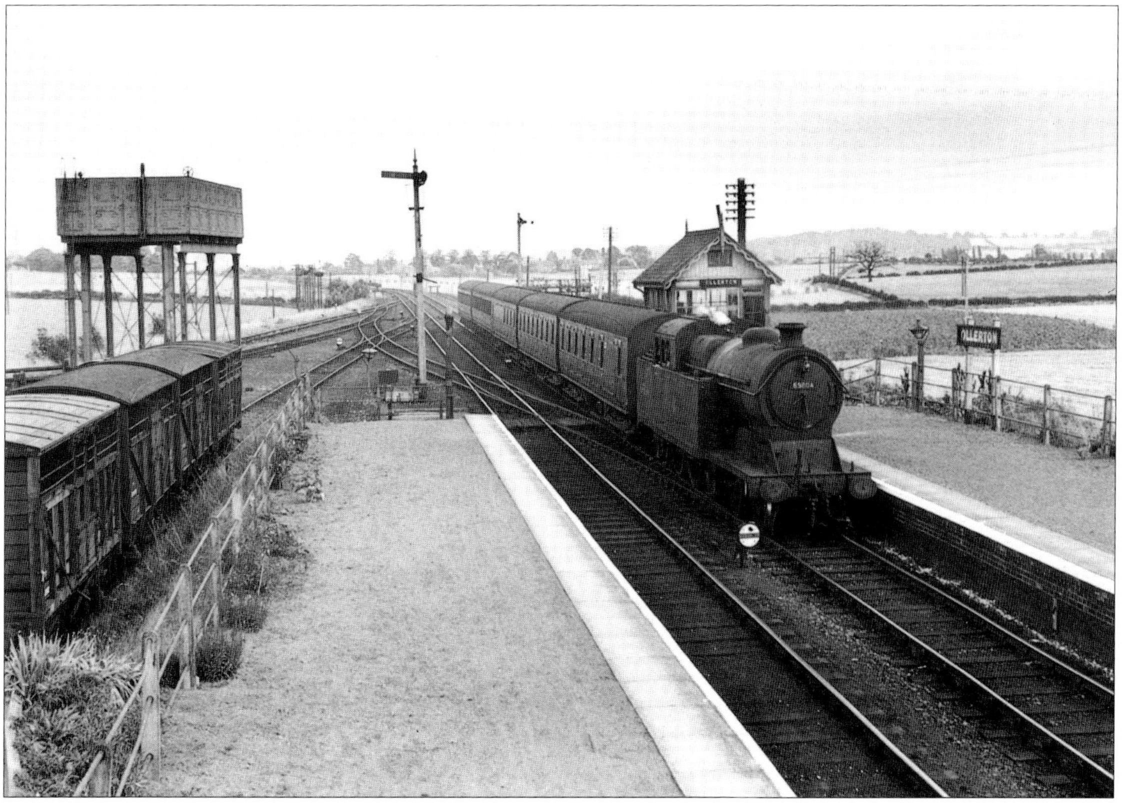

The Great Eastern Railway had Wolferton and the Great North of Scotland had Ballater, but the LD&EC boasted its own royal station, at Ollerton. It was here that Edward Prince of Wales, later King Edward VII, boarded a special train for Doncaster Races, having stayed with Lord and Lady Savile at nearby Rufford Abbey. LD&EC 0-6-2T No.26, normally employed on coal trains, was the royal locomotive. In less happy times, A5 No.69804 rolls into Ollerton with a Lincoln Central-Shirebrook North train on 17th September 1955, the last day of regular passenger services. Photograph Jack Cupit.

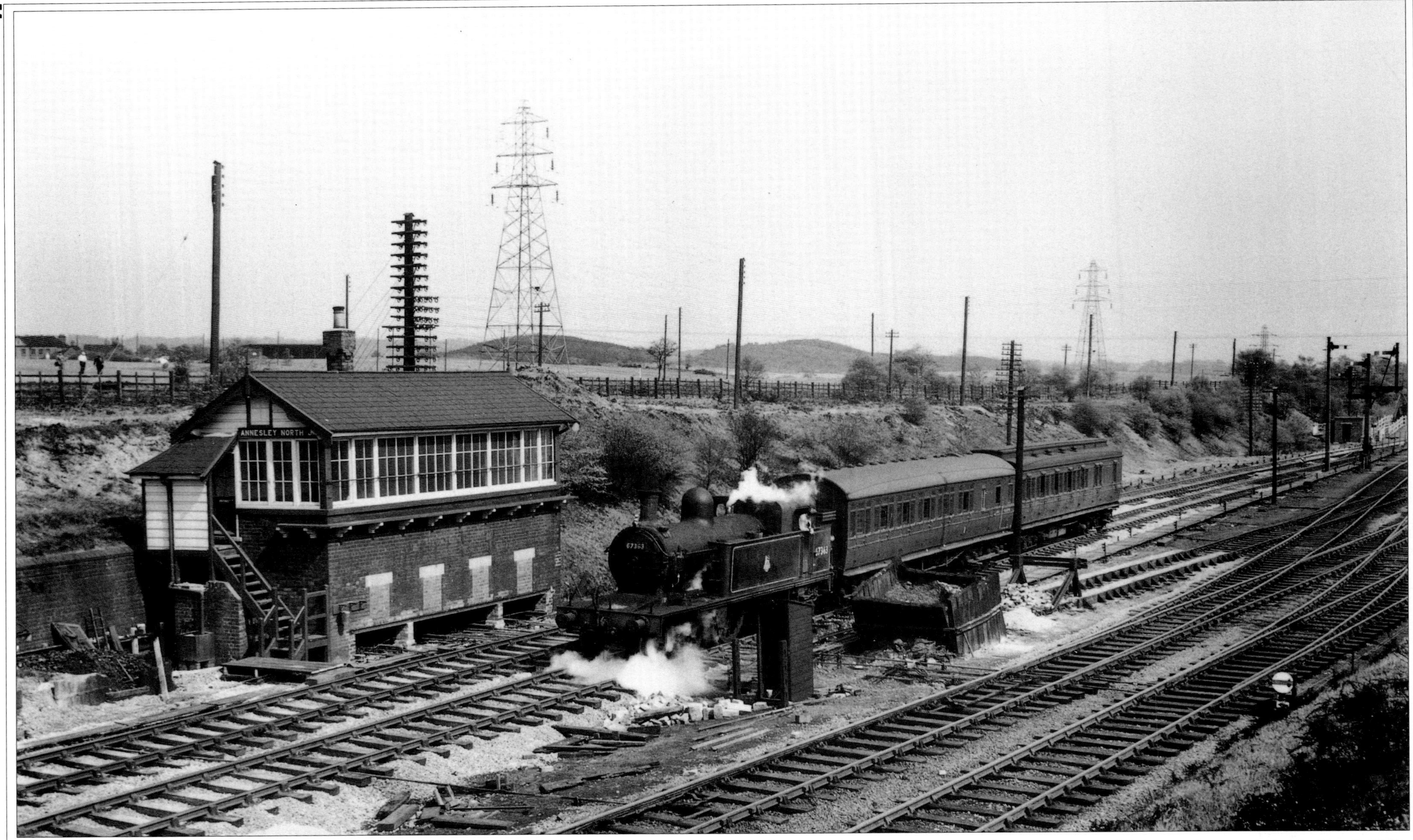

As originally envisaged, the Leen Valley Extension was literally a continuation of the existing Leen Valley branch beyond Annesley, thus requiring a third tunnel through Robin Hood's Hills. Fortunately, a new spirit of co-operation with the Great Central meant that the point of divergence was moved beyond the ridge. Close to what might have been the junction for Shirebrook, push-pull fitted C12 4-4-2T No.67363 of Annesley shed is in charge of the 'Dido' at Annesley North Junction signal box on 12th May 1956. This unadvertised train ran purely for railway staff, to Bulwell Common from either Newstead GN or a dedicated platform on the GC main line. Photograph Jack Cupit.

Chapter 8

LEEN VALLEY EXTENSION

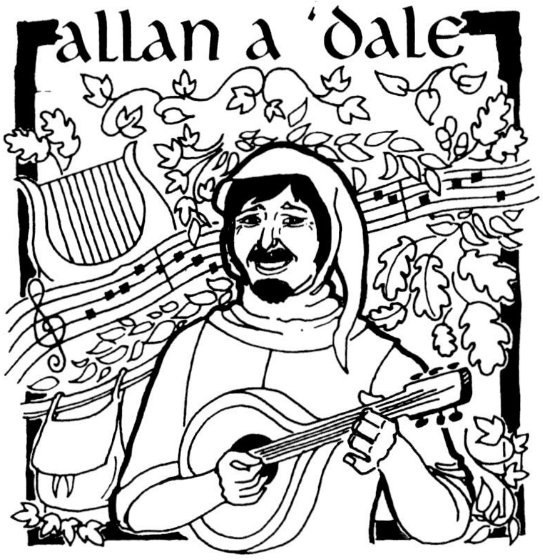

Early attempts to threaten the Midland's lucrative monopoly of coal traffic around Mansfield emanated mainly from the Great Northern to the east and were effectively quashed by the Worksop and Southwell extensions, as noted in Chapters 4 and 5. When the Great Northern attack eventually materialised it came from the south.

Like so many chance developments in railway history, the seeds for the invasion were set when a benefactor with foresight acted in his company's interest. As a result, the Great Northern gained a firm foothold in Nottingham, from which it was able to penetrate the Erewash and Leen valleys. Having reaped rich rewards from these exploits, the intruder decided to venture further north in order to tap the collieries west of Mansfield, although the resulting Leen Valley Extension through Sutton in Ashfield and Pleasley to Langwith was partly a response to MS&L ambitions to reach London. It was also the line of the limestone, burrowing through the Magnesian outcrop throughout its length and employing the greyish-white stone for its buildings and bridges.

Besides the sensible projects erupting from the Railway Mania of 1844-45, there were numerous madcap schemes with bloated ambitions and cumbersome names. Most of them soon evaporated, but a few eventually materialised in truncated form. In this category were the Manchester, Buxton, Matlock & Midland Junction Railway and the Ambergate, Nottingham & Boston & Eastern Junction Railway. Together, they would form a line of communication between Lancashire and the Lincolnshire coast, meeting at Ambergate on the North Midland route of the Midland Railway. Boston, fearing the potentially disastrous consequences for its docks upon the opening of the north-south Great Northern line, was overjoyed by the prospect of an east-west link to the Midlands. Nottingham, frustrated by its position at the end of a Midland branch, embraced both projects and urged that they be combined to form a Grand Union Railway trunk route. The Manchester company only managed to build a modest eleven mile line between Ambergate and Rowsley, but the so-called Ambergate company at least provided a twenty mile link between Grantham and the outskirts of Nottingham.

Authorised in July 1846, this bucolic railway from the canal basin at Grantham to Carlton Junction, Colwick, on the Midland's Lincoln branch, opened during July 1850. Prior to this, the Great Northern had made two attempts to acquire it, but the local company remained

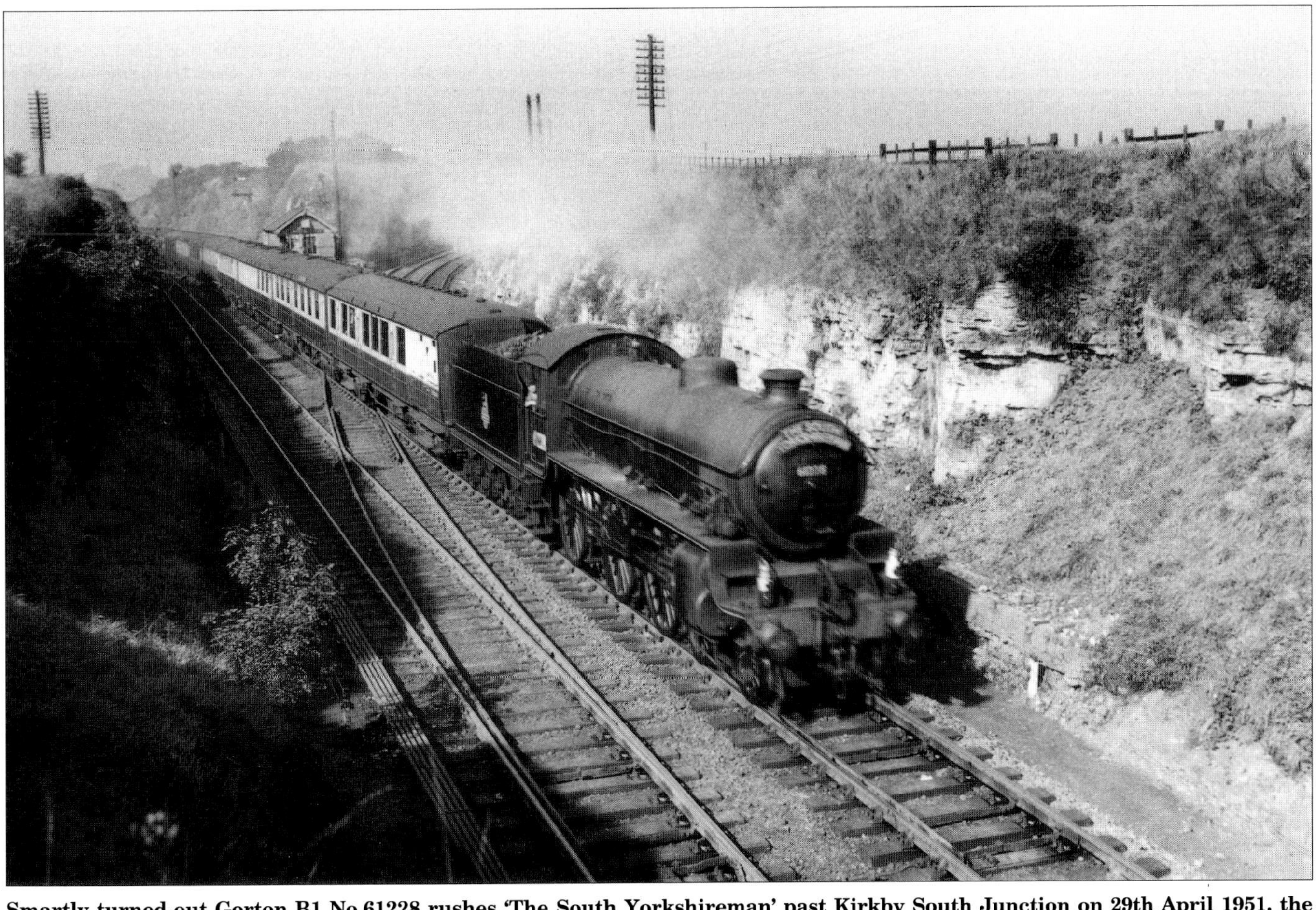

Smartly turned-out Gorton B1 No.61228 rushes 'The South Yorkshireman' past Kirkby South Junction on 29th April 1951, the Marylebone express being largely composed of Gresley coaches in 'blood and custard' livery. 'The Master Cutler' covered the same route through the East Midlands, but these were the only named trains in the Mansfield area. Despite the rock cutting, this spot was chosen as the springing point for the Great Northern Leen Valley Extension, which can be seen curving away beneath the first coach. Photograph Jack Cupit.

obstinately independent. The Midland was well placed to make a bid for the Ambergate and did so in 1851. Unfortunately, it had reckoned without Graham Hutchison, a director and major shareholder in the Great Northern who saw the strategic importance of this probe towards the East Midlands coalfield. Hutchison managed to purchase copious amounts of Ambergate shares and thwarted Midland aspirations. When further overtures were made by the Great Northern in the spring of 1852, his influence ensured that a working agreement was signed in time for the opening of the 'Towns Line' between Peterborough and Retford on 1st August. During the 1854 Parliamentary session, permission to 'work, lease or purchase' the Ambergate track was granted, the leasing option taking effect from April 1855. Independent access to Nottingham was assured when a line from Colwick to a terminus on London Road opened in October 1857. The rather grand buildings here incorporated the headquarters of the company (Nottingham & Grantham Railway & Canal Co. from 1860) until its absorption by the LNER in 1923.

By 1860, the Grantham-Nottingham line had assumed great importance, bearing in mind Midland opposition to an assault on the coalfield from Newark and Retford. The Great Northern accordingly secured permanent possession of the railway during 1861. There was a trickle of coal from local pits via the connection at Colwick, but the Midland refused to quote through rates from highly productive collieries further afield. So, in 1862, a Bill was deposited for a line from Colwick, round the south side of Nottingham, to Codnor Park, in the Erewash Valley. Essentially, this move was designed to force the Midland to acquiesce, which it did. Rates were agreed in January 1863, the Codnor Park plans then being dropped. However, with the opening of its London Extension from Bedford to St Pancras in 1868, the Midland no longer depended on the Great Northern for access to the capital via Hitchin. It therefore scrapped the 1863 agreement in 1871, effectively excluding its rival from the Erewash Valley. The Great Northern could either admit defeat or build its own line, and chose to do the latter.

The company acted quickly and came up with plans far more wide-ranging than the Codnor Park scheme. From Colwick, a line would sweep round the north of Nottingham then pass through Basford, Kimberley, Ilkeston and Derby before joining the North Staffordshire Railway at Egginton Junction. That all-important access to the Erewash Valley would be provided by a branch from Awsworth Junction to Pinxton. Every town along the route welcomed the project with open arms and Parliament sanctioned it on 25th July 1872. The railway was an expensive one, largely cutting across the grain of the country and requiring a profusion of viaducts, tunnels and substantial earthworks. Mineral traffic over the Pinxton-Awsworth Junction-Kimberley-Colwick section commenced at the end of August 1875, allowing the Great Northern back into the coalfield after an absence of 4½ years. The venture was an immediate and resounding success. Passenger services from Pinxton to Nottingham London Road began on 1st August 1876, Colwick sidings and eng shed being established three years la to deal with the burgeoning traffic.

By the time the Derby line openec April 1878, several collieries had be sunk along the Leen Valley and the Gr Northern turned its attention to this p tential source of revenue as well. The li from Basford to Annesley was authoris on 6th August 1880 and coal traffic ov the first couple of miles to Bestwood Co liery began in July 1881. Mineral traff over the remainder commenced durin October 1881 and a passenger service to Nottingham London Road started on 2nd October 1882. The Annesley tracks pursued a snaking course up the Leen Valley, involving several sharp curves and two crossings of the Midland near Hucknall. Again, the expenditure proved more than justified and by the turn of the century, the branch had been extended through the coalfield west of Mansfield. However, this development was associated with moves by the Manchester, Sheffield & Lincolnshire Railway, whose invasion of the area came from the north.

Edward Watkin became General Manager of the MS&L in 1853 and its Chairman eleven years later. For the rest of the century he was a force to be reckoned with in British railway politics. As seen in Chapter 4, his company's reaction to Midland plans for an extension from Mansfield to Worksop was fairly docile at first, but that soon changed and the 'liberation of the South Yorkshire coalfield' became an obsession. During 1871 the MS&L had discussions with the London & North Western about a line from Doncaster to Market Harborough via Worksop and in 1873 plans for a similar

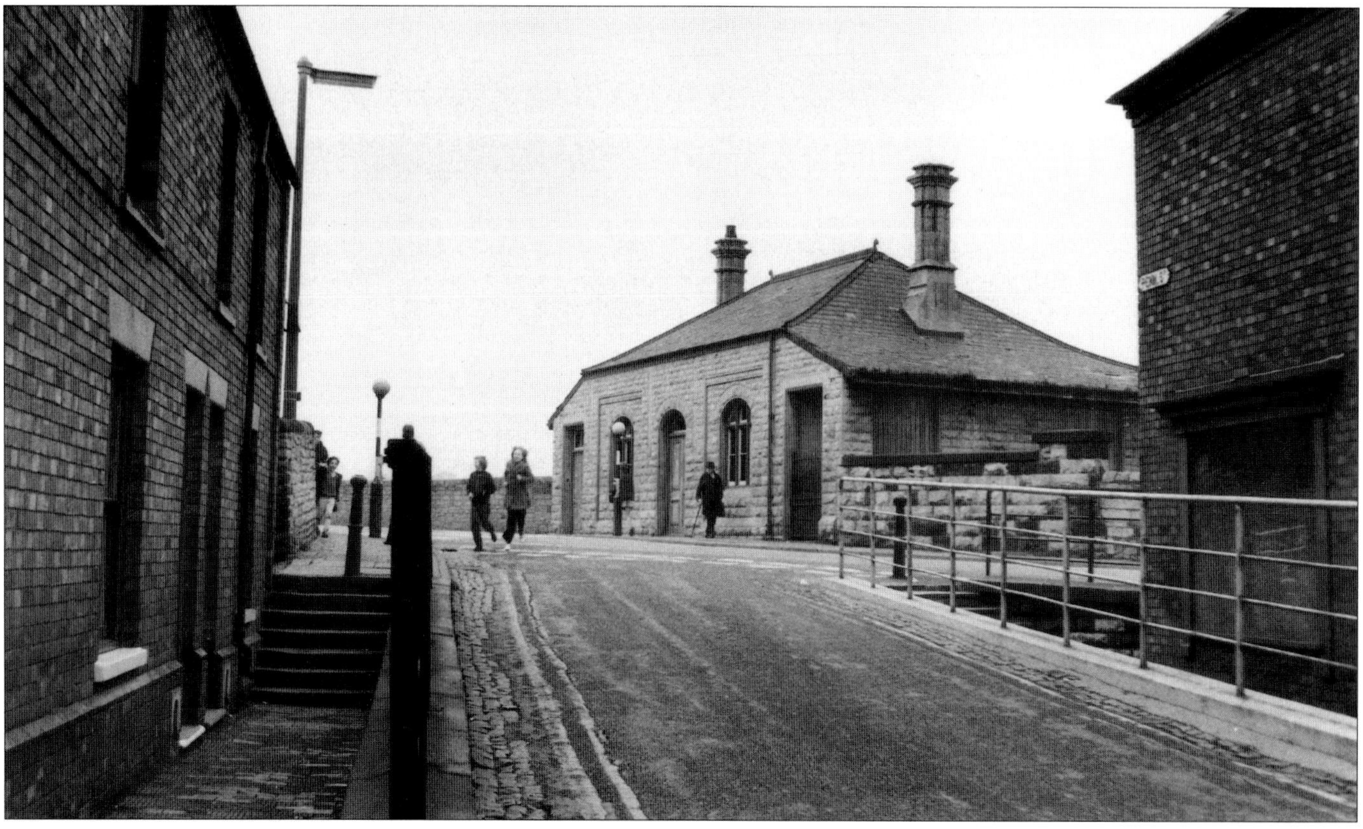

The Great Northern station at Sutton in Ashfield was in the town centre, but construction of the railway disrupted a long-established street layout. Although the line itself was in a cutting, an overbridge carrying the entrance building meant that Outram Street (subsequently known locally as Northern Bridge) had to be raised. Penn Street, from where this view was taken in October 1971, also had to be modified, as indicated by the steps and railings alongside the earlier terraced houses. By this time, the surprisingly elegant GN facilities were very derelict. Photograph Paul Anderson.

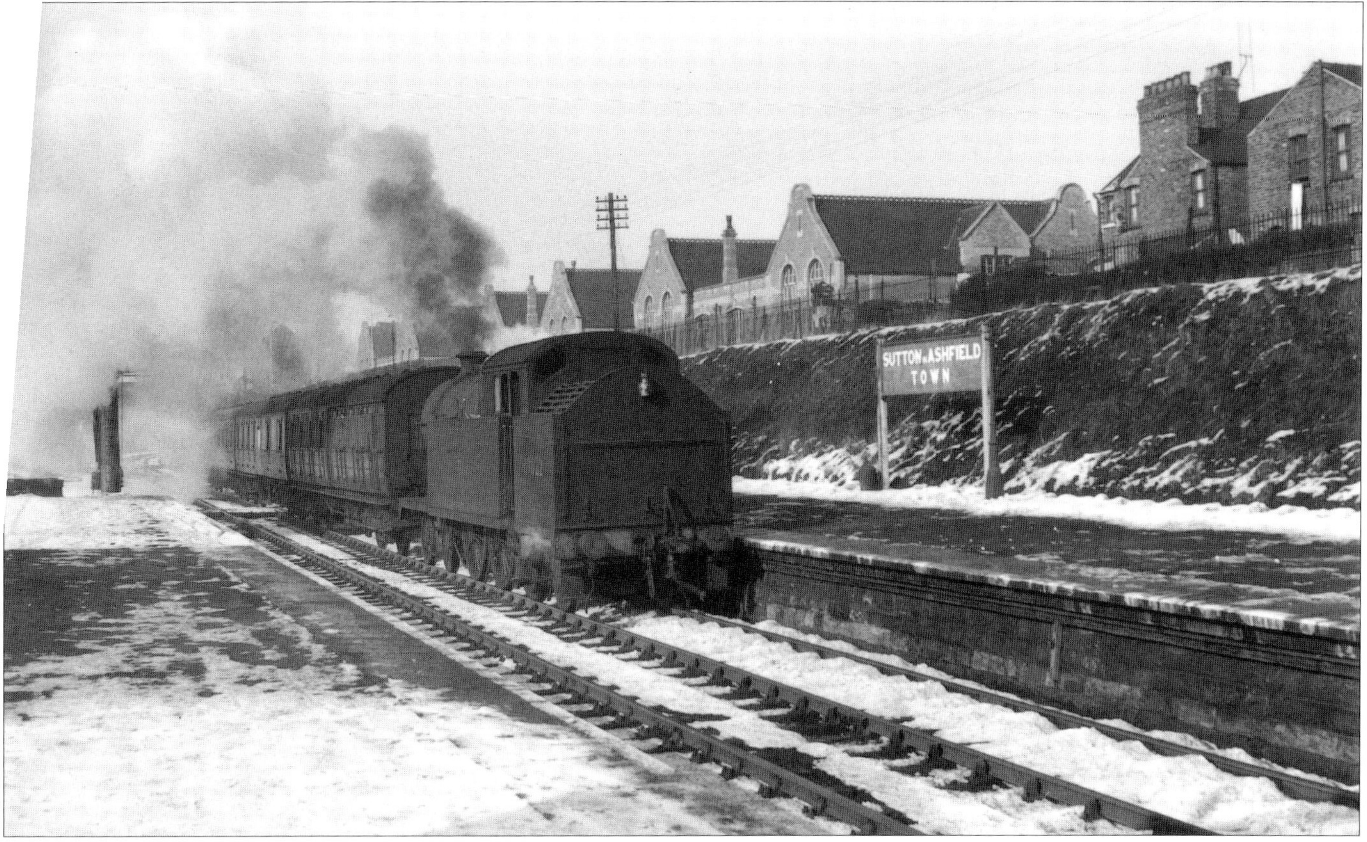

Although regular passenger services over the former Great Northern line through Sutton in Ashfield ceased in 1931, the station was well maintained for holiday trains and other specials, which continued to run for over thirty years. Then, in February 1956, regular workings to Nottingham Victoria were reintroduced, following closure of nearby Sutton in Ashfield Central on the Mansfield Railway. There were numerous complaints about inconvenient timings and it seems that the venture was never intended to succeed. On the bleak morning of 25th February 1956, Colwick A5 4-6-2T No.69822 draws its non-corridor stock into Town station, to await no more than a handful of passengers. Photograph Jack Cupit.

route from Conisborough to Northamptonshire jointly with the Midland actually reached Parliament, but nothing came of either scheme. As early as 1875, the Great Northern conceded that Nottingham was a legitimate target for the MS&L and watched as the Sheffield company launched unsuccessful schemes to reach the town, using running powers, during 1884 and 1888. Eventually, the MS&L decided to build most of the line itself. The Great Northern was highly suspicious of its neighbour's long term objectives, but realised that the Bill would probably pass anyway and granted access to Nottingham in return for running powers to Sheffield. On 26th July 1889 the MS&L branch from Beighton to Annesley was duly authorised.

Mineral workings from Woodhouse Junction on the Sheffield-Worksop line to Staveley Works began in December 1891, followed by a passenger service to Staveley on 1st June 1892. The remainder of the line to the end-on junction with the Great Northern at Annesley opened on 24th October 1892, finally giving the MS&L access to Nottingham for coal and goods. Sheffield-Nottingham passenger trains commenced on 2nd January 1893, the Great Northern reciprocating with a Nottingham-Staveley service on 28th January 1893. The latter only lasted for a few months. Before long, no less than seventeen mines were served by the new route.

From a mere 150ft above sea level at Beighton in the Rother Valley, the line climbed relentlessly through Killamarsh, Renishaw, Staveley, Duckmanton and Heath, to over 550ft at Pilsley. A twisting course across the coalfield

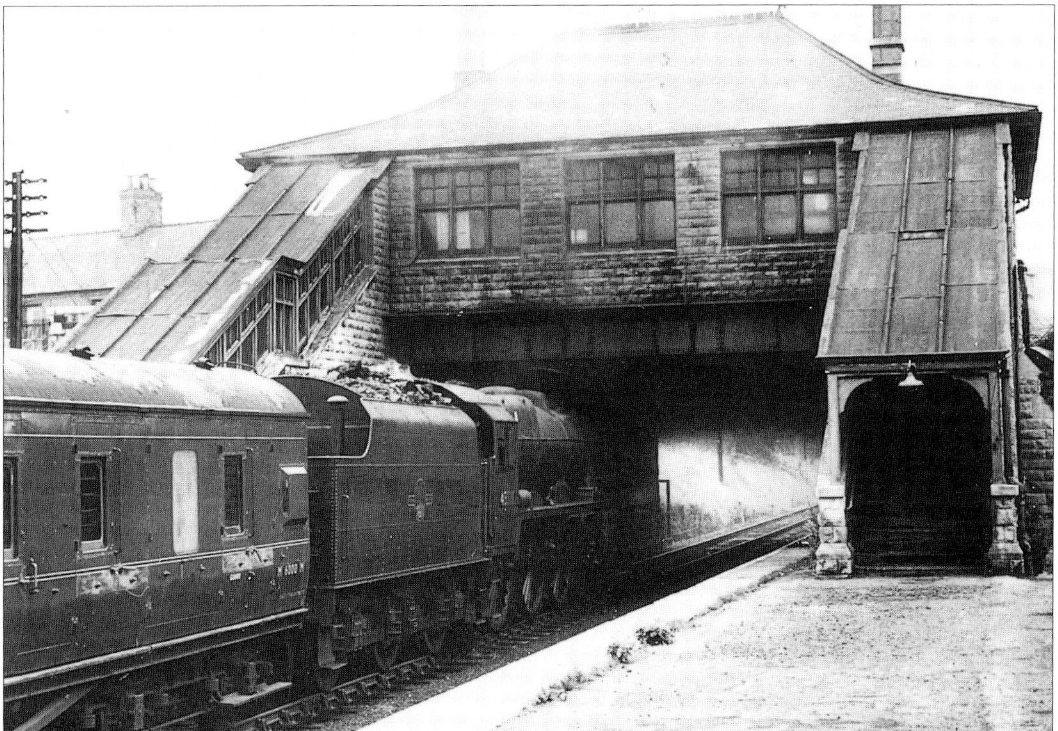

Sutton in Ashfield Town did have its moments! Liverpool Edge Hill's Rebuilt Patriot 4-6-0 No.45531 SIR FREDERICK HARRISON pauses at the station with a special for Oxford on 18th July 1963. The ample entrance building with its sophisticated sweeping roof rears above both platforms. Photograph H.B. Priestley.

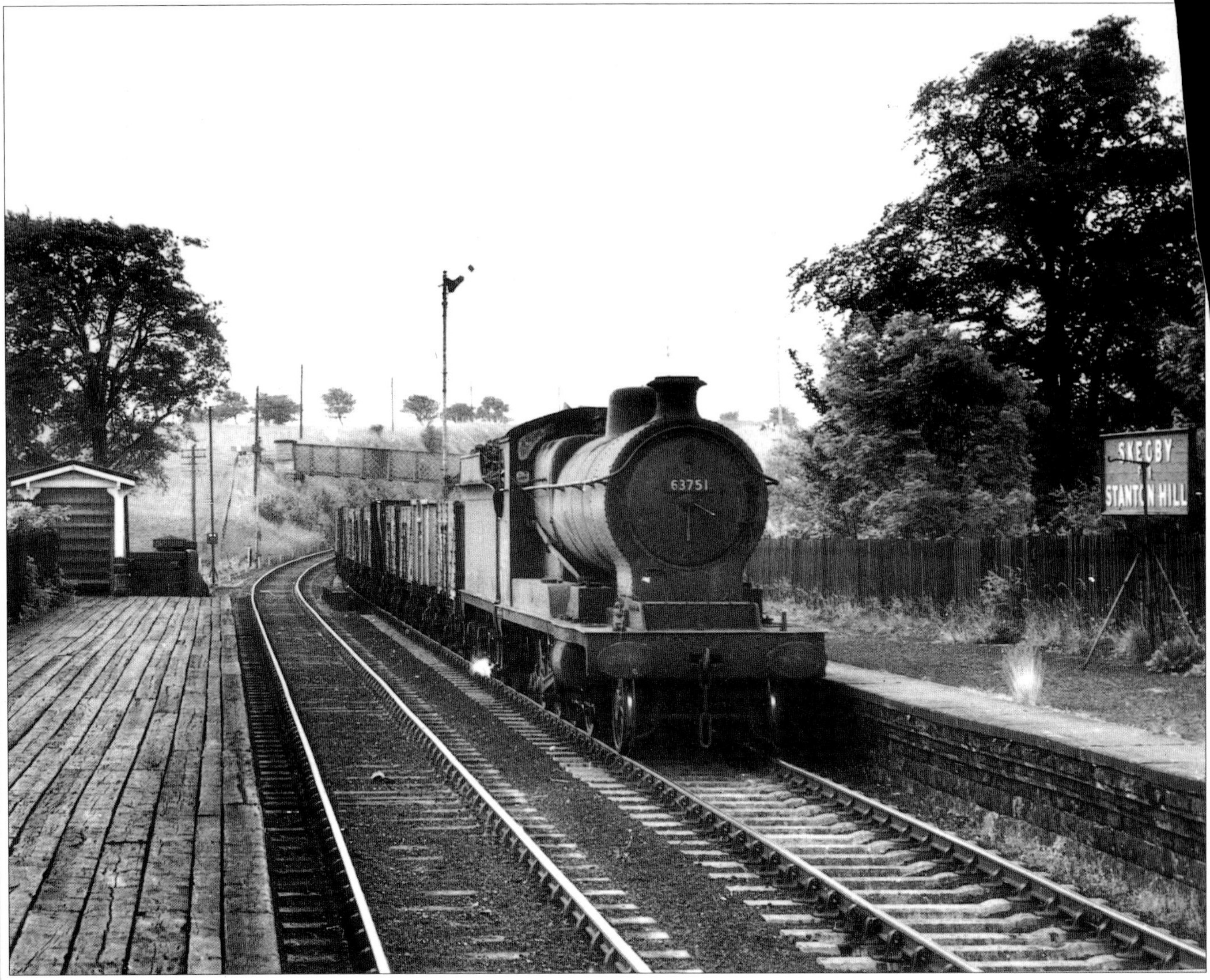

Skegby was a quiet farming village, devoid of collieries and more or less oblivious to the development of the surrounding coalfield, until the Great Northern opened a line through the middle of it in 1897. For seventy years, an endless procession of coal trains were audible from the ancient parish church, inns and limestone cottages. Robinson ROD class O4/3 No.63751 of Colwick shed does its bit to disturb the rural peace as it trundles north through Skegby with mineral empties, on 2nd July 1955. The little 'confessional' at the end of the platform is actually a stairway from the booking office at street level. Photograph H.B. Priestley.

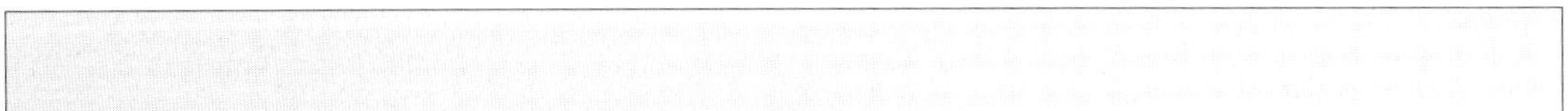

The platforms at Skegby were something of a hotchpotch, comprising both timber construction and ash filling behind stone edging. Fortunately, the neat little buildings provided ample compensation. WD 2-8-0 No.90000, a long-term Colwick resident, rumbles south with a loaded coal train on 2nd July 1955. Photograph H.B. Priestley.

hills took the railway past Tibshelf and Blackwell to 450ft in the Erewash headwaters just south of Kirkby in Ashfield. Ahead lay Robin Hood's Hills, which had caused the Midland some expense forty-five years earlier. The MS&L tracks were somewhat lower than the Nottingham-Mansfield line and the new Annesley Tunnel, parallel to the Midland and slightly to the east, was 1,001yds long. It was preceded by a deep and lengthy rock cutting through Magnesian Limestone, but the southern portal revealed open country bordering the grounds of Newstead Abbey. In order to reassure the Great Northern that this line was not the start of a trunk route to London, the proposed stations were to be 'of ordinary character'. They were built of timber and, indeed, a lot less substantial than those recently erected on secondary lines further north. Kirkby in Ashfield was typical. A low building clad in horizontal boards and finished off with a pitched slate roof parallel to the tracks was enhanced by a fairly generous platform canopy consisting of five glazed gables.

Back in 1889, Watkin had written to the Great Northern suggesting a joint line to London, but the response from an alarmed King's Cross board was negative. So the MS&L Chairman replied, 'The work is inevitable and it will be done without you, if it cannot be done with you'. This was despite assurances the same year that there was no intention of extending the proposed Beighton-Annesley branch, a hollow sentiment as it turned out. MS&L plans for a ninety-two mile route from Annesley to the Metropolitan Railway at Quainton Road in Buckinghamshire were announced in the autumn of 1890 and the Great Northern (with the Midland and LNW as allies) prepared itself for a Parliamentary battle the following session. The Great Northern also introduced its own Bill for an extension of the Leen Valley branch to Shirebrook. In June 1891, a House of Commons Committee found the MS&L plans somewhat wanting and threw out the London Extension, to Watkin's indignation. Shortly afterwards, the Great Northern withdrew its Leen Valley Extension Bill.

The MS&L Chairman was determined to re-introduce the London project during the next session and again invited the Great Northern to participate, putting the latter in a dilemma. There was much debate at King's Cross as to whether to keep up the fight or enter into an agreement over running powers and other arrangements, such as a joint station at Nottingham. Free competition was becoming fashionable and the MS&L Bill was very likely to pass at the second attempt, so with resignation the Great Northern decided to co-operate. The company also decided to submit its Leen Valley Extension again. Although the trunk route to London had passed most stages by June 1892, Parliament was dissolved before the process had been completed, so the Act was not passed until 28th March 1893.

Meanwhile, the Leen Valley Extension had been authorised, on 20th June 1892, allowing the Great Northern to extend its Annesley branch to Kirkby in Ashfield, Sutton in Ashfield, Skegby, Teversal, Pleasley and Shirebrook. By this time, relations with the MS&L were improving and an Act of 29th June 1893 sanctioned running powers over the newly opened Beighton line to a proposed Kirkby South Junction, thus eliminating the need for a third tunnel through Robin Hood's Hills. Because of heavy commitments elsewhere, work did not begin until June 1895 and only then after potential customers told the King's Cross board to hurry up. The Great Northern had taken an interest in the Lancashire, Derbyshire & East Coast since its inception and an Act of 29th July 1896 authorised a short extension from Shirebrook to Langwith Junction on the East to West.

Summit Colliery at Kirkby was reached in September 1896 and single track working to Silverhill Colliery, on what became the Teversall branch, commenced on 8th February 1897. A further section of the main line, from Skegby to Pleasley Colliery, opened for minerals on 1st March 1898. The inauguration of passenger services between Nottingham London Road and Skegby on 4th April 1898 was used to celebrate the building of the line, invited guests travelling on special trains from London King's Cross and Nottingham. Pleasley to Shirebrook Colliery opened on 26th November 1900 and the connection with the LD&EC was commissioned on 29th May 1901. By this time, the new railway had proved itself yet another highly lucrative probe into the coalfield. Passenger services were extended to Shirebrook on 1st November 1901.

The Leen Valley Extension had no level crossings and neither tunnels nor viaducts, but nevertheless was heavily engineered to maintain reasonable gradients for moving bulk coal traffic. Embankments and rock cuttings abounded and there were numerous stone or girder bridges. At Kirkby South Junction, 450ft above sea level, the MS&L was in a substantial limestone cutting and the Great Northern had to carve a passage out of this to reach the upper Erewash Valley. A bridge over the Midland's Pye Bridge line comprised two deck girder spans to allow widening of the earlier route to four tracks if necessary. Beyond it, an embankment and cutting on the opposite side of the valley marked the course of a west-north spur which trailed in from the MS&L main line at Kirkby North Junction. A shallow cutting through friable strata carried the line through Kirkby in Ashfield and on to the rather featureless River Maun watershed, dominated by Summit Colliery.

Following a bridge under the short Midland branch from Sutton Junction, another excavation through Sutton in Ashfield (2¾ miles from Kirkby South Junction) facilitated a gentle two mile descent to the Meden Valley. Just north of

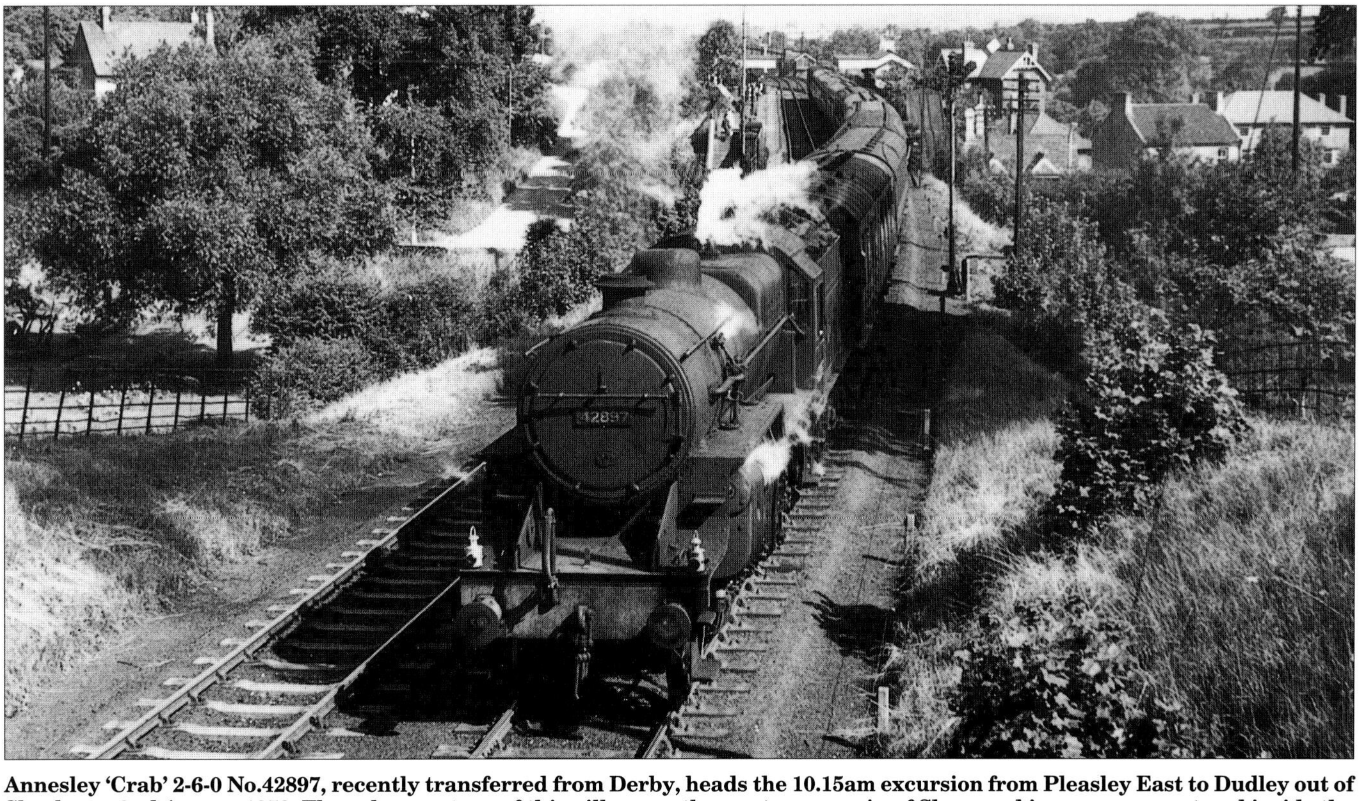

Annesley 'Crab' 2-6-0 No.42897, recently transferred from Derby, heads the 10.15am excursion from Pleasley East to Dudley out of Skegby on 2nd August 1959. The sylvan nature of this village on the western margin of Sherwood is very apparent and inside the parish church there is a tangible reminder of its woodland past, in the form of an effigy of a 14th century forester. Slung by his side is his official badge of office, a hunting horn. Even the Great Northern managed to penetrate the territory of Robin Hood! Photograph R.J. Buckley.

Skegby (4 miles) the 1¼ mile Teversal branch veered off to the west, whilst the main line ran through undulating ground overlooking the River Meden, requiring a succession of cuttings and embankments. Beyond Pleasley (6¼ miles) another embankment was punctuated by a bridge across the Midland tracks from Mansfield Woodhouse to Westhouses, followed by the mightiest excavation of all. The descent from 400ft at Pleasley Park to 300ft at Shirebrook (8½ miles) passed through the Meden-Poulter watershed and demanded a 1¼ mile sheer rock cutting up to 40ft deep. Finally, a high embankment punctuated by several bridges curved round the west side of Shirebrook and led to the LD&EC at Langwith Junction, 9½ miles from Kirkby South Junction.

The Great Northern gained a reputation for its ample yet architecturally impoverished stations. On the Derbyshire lines, large red brick buildings with blue brick courses, steeply-pitched roofs and tall chimneys were the norm. Long-demolished Pinxton was typical, and a good example survives at Kimberley. There was a variation at road overbridges, where a painfully undistinguished block sat on a girder deck over the tracks, as at Linby in the Leen Valley. Fortunately, the Leen Valley Extension fared somewhat better, partly because rough-hewn limestone was employed. Indeed, Sutton in Ashfield was quite impressive and furthermore, it was right in the town centre. The street level building had an unusual hipped roof, which swept out almost to the horizontal on three sides. A pair of Tudor chimneys, reminiscent of 1840s fashion, added a touch of elegance. Covered stairways led down to the platforms, where substantial waiting rooms sported generous canopies.

Skegby station stood on an embankment, wooden planking being used for part of the up platform. Neat little timber buildings with flat canopies were provided at this level, whilst the office block was a small but complex single-storey stone structure tucked away against the embankment. Gable ends, either chamfered or treated with prominent bargeboards seemed to dominate it. An enclosed passageway passed through its own bridge under the tracks and covered stairways led to the platforms. The slightly later stations at Pleasley and Shirebrook had conventional side buildings with stubby chimneys and, if anything, an even rougher finish to the limestone. Teversal had a single-platform station featuring a plain brick structure with tall chimneys. There were no timetabled services, only miners' trains and pit holiday excursions. However, the main line enjoyed a generous and, as it turned out, over-optimistic passenger service of ten trains each way between Nottingham Victoria and Shirebrook from November 1901.

On 1st August 1897, when the huge task of building the London Extension was well advanced, the MS&L changed its name from Manchester, Sheffield & Lincolnshire to Great Central Railway. Coal traffic commenced on 1st July 1898 and regular passenger services began on 15th March 1899. The new route exuded confidence, a culmination of seventy years of main line railway construction. From Annesley it swept down the Leen Valley, round the back of Hucknall and across the Midland at Bulwell on a magnificent blue brick viaduct. Beyond Basford, tunnels led to the huge Nottingham joint station, opened on 24th May 1900 and christened Victoria three weeks later. Connecting lines between the Great Central and Great Northern were built at Bulwell, Basford and Nottingham London Road, reflecting the new spirit of co-operation between the two companies.

Extensive yards and a large engine shed were built at Annesley, echoing the arrangements at Colwick on the Great Northern. Passenger stations at Hucknall, Bulwell and Basford had island platforms, a characteristic feature of the London Extension. The Great Central route was the only true main line in the Mansfield area and sumptuous restaurant car expresses from Manchester to London Marylebone added a touch of class to the coalfield from the outset. In fact, Robinson's handsome 4-4-0s, Atlantics and 4-6-0s in bright green and deep red, hauling chocolate and French grey or varnished teak coaches were an almost incongruous sight in the grimy setting of Kirkby and Annesley during the early 1900s. More in keeping with the surroundings was the relentless flow of coal, steel and general goods traffic. However, it is worth noting the view of a contemporary historian who described the London Extension as 'a belated and almost entirely superfluous product of the original era of fighting construction'.

The Leen Valley Extension was built for coal and while there was an abundance of this once vital commodity to be moved, the line flourished. Its appendages gradually fell by the wayside, however. The west to north spur from Kirkby North Junction on the Great Central saw precious little use, despite its high construction costs. It was virtually moribund by 1905, completely disused by 1918 and dismantled about 1922. Passenger traffic had always been a financial liability and the LNER withdrew services between Shirebrook South and Nottingham Victoria on 14th September 1931. The

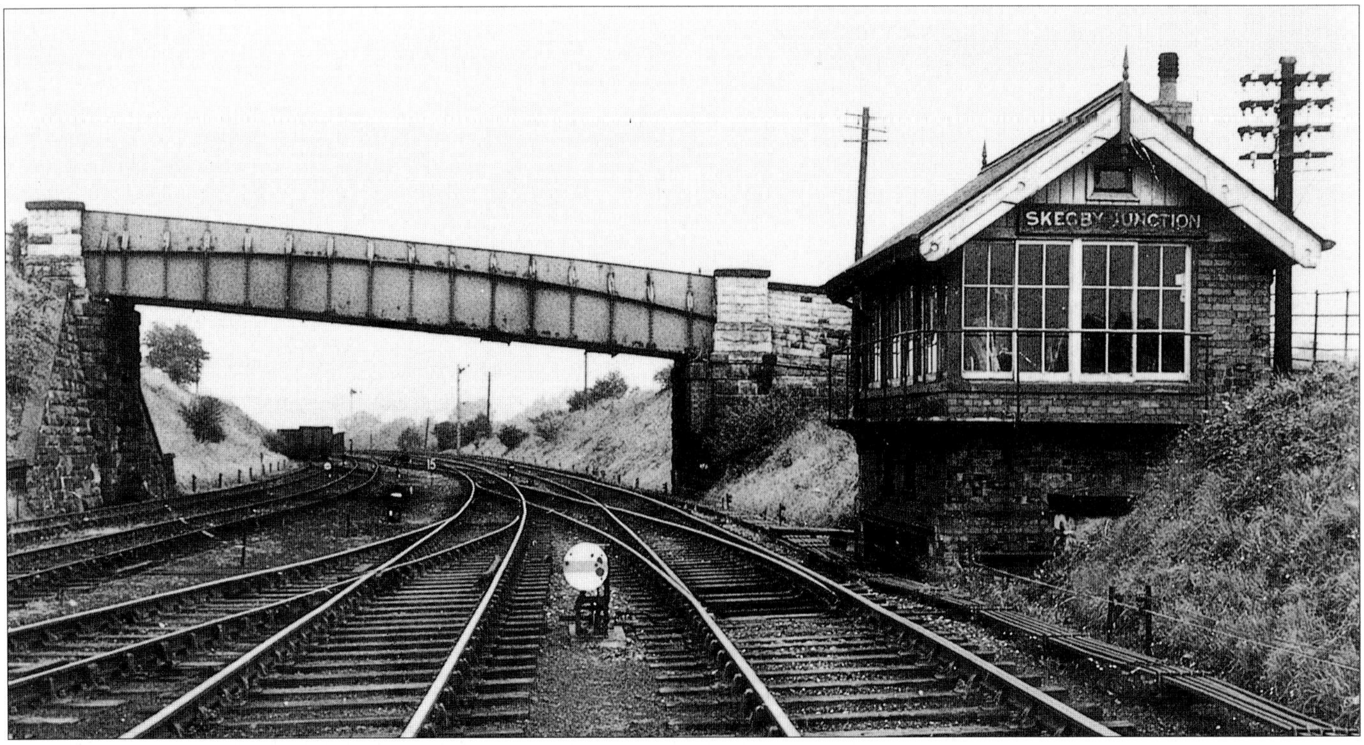

Skegby Junction signal box, on 14th August 1965. It controlled the divergence of the Teversall branch from the Leen Valley Extension proper. The cabin is characteristic of late nineteenth century Great Northern practice, while the occupation bridge beyond it was typical of such structures on this line. Shallow bowstring plate girders with extended metal sidewalls rested on limestone abutments. This particular example still stands and another good example carries the main road adjacent to the present Kirkby in Ashfield station. Photograph H.B. Priestley.

goods yards at Teversall and Skegby closed on 1st October 1951 and 4th August 1952 respectively. Shirebrook South retained its facilities until 4th February 1957. Meanwhile, passenger trains serving Sutton in Ashfield Central had ceased (see Chapter 9) so British Railways reintroduced services from the former Great Northern station at Sutton in Ashfield Town to Nottingham Victoria, on 20th February 1956. The experiment was accompanied by the warning, 'use it or lose it'. As a result of poor loadings, they lost it, although local people often complained of inconvenient timings, especially during the evening. Nevertheless, the Leen Valley Extension, in conjunction with the former LD&EC branch from Beighton to Langwith Junction, remained an important diversionary route when the main line was closed for engineering work. Excursions to the seaside, London and other destinations continued to run until the mid-1960s.

During the 1950s, named trains such as the 'Master Cutler' and 'South Yorkshireman' attempted to maintain the proud tradition of the former Great Central main line, despite its questionable future following the creation of a unified national railway network in 1948. But the once-cherished Manchester-Marylebone expresses, hauled by Gresley A3 Pacifics until September 1957, finished in 1961. The half a dozen languid stopping trains between Nottingham Victoria, Chesterfield Central and Sheffield Victoria finished on 4th March 1963, resulting in the closure of wayside stations such as Kirkby Bentinck (which had gained its local suffix in 1925). When residual cross-country trains, notably the diesel – hauled Bournemouth-York, were diverted to the North Midland route on 5th September 1966, the Great Central main line was destined to become a siding from Staveley to Arkwright Colliery. Further inroads into Leen Valley Extension facilities were also taking place, Pleasley goods depot closing on 2nd October 1963, followed by the yard at Sutton in Ashfield on 1st February 1965. With rationalisation rampant in the coalfield, the route between Langwith Junction and Kirkby South Junction closed completely on 27th May 1968. Fortunately, that was not the end of the story for this former Great Northern line. Today, the track through Kirkby in Ashfield is carrying no less than 52 passenger trains on Saturdays *(see Chapter 10)*.

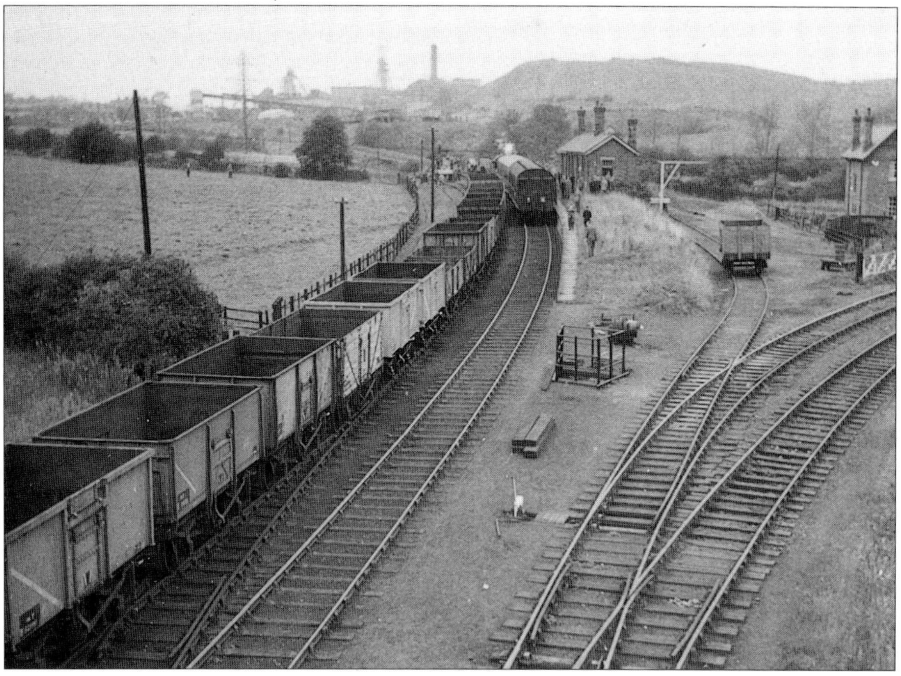

Teversal has a long history, as revealed by its fine Norman church. More recently, it was the fictional home of D.H. Lawrence's Lady Chatterley. On a more prosaic level, the village was dominated by Teversal and Silverhill collieries for over a century, the latter forming a backdrop to the Great Northern terminus in this view taken from the Midland embankment on 19th September 1959. A railtour stands at the single platform station, which had a fair-sized building but saw no advertised services, just miners' trains and excursions. The tracks going off to the right, past the goods yard and stationmaster's house, leads to Teversal Colliery. Photograph Robert Humm Collection.

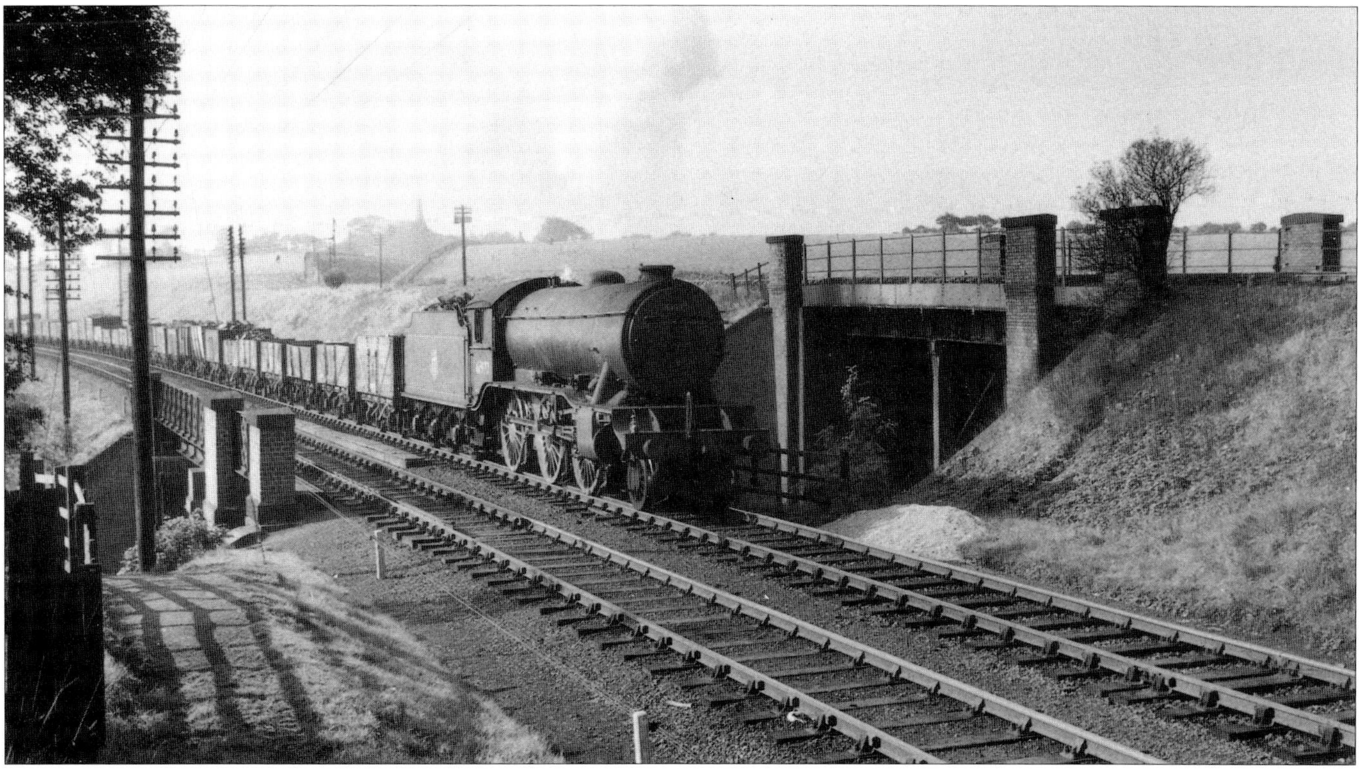

Annesley K3 2-6-0 No.61977 heads along the Great Central main line towards Kirkby South Junction with an up mineral working on 29th September 1951. The sheer complexity of the railway system at this point was quite remarkable. Prominent on the right is the Mansfield Railway, firstly on an embankment, then curving away through a cutting towards Kirkby in Ashfield. Although the Great Northern is away to the right, its long-disused north to west spur passed beneath the Mansfield Railway just this side of the cutting. The plate girder bridges cross the Midland route to Pye Bridge, while the original Mansfield & Pinxton formation lies beneath the earthworks in the immediate foreground. Photograph Jack Cupit.

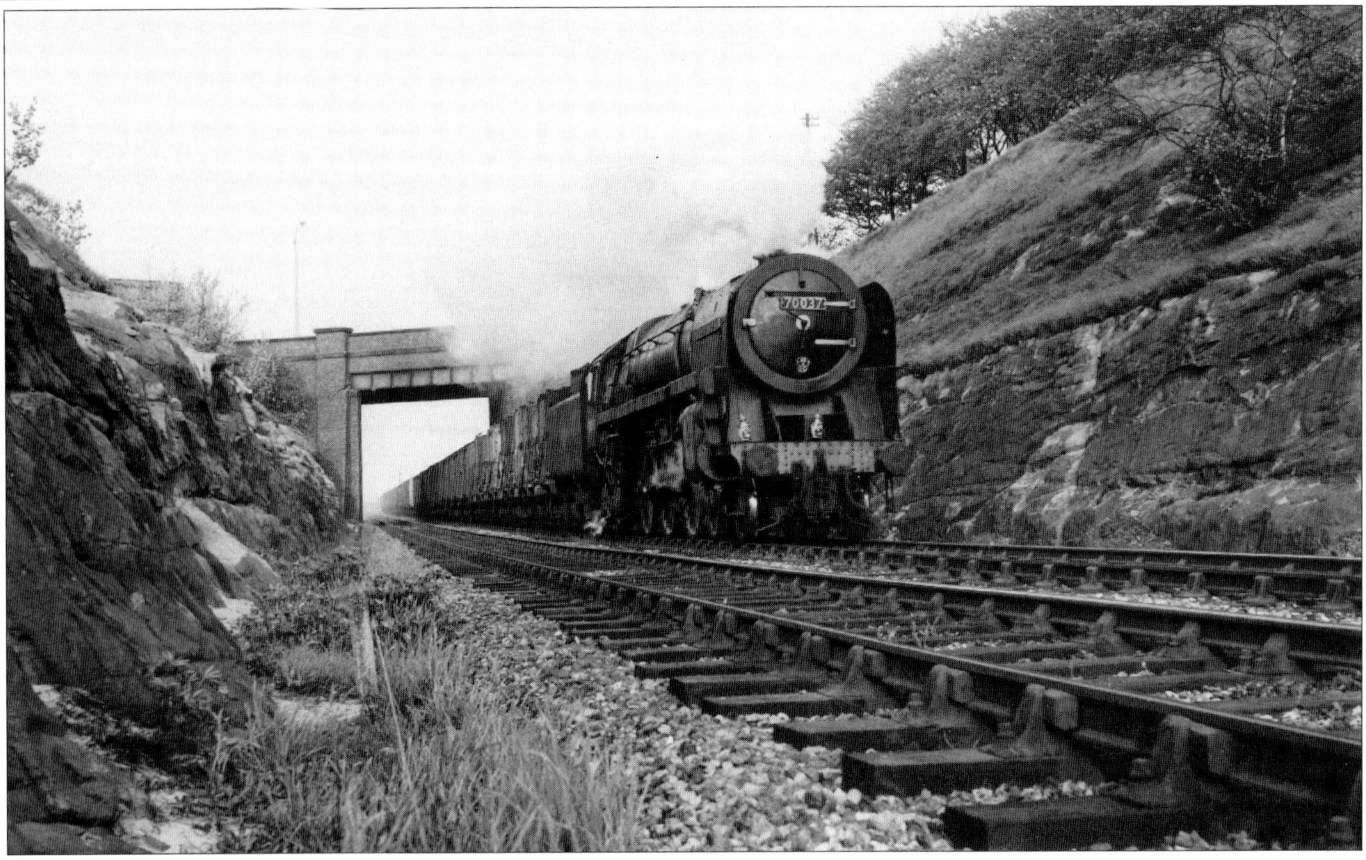

Britannia Pacific No.70037 HEREWARD THE WAKE, recently transferred from Norwich to Immingham, lifts the Grimsby-Whitland fish up the last few yards of the 1 in 200 ascent from Forest Town on 16th May 1962. Freights not calling at Mansfield took a run at the bank in order to gain momentum for the climb to Sutton on the far side of the Maun Valley. In the middle distance, Clipstone Road bridge spans the deep sandstone cutting. Photograph Jack Cupit.

On 3rd August 1958, B1 4-6-0 No.61177 climbs out of Mansfield and plunges into the sandstone cutting at Windmill Ridge with a Kirkby in Ashfield Central-Mablethorpe excursion via the LD&EC, Lincoln and Firsby. The bridge carrying a lane to Ravensdale Estate was a favourite childhood haunt of the photographer. Although No.61177 was a Colwick engine at the time, it had been at Stratford and Lincoln sheds since its construction in 1949. Photograph Jack Cupit.

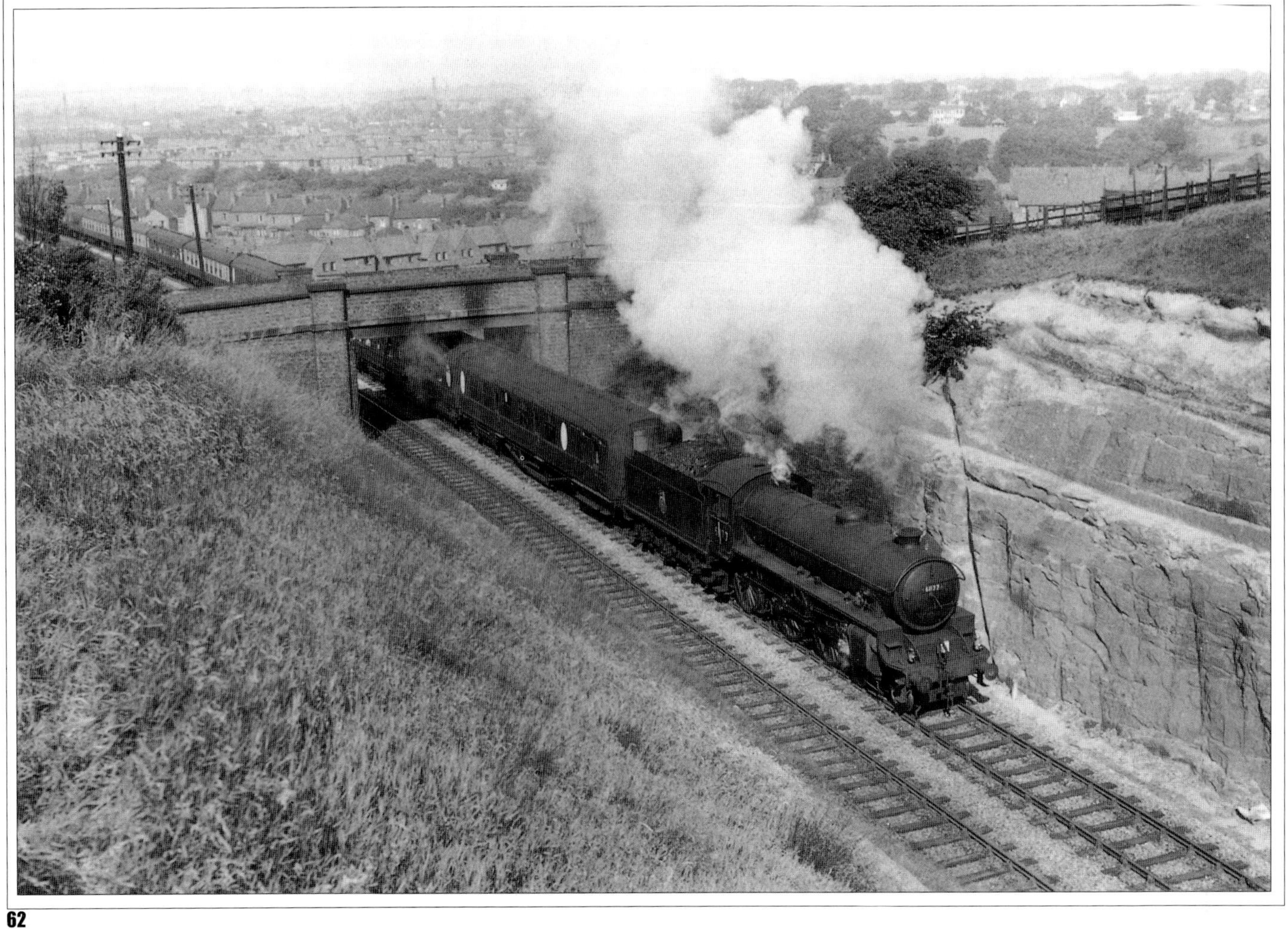

Chapter 9

THE MANSFIELD RAILWAY

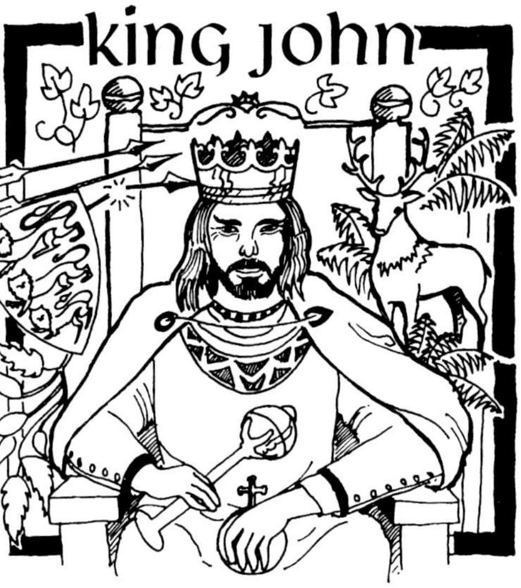

Around 1809, coal owners in the upper Erewash Valley were eager to build a railway to Mansfield, their enthusiasm resulting in the formation of the Mansfield & Pinxton company, as described way back in Chapter 2. A century later, the proprietors of new and proposed collieries east of Mansfield joined forces with prominent local residents to promote an independent railway to serve the district, proof at the time that there really was 'nothing new under the sun'. The Mansfield Railway was one of the last conventional steam-operated lines offering both goods and passenger services to be built in Britain. It gave the town a second through station, not the most attractive in the area but certainly the most remarkable. Traffic was far more varied than that over the Midland route and included long distance freight, making the Mansfield Railway, in effect, a secondary main line. In later years, there were even regular workings by BR Britannia Pacifics.

Despite a peripheral incursion by the MS&L from Beighton and the presence of the Great Northern at Pinxton and Annesley, the Midland seemed to be fairly complacent about its monopoly around Mansfield. Rates for coal and goods traffic were deemed unreasonably high and passenger services were the subject of a constant stream of complaints. Furthermore, the long-awaited deep mines in Sherwood Forest were about to become a reality by 1890, with the Mansfield-Southwell line ideally placed to tap them. With promotional activity concerning the Leen Valley and London extensions in full flow, Mansfield Town Council approached both the Great Northern and MS&L during 1891-92 in the hope of getting a branch line, but neither showed the slightest interest. Shortly afterwards, a body known as the Mansfield Railway Commissioners was established. Although this organisation managed to shame the Midland into improving passenger services, what the town really wanted was an alternative railway.

A great deal of lobbying took place during 1895. In July there was talk of sending a deputation to King's Cross to meet the Great Northern Board. In October, the Town Clerk heard of a scheme to build a line from Sutton in Ashfield to Warsop on the LD&EC and asked the Great Northern to become involved. Later that month, King's Cross was urged to alter the course of its Leen Valley Extension to pass through Mansfield. During November, much excitement was generated by a proposed railway from Burton on Trent to Retford via Ashbourne, Cromford, Clay Cross and Mansfield, but that scheme soon faded away. At last, in autumn 1896, Parliament approved an LD&EC branch from Edwinstowe to Mansfield. However, the Commissioners were upset by the prospect of a level

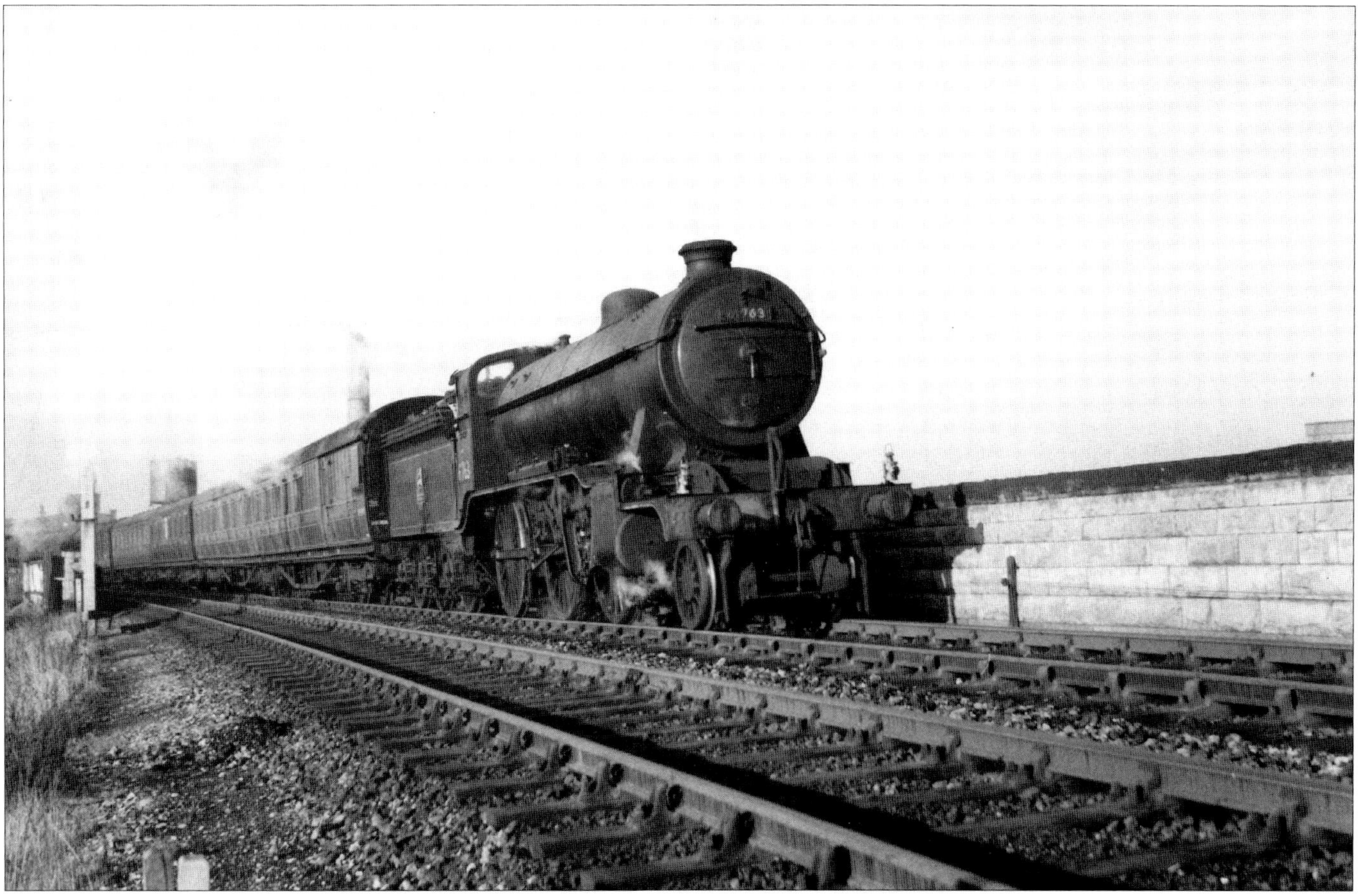

Class K2/2 2-6-0 No.61763, one of Colwick's seemingly permanent residents, heads a Summer Saturday Nottingham Victoria-Mablethorpe holiday train out of Mansfield Central on 6th September 1952. As was customary during the 1950s, the articulated twin behind the engine has its depot and set number painted on the end, in this case Basford 16. Immediately north of Ratcliffe Gate, the formation was a sloping embankment on the east side and a vertical retaining wall to the west, as can be seen in the foreground. Photograph Jack Cupit.

crossing at Pelham Street near the intended terminus and actually withdrew their support! Because of its parlous financial state, the LD&EC was more than happy to abandon the whole idea. There was a half-hearted attempt to promote a link from the Potteries to Retford via Ashbourne and Mansfield in January 1897, but needless to say, this too came to nought. A lull followed, frustration no doubt having sapped the energy of the Commissioners.

With the Bolsover Colliery Company's huge Mansfield Crown Farm mine drawing its first coal in 1905, the need for an alternative to the Midland assumed considerable importance once more. From the end of 1906, relentless pressure was put on the Great Central to build a line from Annesley to Clipstone through the eastern outskirts of Mansfield. Even the vaguest of rumours that a branch from the main line north of Kirkby to Sutton in Ashfield and Mansfield was being considered prompted enquiries and resulted in a deputation visiting Great Central headquarters at Marylebone. The Mansfield contingency urged the GC Board to alter its starting point to Annesley, but this argument proved totally irrelevant, for with depressing predictability the scheme fell through. Such indifference on the part of established companies was baffling. Crown Farm was destined to become the largest pit in the country, with an estimated output of 1,200,000 tons of coal a year, while the proposed collieries at Rufford and Clipstone would most likely produce 1,750,000 tons between them. Nevertheless, it was now abundantly clear to the worthies of Mansfield that if they wanted an alternative railway they would have to build it themselves.

Landowners, notably the influential Duke of Portland, gave their unequivocal support when the Mansfield Railway Company was formed. The Chairman was J. Plowright-Houfton JP, Managing Director of Bolsover Collieries, and among the directors were R.M. Knowles, Chairman of the Bolsover Company and W.J. Chadburn, a well known Mansfield businessman. Before long, the Great Central began to take a keen interest in the project, especially when it realised that half a million tons of coal a year from Crown Farm and Rufford would be exported through Immingham Docks. Furthermore, the new line would shorten the distance from Grimsby and Lincoln to Nottingham, Leicester and London by five miles. In turn, Mansfield councillors were delighted by the prospect of their town enjoying main line status. Parliament brushed aside Great Northern and Midland objections and sanctioned the route from Clipstone to Kirkby in Ashfield on 26th July 1910. Requests by the Great Northern and London & North Western for running powers were also dismissed. The Great Central had already promised to work and maintain the line for 60% of gross receipts, but wanted further guarantees. An agreement dated 28th October 1910 restrained the local concern from granting running powers or selling, leasing or amalgamating with other companies without the explicit agreement of Marylebone. How the worm had turned!

Construction work on the easiest and potentially most lucrative section, from Clipstone to Mansfield Colliery, began in 1911. The first coal train for Immingham left that pit on 6th June 1913 and regular traffic began ten days later. A 'model village' known as Forest Town was erected by the Bolsover Company on the edge of Mansfield, its houses providing miners and their families with far better accommodation than the terraced streets built thirty years earlier, at Newstead in the Leen Valley for example. With the completion of several substantial earthworks, the line was extended through Mansfield to a large goods depot, on 2nd June 1914. The company then went back to Parliament and on 8th July 1914 obtained an Act for the Clipstone and Rufford colliery branches, a south to west curve at Clipstone and modifications to the junction at Kirkby in Ashfield. Progress was hampered by the war, although the mile long Clipstone branch opened on 13th June 1916, together with a half mile spur to Clipstone Camp. The latter was built by the War Office and the camp itself had a platform for troops, horses and stores. A passenger service operated to and from Mansfield. The remainder of the main line, from Mansfield to Kirkby South Junction, opened for goods on 4th Sep-

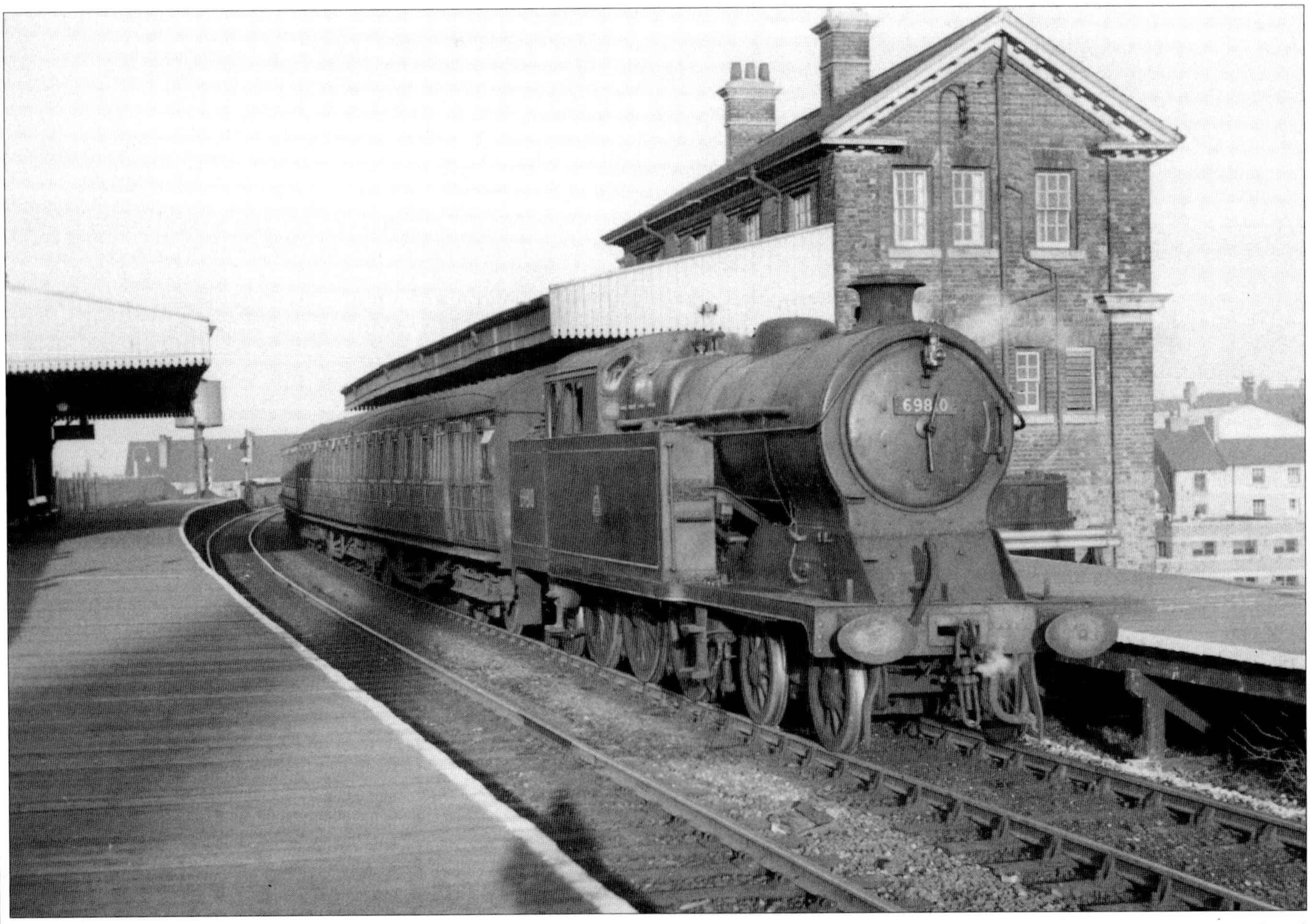

Class A5/1 4-6-2T No.69810 simmers in low evening sunshine and long shadows as it waits to leave Mansfield Central with a local train for Nottingham Victoria in the autumn of 1955. Although the refreshment room never served a single cup of tea, there were watering facilities for locos and many goods trains stopped here for the purpose. Typical GC water cranes stood at either end of the station – the one at the end of the down platform is visible in the distance. Photograph T.G. Hepburn.

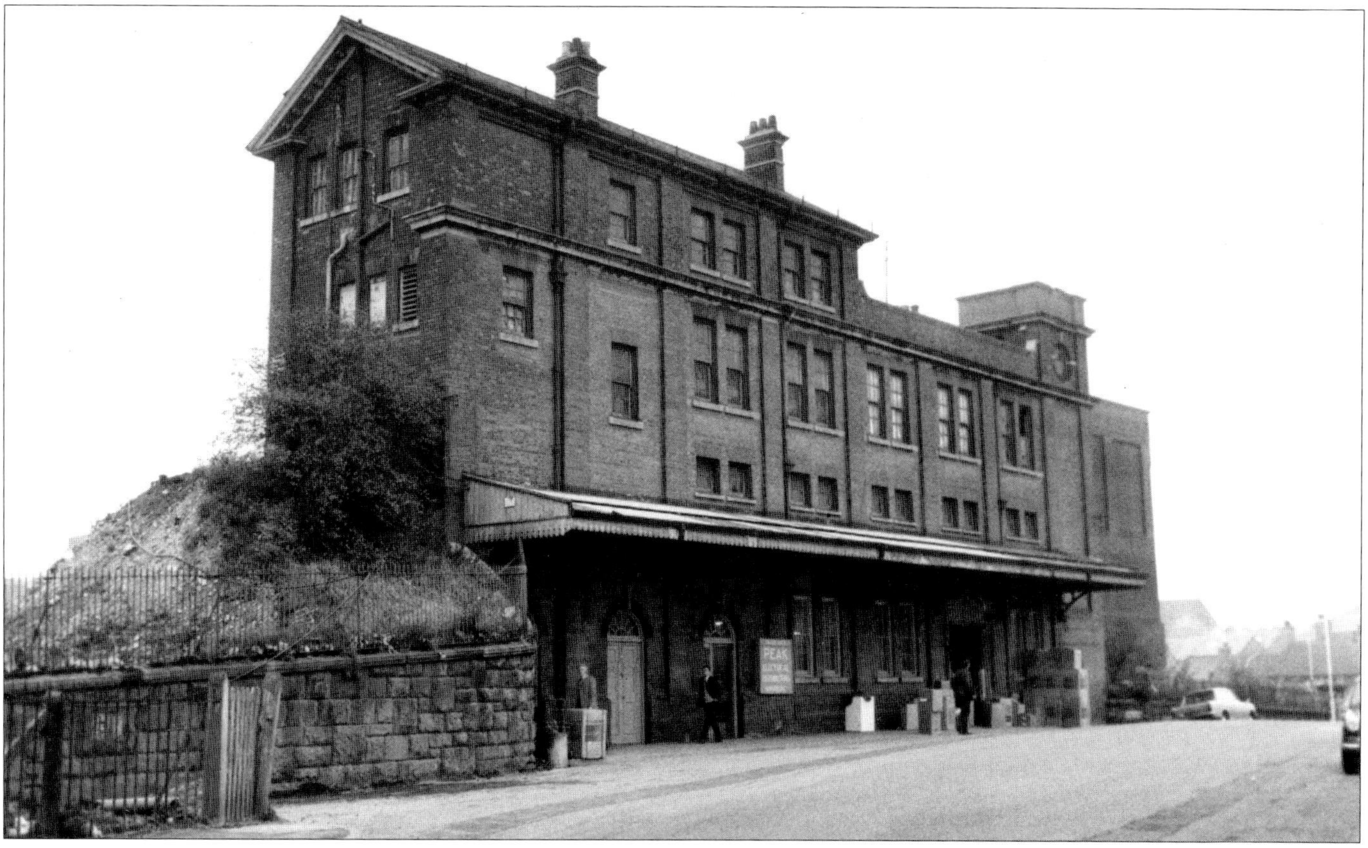

The gaunt pile of Mansfield Central rears above Great Central Road on 17th August 1971. By this time the embankment had been removed, making the building appear even more stark and towering than when it was in use for passenger traffic. The upper storey windows in the second and third bays from the right, distinguished by their lighter appearance, identify the refreshment room which never opened. Photograph Paul Anderson.

tember 1916. It was followed by Clipstone west curve on 18th March 1918 and the two mile Rufford Colliery branch on 8th July 1918. By this time the coal concentration sidings just south of Clipstone Junction were in operation. Initially, there were five roads for empties and five for full loads destined for Immingham, Doncaster and elsewhere, each siding having a capacity of eighty wagons.

In the cramped confines of the Magnesian Limestone cutting at Kirkby South Junction, the Mansfield Railway carved a passage away from the Great Central main line immediately north of the signal box controlling the divergence of the Leen Valley Extension. From 450ft above sea level, the Clipstone route climbed at 1 in 126 out of the Erewash headwaters to Kirkby in Ashfield (¾ mile from Kirkby South Junction), the ascent incorporating a lofty girder bridge across the Midland's Pye Bridge line, a somewhat unnecessary span over the already derelict Great Northern north to west spur and a deep excavation through the flanks of Castle Hill. The formation from Kirkby in Ashfield to Sutton in Ashfield (2½ miles) was just below 500ft and more or less level, but it proved a nightmare for the contractor. A long cutting was required and solid rock was expected. However, friable marl and saturated sand were discovered, demanding masonry retaining walls up to 9ft thick. A metal skew bridge followed by a 138yd brick tunnel carried the Great Northern and Midland respectively across the Mansfield Railway just south of Sutton in Ashfield. Beyond here, the

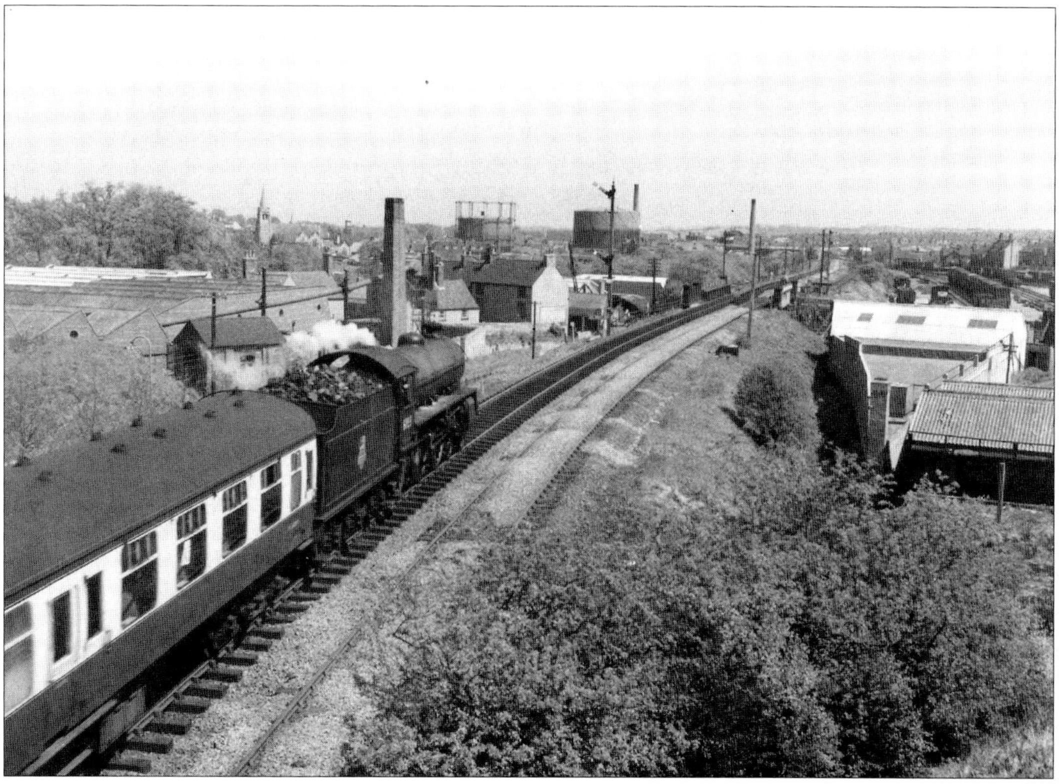

Anticipation of a day at the seaside probably preoccupied most families on this Kirkby in Ashfield-Mablethorpe special as it drifted down to Mansfield Central on 21st May 1955. Colwick B1 No.61163, an exile from GC main line work at Neasden, approaches Central's down outer home signal and Nottingham Road bridge. From left to right, the Maun Valley skyline is punctuated by Nottingham Road Methodist Church, Mansfield Gasworks and, almost, by Mansfield Central station just to the left of the isolated chimney. Photograph Jack Cupit.

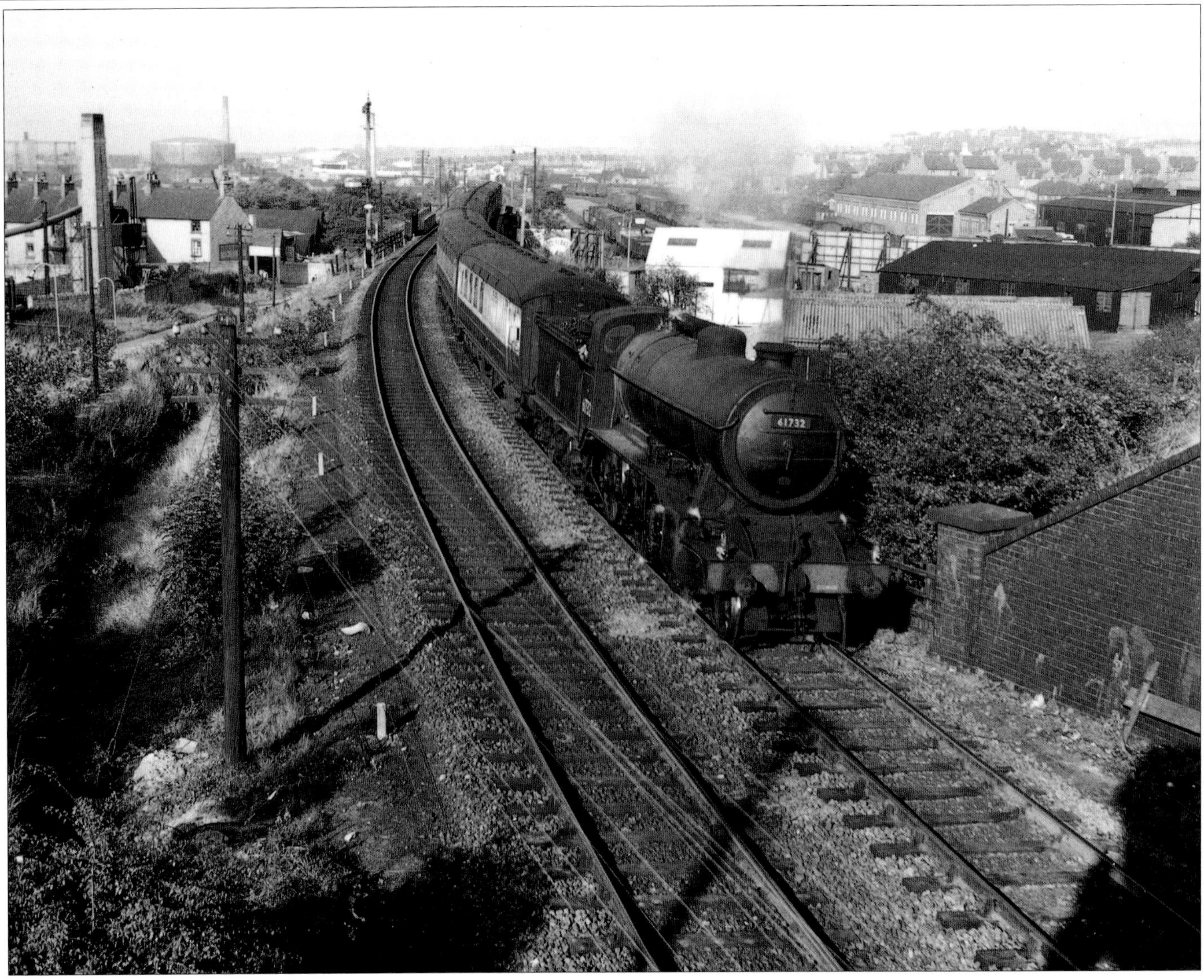

The sun sinks in the west and parents aboard an excursion returning from Skegness to Nottingham Victoria on 17th September 1953 no doubt relax as exhausted children doze after a hectic time at the coast. K2/2 No.61732, another long term resident of Colwick, lifts the train out of Mansfield Central across Nottingham Road bridge. In the background of this view from the Midland's Mansfield-Southwell line overbridge, the GC goods yard is full of wagons, a healthy yet hardly profitable traffic. Photograph Jack Cupit.

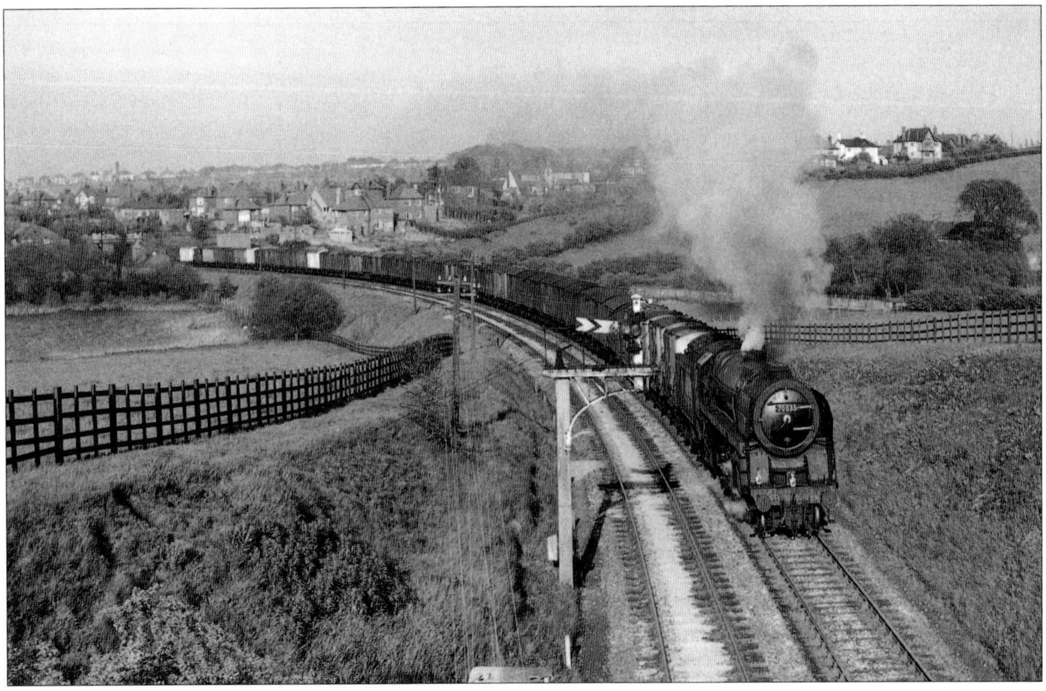

During the early evening of 23 May 1962, Britannia Pacific No.70035 RUDYARD KIPLING, in charge of the Grimsby-Whitland fish, is well into the climb out of Mansfield towards Sutton in Ashfield. In this classic view of a train in the landscape, the mill reservoir known locally as 'The Duckpond' features prominently. Despite the encroachment of new houses on the southern outskirts of Mansfield, this spot remained a favourite place for recreation, the artificial lake having its own resident pair of swans, oblivious to the railway. Photograph Jack Cupit.

line dropped at 1 in 107 past the western end of King's Mill reservoir before passing beneath the Midland's Nottingham-Mansfield line in a rock cutting.

The new railway had to pick its way through the partially built-up eastern outskirts of Mansfield and for two miles earthworks and other engineering work proliferated. First came a sweeping curve across the Cauldwell Brook valley. This modest cleft contained Bleak Hill reservoir, known locally as the Duckpond, which the line crossed by means of a 12ft high embankment. Cuttings on either side completed what was a very picturesque section of the route. A bridge under the Midland's Southwell branch heralded nearly a mile of embankment, the first part of which incorporated a large plate girder span with no less

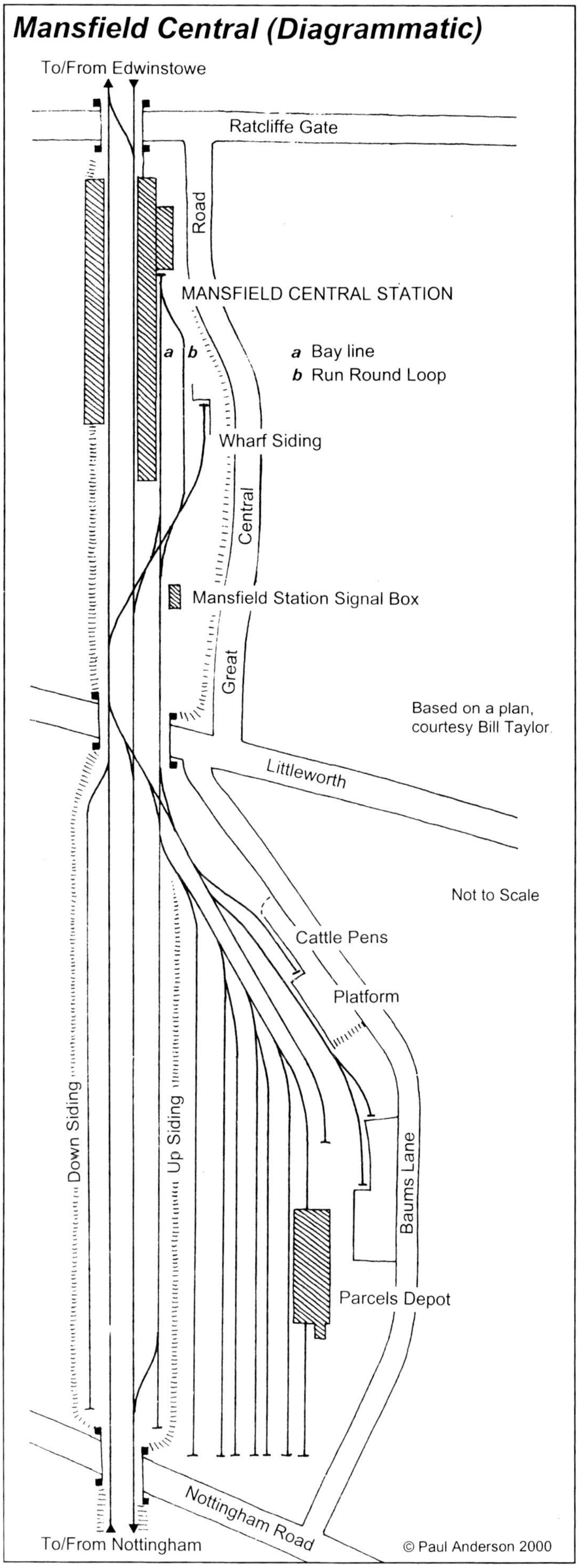

than 17ft headroom to accommodate the electric trams along Nottingham Road. Beyond Ratcliffe Gate near the centre of Mansfield (5½ miles) an existing building was so close to the formation that one side of the embankment had to consist of a vertical wall in concrete and masonry. A steady ascent at 1 in 200 took the tracks through a deep sandstone cutting at Windmill Ridge and they continued along a high embankment near Sherwood Hall. From 350ft next to Crown Farm Colliery to just above 200ft at Clipstone (11¾ miles) the gradient steepened to 1 in 120 and 1 in 130, although earthworks were minimal. For most of the way, the railway overlooked Vicar Water and was in turn overlooked by the sandy heathland of Rufford Forest and Clipstone Forest in the heart of Sherwood.

Although an endless succession of coal trains from collieries to the Concentration Sidings and Annesley Yard dominated workings over the Mansfield Railway, there was a fair amount of through freight, notably fish from Grimsby and steel from Scunthorpe. Three local goods depots were provided. Kirkby and Sutton each had four sidings, one of them serving a coal yard with a loading bank. The facilities at Mansfield were on a much larger scale and occupied a broad swathe of land between Nottingham Road and Littleworth, somewhat lower than the main line. There were seven main sidings, each with a capacity of forty or more wagons. One of the tracks led to a substantial warehouse with goods offices, an internal platform, two cranes and four bays for road vehicles. A cattle dock and timber yard stood adjacent to Baums Lane.

Regular passenger services over the Mansfield Railway commenced seven months after the line had been completed, quite a remarkable development in the circumstances. Numerous passenger workings throughout the country had just been withdrawn as a wartime economy measure – Sutton Junction to Sutton in Ashfield and Nottingham Midland to Ilkeston via Kimberley locally, for instance. Furthermore, the area was already well provided with stations on parallel Great Northern and Midland routes. Finally, by this relatively late date, motor buses were already in the ascendancy, although their future impact could hardly have been foreseen at the time. Nevertheless, the first train to Ollerton via Mansfield duly left Nottingham Victoria at 7.30am, on 2nd April 1917. The day began with a blizzard, but that did not deter directors of the Great Central and Mansfield Railway from travelling on a special later in the day to celebrate the occasion. After a dinner at the *Hop Pole* in Ollerton, there were several speeches involving not a little self-congratulation. The Great Central representatives, for example, actually stressed how helpful they had been in bringing the line into being! Initially, the passenger service consisted of three trains each way, all of them providing London Marylebone connections at Nottingham.

Stations were built at Kirkby in Ashfield, Sutton in Ashfield and Mansfield, of which Mansfield Central was an extraordinary place by any standards. Incidentally, the suffix never actually appeared on its nameboards, but remained in common use long after the Great Central ceased to exist. The term was certainly not a description of the location, the long established Midland facilities being far more convenient for the town centre and, for that matter, most of Mansfield. However, the local company insisted that the station would 'serve the side of the town which is now being principally developed'. A combination of its position, on the substantial embankment south of Ratcliffe Gate, and contemporary architectural trends gave the station its unique character. The site meant that subsidiary buildings on the down (Ollerton) side were supported by piers, whilst the main structure on the up (Nottingham) side was a towering four-storey edifice built up from ground level and fronting a new thoroughfare called, inevitably, Great Central Road. By late Edwardian times, the 'Domestic Revival' movement was mimicking early 18th century Georgian styling and the largely red brick facade of Mansfield Central incorporated elements of this fashion, although the overall specification clearly demanded austerity. A smaller building in the same style had been erected at Barnetby in north Lincolnshire during 1915.

Seen from Great Central Road, the northern end of the frontage was dominated by a gaunt tower for the parcels lift and a sheer brick wall reminiscent of a fortress. The southern aspect was slightly more welcoming, although the gabled section finished off with broken pediments looked like a modest house which had been hoisted up to an elevated position. A prominent stone cornice and a full length canopy emphasised the length of the disproportionately narrow building. The entrance had a touch of fanciful stonework and *Art Nouveau* iron-work, while high above were four stained glass windows belonging to a refreshment room which was never commissioned. Inside, a lofty and rather gloomy booking hall led to stairways up to rail level, with the one on the down side reached by a subway lined in glazed white bricks. The somewhat bleak platforms were on a reverse curve and consisted of timber planking, although generous canopies provided plenty of shelter. A bay was provided for southbound local services starting at Mansfield. Kirkby and Sutton had neat and certainly more conventional single-storey brick buildings, each featuring a charming semi-circular hood porch over the main doorway.

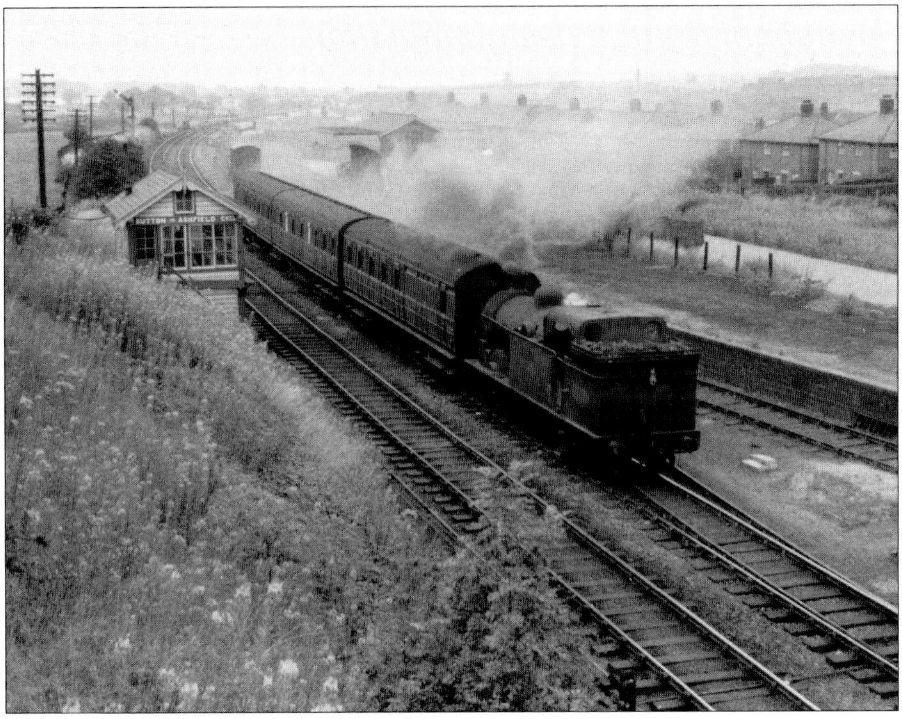

The demanding engineering work required at Mansfield was not necessary further south, the layout at Sutton and Kirkby stations being both conventional and spacious. With a typical GC signal box on the left and the sizeable goods shed almost obscured by smoke, N1 0-6-2T No.69481 ambles into Sutton in Ashfield Central with a Mansfield Central-Nottingham Victoria train on 6th August 1955. The Colwick engine was a refugee from Kings Cross suburban duties at Hornsey shed. Photograph Jack Cupit.

The Mansfield Railway, along with the Great Central, was absorbed by the London & North Eastern Railway on 1st January 1923 and that company instigated several developments over the next decade or so, most of them concerned with coal traffic. Prior to grouping, the Midland had gained access to Mansfield and Rufford collieries by means of branches from its Mansfield-Southwell line, inherited by the London Midland & Scottish Railway. Soon after its formation, the LMS acquired powers to extend the Rufford branch to Clipstone Colliery, which had started to draw coal in 1922, and even to the proposed Welbeck Colliery, which was north of the former LD&EC tracks. Meanwhile, the LNER had secured Parliamentary approval to extend its Rufford branch to Blidworth Colliery beyond the former Midland route to Southwell. Both companies obviously relished access to the highly productive deep mines in the concealed coalfield. They decided to co-operate when it came to the new collieries at Ollerton (opened in 1925) and Bilsthorpe (scheduled to open in 1928), together with the proposed pits at Calverton, north of Nottingham and Checker House and Bothamsall, south west of Retford. Consequently, the twenty-four mile LNER/LMS Mid-Nottinghamshire Joint Railway from Checker House on the Worksop-Retford line to Bestwood, near Hucknall in the Leen Valley, was authorised in 1926. There was no question of providing passenger services, bus companies having firmly established themselves in rural areas by then.

In June 1927 there was a meeting of the LNER Traffic Committee at Marylebone concerning Mansfield Concentration Yard. It was reported that the five sidings on the up side for receiving empties could barely cope, whilst the four sidings and reception road on the down side were overwhelmed by the flow of 550 loaded wagons a day. With several new collieries proposed or about to open, the 1½ million tons of coal a year handled by the yard would eventually rise to no less than 3½ million tons. Therefore, an additional reception road and fifteen new sidings were sanctioned, ten of the latter being on the down side. Coaling and watering facilities were also to be provided, thus ending wasteful light engine movements to Ollerton. The seven miles of Mid-Notts Joint line between New Ollerton and Farnsfield opened in 1931. This development afforded the LMS access to Bilsthorpe and Ollerton Collieries but was of little use to the LNER. By this time the Depression had postponed further development of the coalfield and no more of the line was built. On the passenger side, Mansfield Central had fourteen trains a day to Nottingham Victoria and twelve from the city by 1939. There were extras on Saturdays. A Leeds-Bournemouth express was also routed this way during the 1930s.

Mansfield Central had a particularly gloomy and neglected air about it in the 1950s. The stairways were grimy and uninviting, both platforms emulated the waves of a gentle sea because of warped timbers and the canopies sagged. There was also a distinct aroma of fish, no doubt caused by slight but relentless water spillage as daily trains to and from Grimsby docks negotiated the curves through the station. For a while after Nationalisation, former Great Central motive power maintained a strong presence. An N5 0-6-2T from Langwith shed was the station and goods yard pilot, while Langwith O4 2-8-0s and J11 0-6-0s worked mineral and other through goods traffic. Class A5 4-6-2Ts redeployed from Marylebone suburban services regularly worked local passenger trains, along with ex-Great Northern J6 0-6-0s and N1 0-6-2Ts from Colwick. Exiles from King's Cross in the form of N2 0-6-2Ts were used, but these were suddenly banished from the Nottingham district after an accident near Forest Town on 2nd September 1950, involving No.69552 on a passenger train. Defective engine springs and faulty track led to a derailment, the loco and two out of three coaches rolling down a low embankment.

In the autumn of 1955 there were eight northbound and seven southbound passenger trains over the Mansfield Railway, the first of the latter being the 7.14am from Mansfield Central to Leicester Central. Unfortunately, they were becoming a financial liability and British Railways decided to withdraw them on and from 2nd January 1956, Kirkby and Sutton goods yards closing at the same time. Scheduled summer Saturday holiday trains survived until 8th September 1956. Seasonal excursions to Scarborough, Cleethorpes, Skegness and Mablethorpe continued for several years, but the railway was doomed. Mansfield goods depot finished on 13th June 1966 and the line south of Crown Farm Colliery closed on 7th January 1968. Mansfield Central station was demolished in 1972 and virtually all traces of the route through the town vanished soon afterwards. Crown Farm Colliery closed in March 1988, followed by Blidworth in April 1989, Rufford in April 1993 and Bilsthorpe in March 1997, the Concentration Sidings having become a memory by this time. However, Clipstone Colliery was scheduled to remain open until September 2000, along with a short section of the undisputedly charismatic Mansfield Railway.

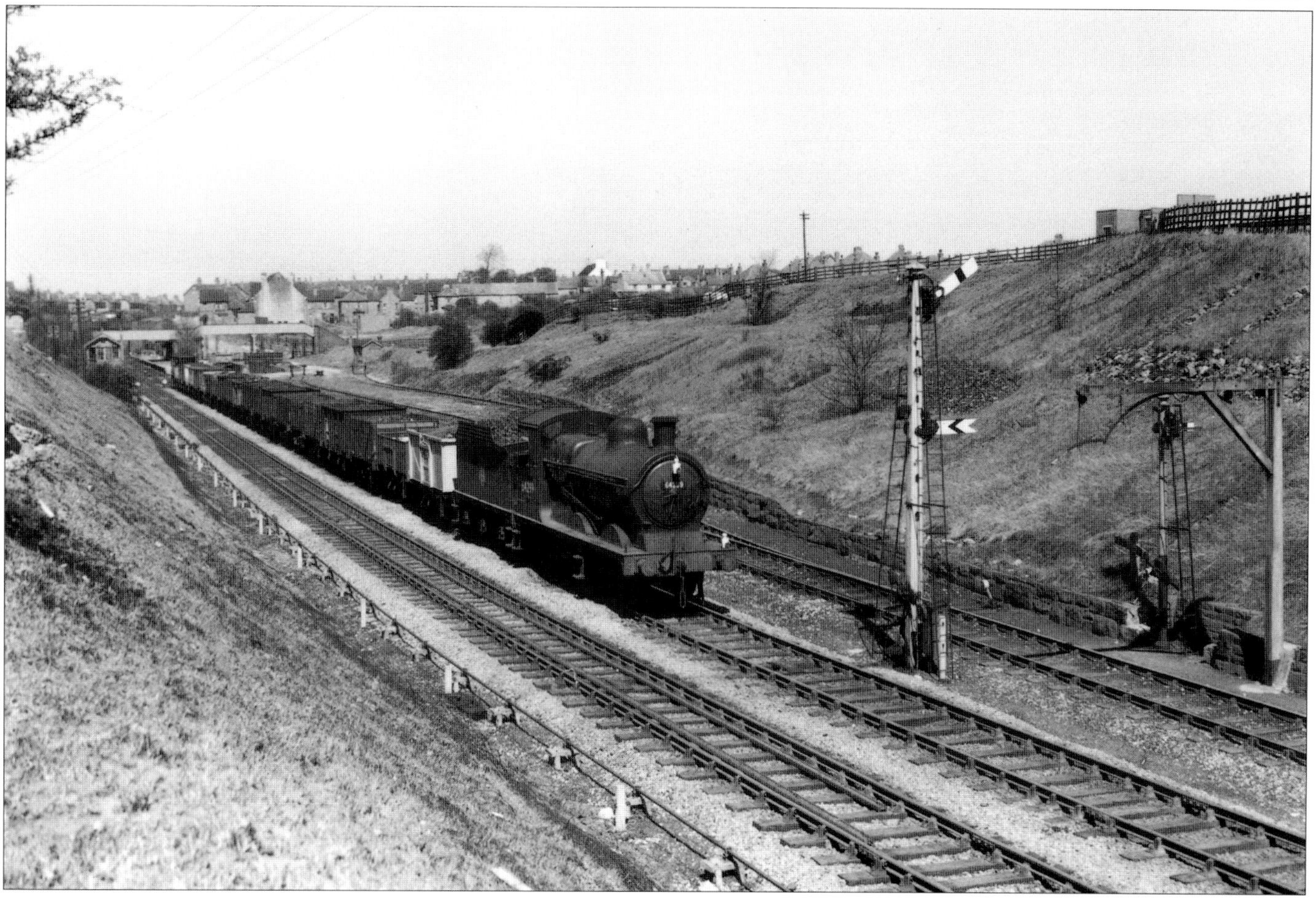

Ex-Great Central J11 0-6-0 No.64299, one of Tuxford's stalwarts, plods south through Kirkby in Ashfield Central with an up mineral train on 2nd May 1953. Along with virtually every other line in the area, coal was the lifeblood of the Mansfield Railway, and it moved in a wide range of wagons before the introduction of the standard 16 ton mineral. This particular train was made up of 21 wagons of no less than eight varieties, including several wooden bodied types, some older steel sided vehicles and four new 16 tonners. In the foreground, Kirkby South Junction's distant signal is below the Kirkby in Ashfield starter. Photograph Jack Cupit.

Kirkby South Junction was less than a mile away from Kirkby in Ashfield Central. On 2nd May 1953 J6 0-6-0 No.64238, another Colwick loco, has just joined the Great Central main line and is crossing the Leen Valley Extension with a Mansfield Central-Nottingham Victoria train. Photograph Jack Cupit.

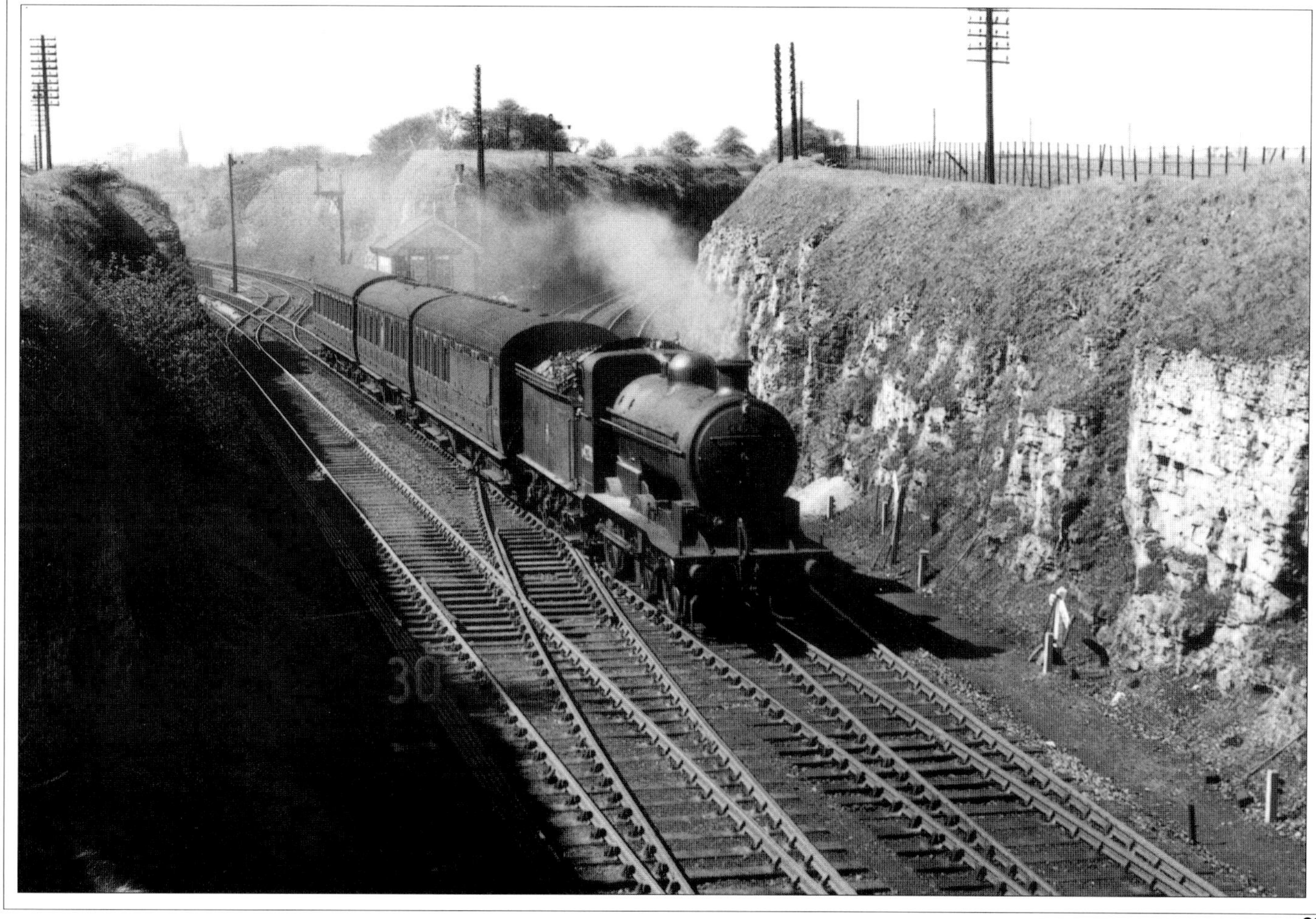

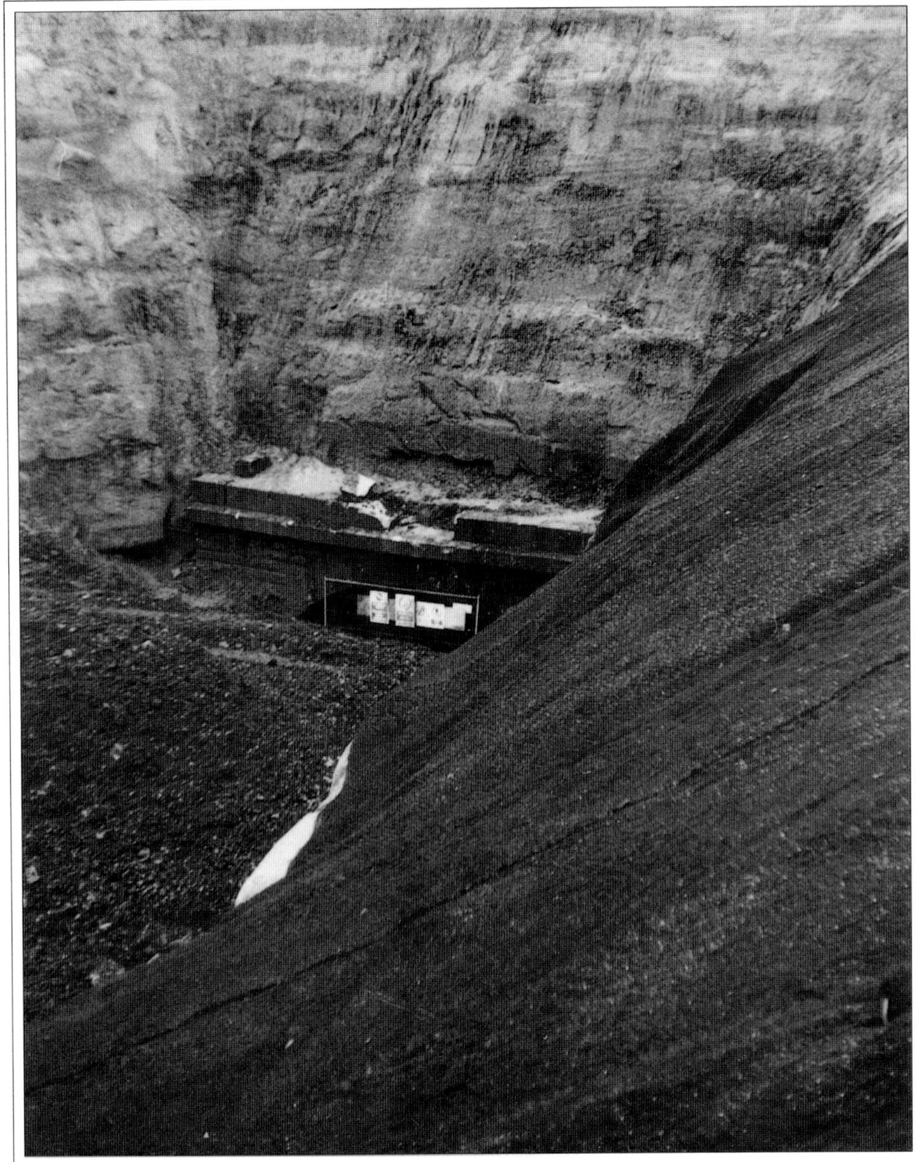

Rebirth of a tunnel. For the Robin Hood line to materialise, virtually everything depended on the condition of Kirkby Tunnel. This had been disused and filled with spoil for over twenty years when exploratory probes began. Fortunately, the early Victorian structure was in excellent condition. Work is underway at the north portal on 13th November 1994 (top) and the south portal on 5th June 1994 (bottom). Photographs Alf Henshaw.

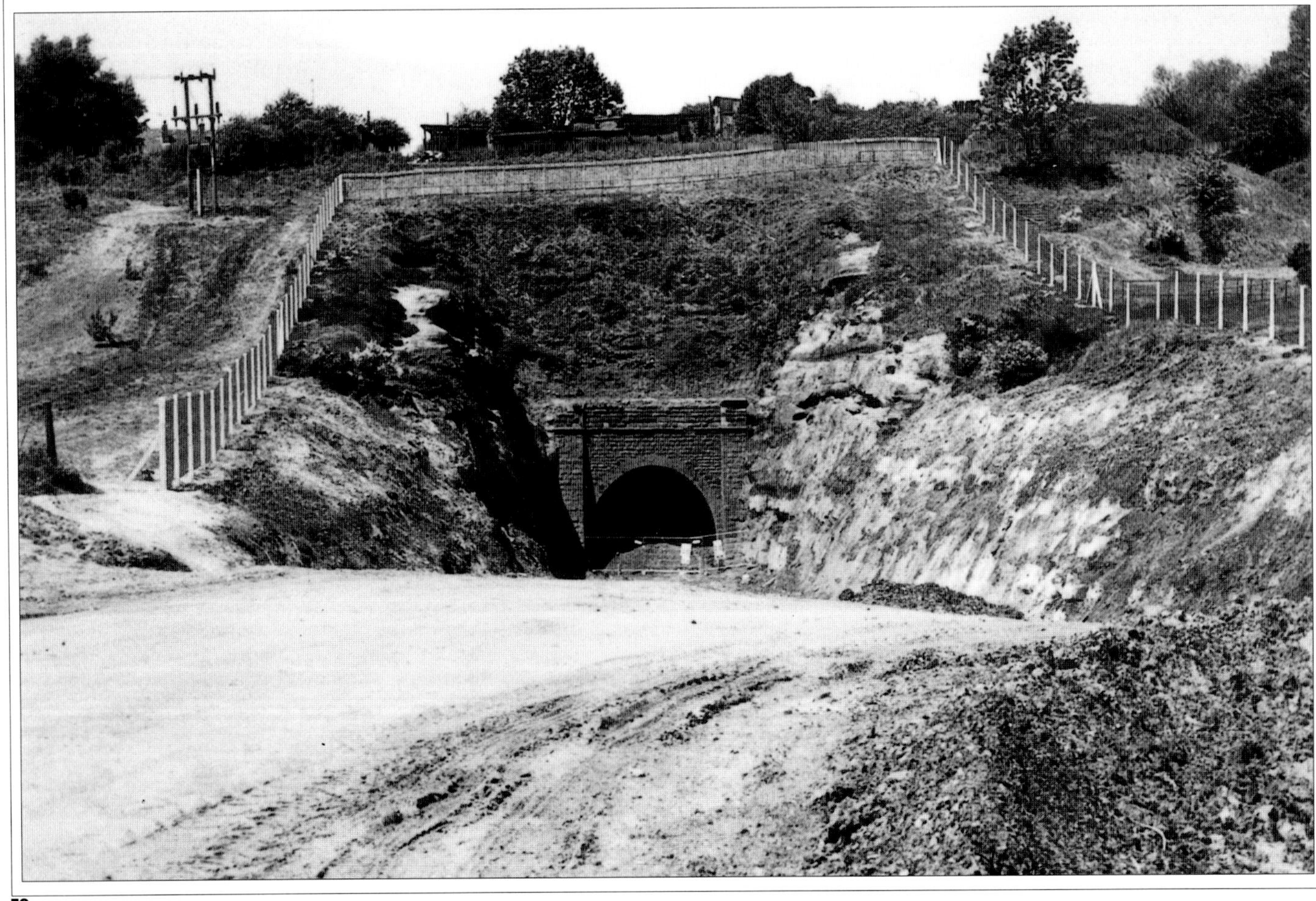

Chapter 10

The ROBIN HOOD LINE

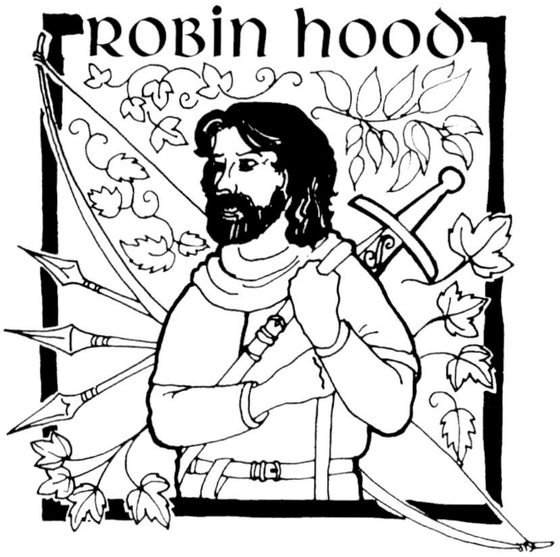

The story of Mansfield's railways over the last fifty years has been one of hectic activity, sudden decline, near annihilation and partial resurrection, in that order. Although the revival only applies to passenger services over the Nottingham-Worksop line of the former Midland Railway, it represents a modest victory of common sense over the headlong plunge into total reliance on road transport characteristic of the second half of the twentieth century. The demise of the Midland's Southwell and coalfield branches, the Great Central main line, the Leen Valley Extension and most of the LD&EC and Mansfield Railway has been described in previous chapters. Apart from the slim possibility of reintroducing passenger trains to Sheffield via Clowne and over the LD&EC to Ollerton, there is very little likelihood – and probably no point – in bringing other parts of the once extensive system back to life. However, the same was said about the direct Nottingham-Mansfield route in the mid-1980s.

Shortly after the formation of British Railways on 1st January 1948, the viability of marginal passenger services throughout the country came under scrutiny. An early casualty was the 'Penny Emma' from Sutton Junction to the town terminus in September 1949, as noted in Chapter 6. There was also the question of adjacent passenger and goods facilities with the same name on different lines, a potential source of confusion in the newly nationalised network. As a result, Shirebrook's former Midland station gained the somewhat enigmatic suffix West on 18th June 1951 to distinguish it from the ex-LD&EC and Great Northern stations nearby, and further west. Similarly, Bulwell Market, Hucknall Byron and Mansfield Town acquired their appendages on 11th August 1952. Annesley closed to both passenger and goods traffic on 6th April 1953, hardly surprising as Newstead station was only ¾ mile to the south and Annesley Woodhouse village was over a mile away up the hill and adequately served by buses. The token passenger service through Clowne finished in July 1954 and Mansfield Central shut its doors to regular customers at the very end of 1955. There was a feeling of optimism when Sir Brian Robertson announced his Modernisation Plan for British Railways in 1955. Diesel locomotives would eventually replace steam on main line passenger and goods services, pick-up traffic and shunting duties, diesel multiple units were to be introduced in increasing numbers for local and commuter services and several electrification schemes were proposed. Mansfield saw very little of this revolution. Stanier and WD 2-8-0s, ex-Great Central O4 2-8-0s and assorted 0-6-0s continued to haul the coal, while the Nottingham-Worksop passenger service remained firmly in the hands of tank engines. Lord Robertson retired in 1961, genuinely saddened by leaving the friends he had made in the railway industry. He was succeeded by Dr Richard Beeching from ICI, by which time the mounting debt of British Railways was causing the government much concern. Furthermore, car ownership was increasing and the M1 motorway was under construction. In March 1963, Beeching's infamous report *The Re-shaping of British Railways* appeared and was accepted by Parliament at the end of April. It was not good news for Mansfield.

A significant proposal in the report was the abolition of local goods yards and their attendant daily 'pick-up'. In many cases the depots had existed for well over a century and, as a common carrier, the railway was obliged to accept almost anything for almost anywhere. Prior to Beeching, Shirebrook West yard closed on 1st May 1962, followed by Kirkby Bentinck (on the former Great Central main line) on 4th

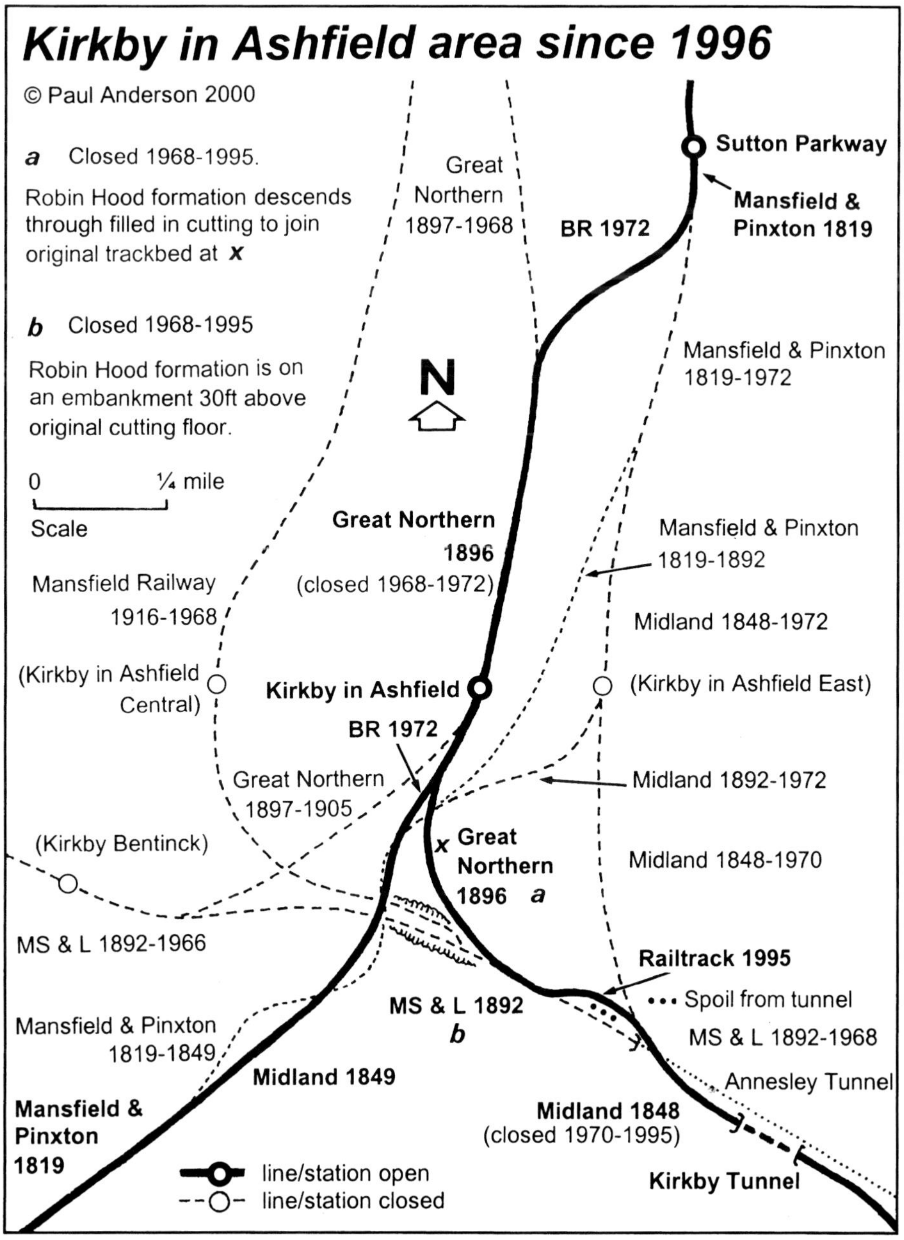

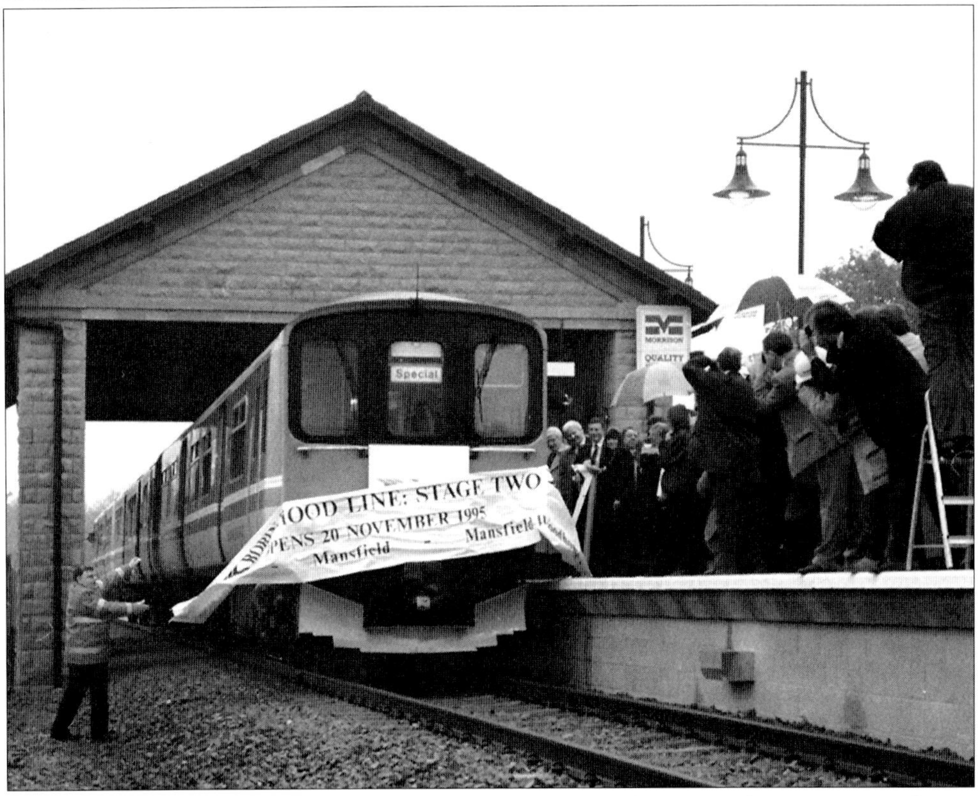

The official opening ceremony marking the long awaited return of passenger trains to Mansfield took place on Friday 10th November 1995 at Mansfield Woodhouse, where a class 150 Sprinter is seen breaking the traditional banner amid a flurry of attention from the press. A 'fun day' followed on Sunday 19th and regular services began the next day. Centro 150s from Tyseley depot in Birmingham monopolised the service at first and they were still making appearances in 1999. Note the former goods shed, now an integral part of the station. Photograph Mansfield Chad.

March 1963. Linby, Newstead, Kirkby in Ashfield East, Sutton Junction, Langwith and Elmton & Creswell goods facilities closed on 6th January 1964, as part of the national cull. However, there was something rather more serious in the air.

Another Beeching recommendation was, of course, the withdrawal of loss-making passenger services; the purely economic criteria for such closures having been a point of contention ever since. Despite their charm, many rural lines just had to go – there was no place for them where roads would always be able to cope. The loss of strategic cross-country routes was far more questionable, but the destruction of lines through built-up areas showed an appalling lack of judgement. The Department of Transport, infatuated with roads in general and motorways in particular was quite happy to see the end of services such as Nottingham-Worksop and Nottingham to Derby via Ilkeston. Public perception did not help. Miniskirts and Austin Minis were 'in' and trains were 'out' during the mid-1960s. A journey from Mansfield Town to Nottingham Midland was not much quicker than the bus and for those with a car it did not even enter the mind. Services were still fairly well used during the morning and evening peaks, but had few patrons at other times. A three-coach set of either non-corridor or corridor stock, the latter of ex-LMS or sometimes BR Standard type, was usually employed. Motive power was provided by Stanier or Fairburn 2-6-4Ts based at Kirkby in Ashfield shed, these engines having been displaced from Neasden, just like the Stanier 2-6-2Ts were exiled from Kentish Town, Leicester, Hellifield and the Birmingham area a decade earlier.

Before the 1968 Transport Act, there was no statutory closure process to go through, so when the intention to withdraw Nottingham-Worksop passenger trains during June 1964 was announced, all that local authorities and other interested parties could do was to register formal objections. These had no

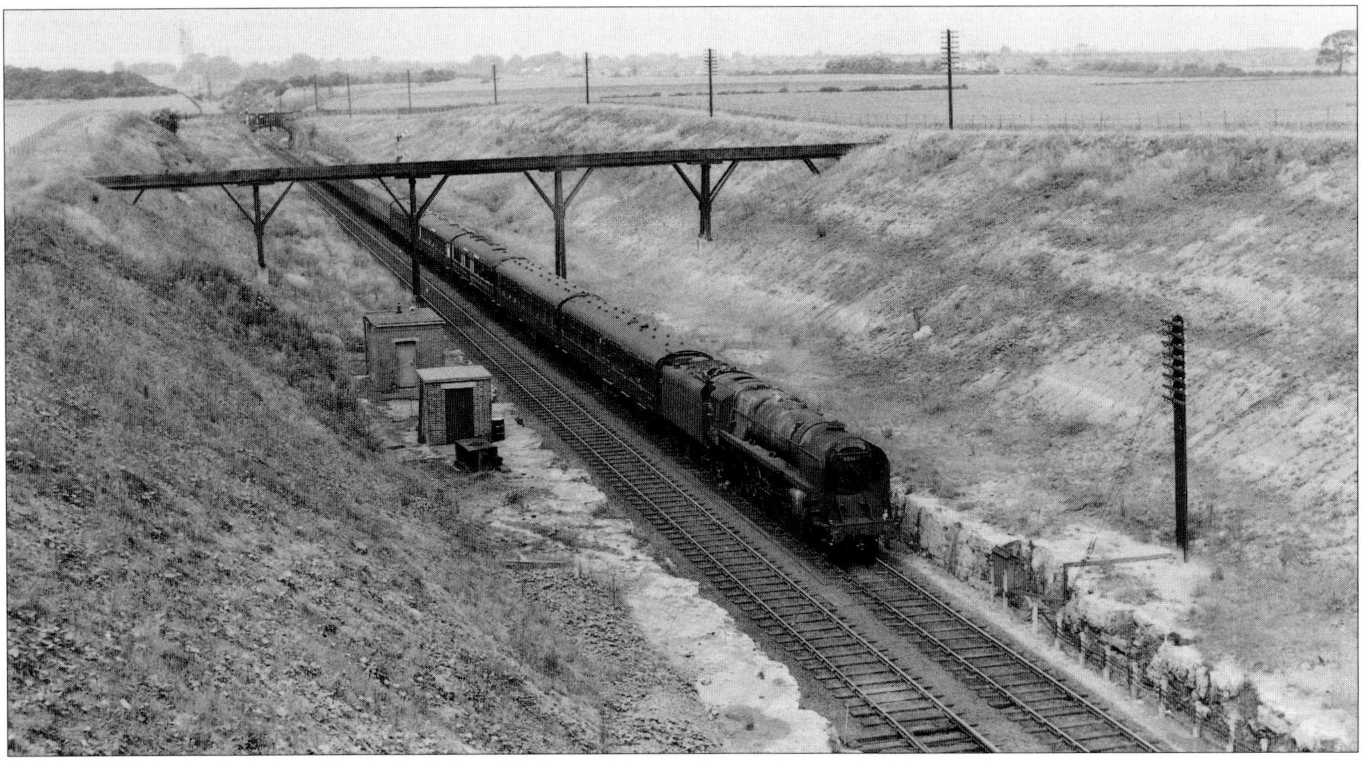

The transformation of the railway landscape south of Kirkby in Ashfield has been truly remarkable over the last forty years. This was the scene on 29th April 1958 as Annesley 9F 2-10-0 No.92069 headed towards Annesley Tunnel with the up 'South Yorkshireman'. In turn, the expresses, local services, through freights, coal trains and former Great Central main line itself disappeared, the cutting then being filled with spoil. Stage 2 of the Robin Hood project saw new track coming in from the right, approximately level with the top of the cutting. It then crossed Lindleys Lane by an overbridge, precisely above the site of the old GC underbridge seen in the background of this view. Photograph Jack Cupit.

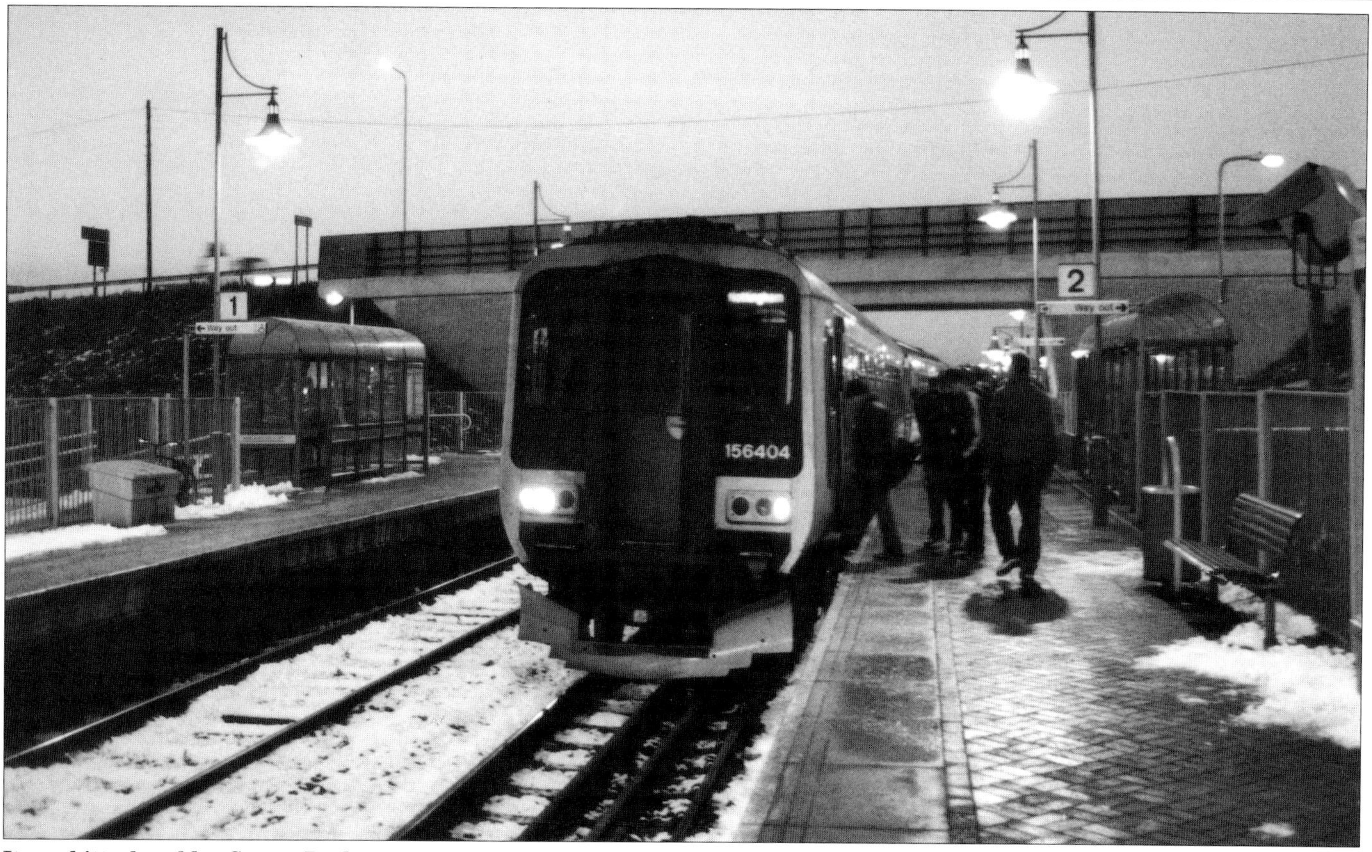

It was bitterly cold at Sutton Parkway on 15th December 1999 as passengers joined the 16.14 to Nottingham, formed of Sprinter 156 404. Sutton in Ashfield had no less than four stations, two on the Midland and one each on the Great Northern and Mansfield Railway, though they were only open at the same time between 1923 and 1931 and had all closed by the winter of 1964. Sutton Parkway opened in 1995 on a new and fifth site, just south of Sutton Junction. Note the distinctive lamps, a characteristic feature of the Robin Hood line. Photograph Paul Anderson.

effect and the government sanctioned closure, although there was a stay of execution until 12th October. With no Sunday service, the last trains ran on Saturday 10th October 1964. The final departure for Nottingham was at 8.51pm and when the 10.25pm from Nottingham to Elmton & Creswell left Mansfield at 11.14pm, exactly 115 years of passenger services to the town came to an end. It was appropriate that the old Mansfield & Pinxton Railway route saw the very last passenger trains in view of the fact that it had carried the very first. The early morning workmen's service to Nottingham via Pye Bridge and late afternoon return were retained, although Kirkby in Ashfield rather than Mansfield became the northern terminus. This working finished on 6th September 1965, normal services having been withdrawn on 10th September 1951.

It has often been stated that Mansfield was the largest town in Britain without a station. This is not strictly true, the dubious honour belonging to Gosport in Hampshire which lost its passenger trains from Fareham during 1953. Gosport has always looked to Portsmouth, a ¼ mile ferry journey away but seventeen miles by rail. However, Mansfield is a focal point in its own right and together with Mansfield Woodhouse, Kirkby in Ashfield and Sutton in Ashfield was by far the largest concentration of population in the country without passenger services. Fortunately, the track was still required for coal traffic and remained in situ, but goods yard closures continued relentlessly: Pinxton & Selston 2nd November 1964; Shirebrook North 4th January 1965; Blidworth on the Southwell branch and Sutton Town on the Leen Valley Extension 1st February 1965; Whitwell 14th June 1965; Mansfield Woodhouse 2nd January 1967; Bulwell Market 7th August 1967.

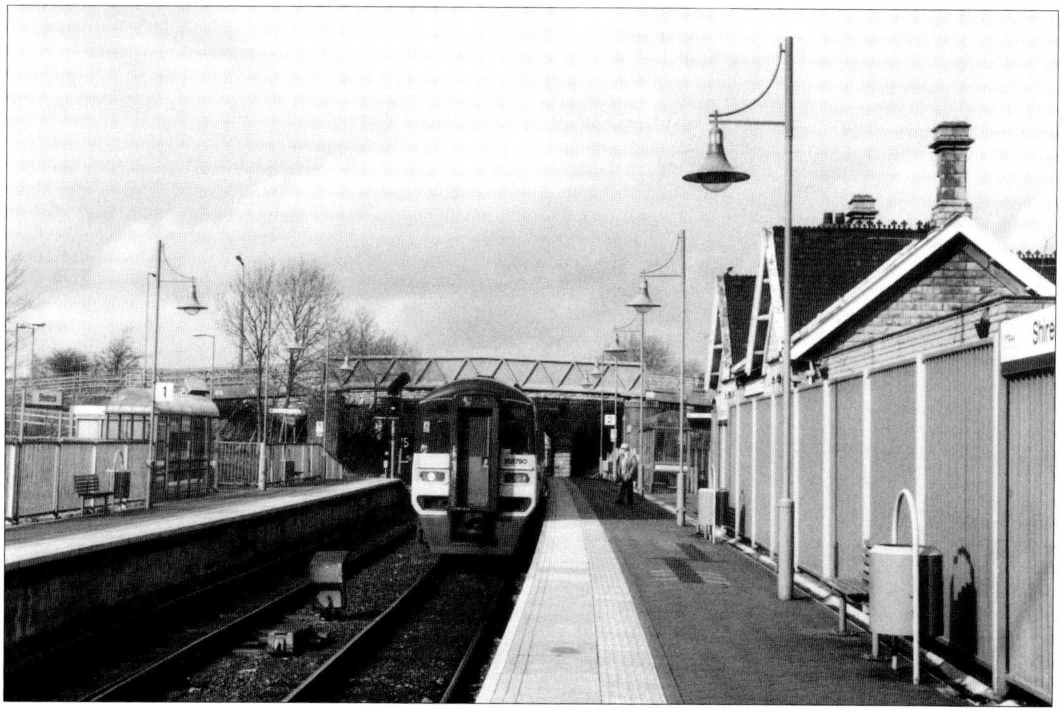

The most pleasing station on Stage 3 of the Robin Hood line is Shirebrook which retains its 1875 Midland Railway building, albeit boarded up at present. Central Trains 158 790 in the new dual green, blue, red and yellow livery calls at Shirebrook on 29th February 2000, forming the 13.36 from Worksop to Nottingham. This colliery town once had two other stations, Shirebrook North (originally Langwith Junction) on the LD & EC and long-closed Shirebrook South on the Great Northern. Photograph Paul Anderson.

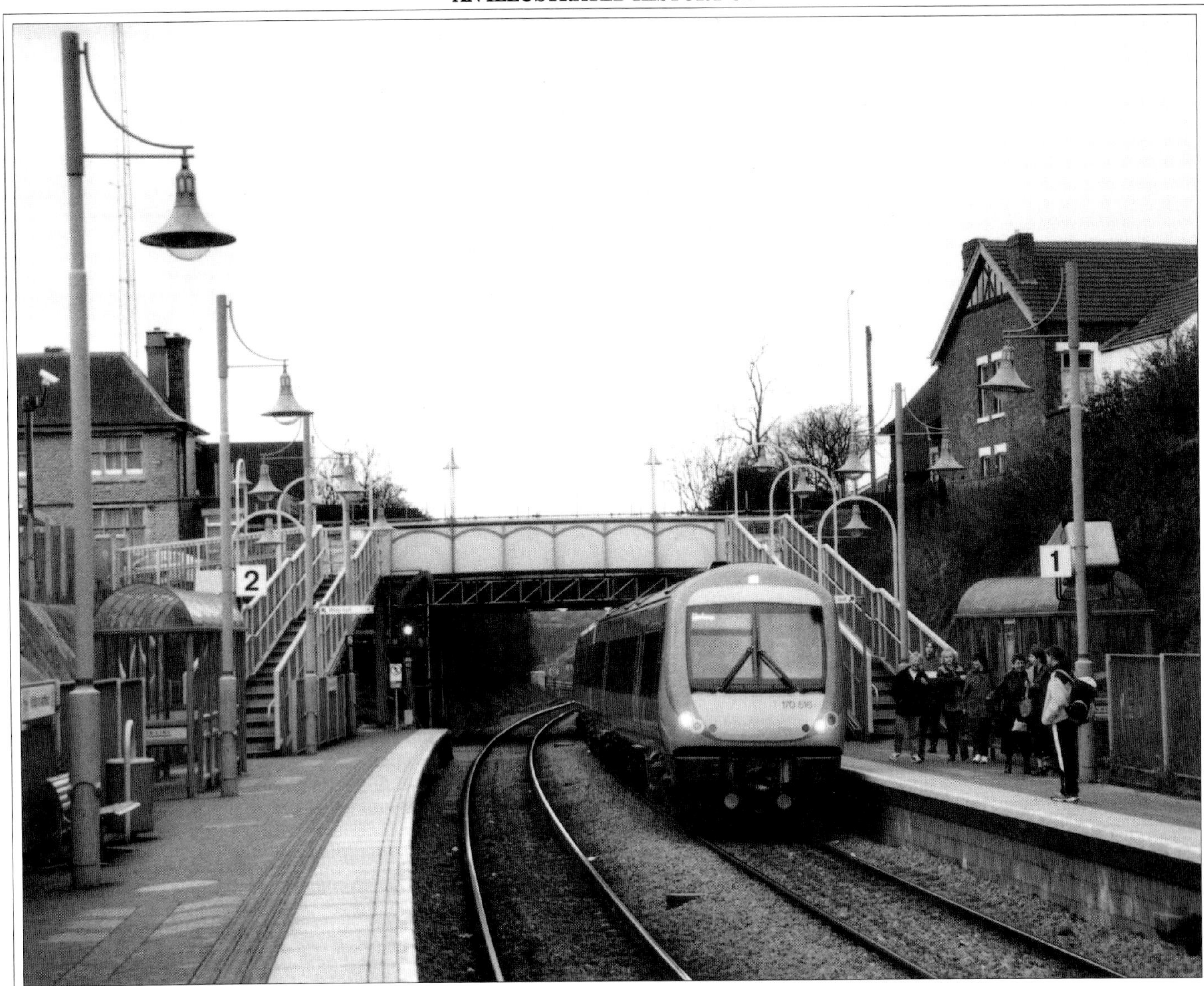

Kirkby in Ashfield once had three stations, on the Midland, Great Central and Mansfield Railway respectively, but the present Robin Hood facilities are on the former Great Northern route where none had existed previously. On 29th February 2000, brand new Central Trains Turbostar 170 516, forming the 16.20 from Nottingham to Worksop, calls at Kirkby in Ashfield. A rush hour short-working to Mansfield Woodhouse followed half an hour later; earlier attempts to cope with peak period demand involved the use of three class 153 single cars coupled together. Photograph Paul Anderson.

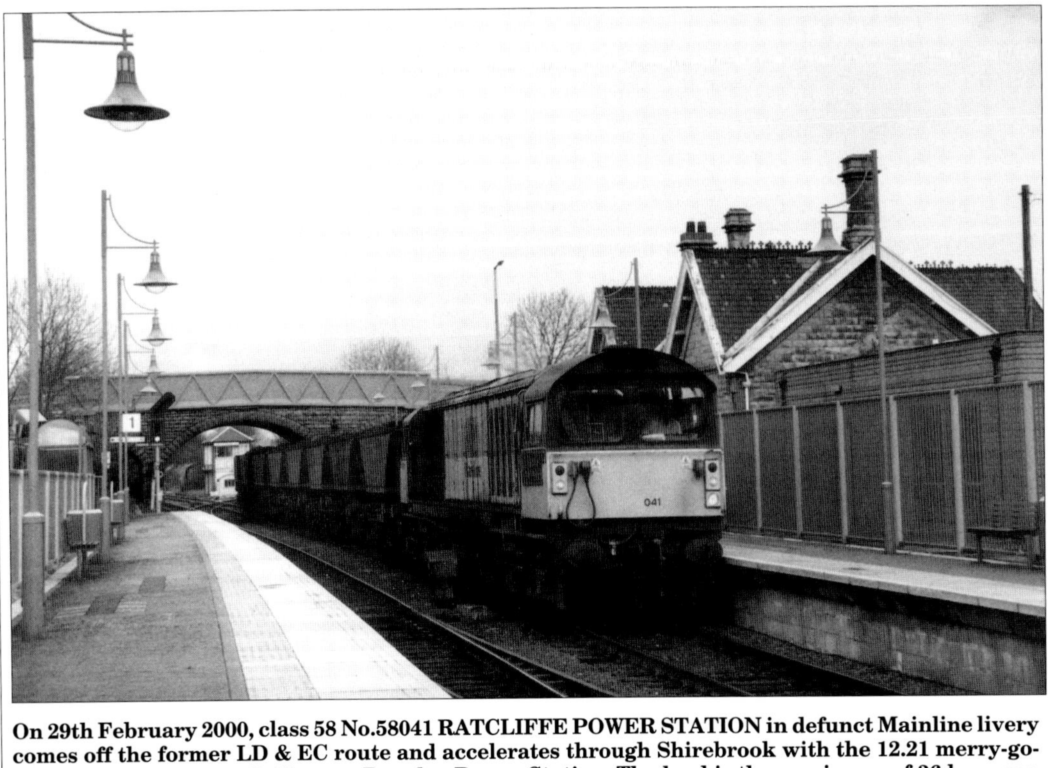

On 29th February 2000, class 58 No.58041 RATCLIFFE POWER STATION in defunct Mainline livery comes off the former LD & EC route and accelerates through Shirebrook with the 12.21 merry-go-round from Thoresby Colliery to Rugeley Power Station. The load is the maximum of 36 hoppers. Some coal trains head east to High Marnham Power Station, whilst others use the east-north spur on their way to Yorkshire destinations such as Drax. Photograph Paul Anderson.

Some of the older collieries expired as well, Bestwood during 1967 and Kirkby Summit in July 1968, for example.

Rationalisation of the Nottingham-Worksop route then took an alarming step forward. When the Leen Valley Extension and former Great Central line down the Leen Valley itself closed in May 1968, Annesley Tunnel and its approach cuttings were gradually filled with spoil and refuse. The Midland formation then suffered the same fate, following closure of the section of track from Kirkby in Ashfield to Annesley on 11th October 1970. In order to eliminate the level crossing at Kirkby in Ashfield and release land for building, a diversion was brought into operation on 4th April 1972. This involved constructing a short spur between the Pye

Bridge line and the former Great Northern route south of Kirkby, reinstating ¾ mile of the Leen Valley Extension through the town, and laying another spur from the site of Summit Colliery to the Mansfield line at Kirkby Hardwick. South of Langwith, an east-north spur between the LD&EC and Midland routes opened on 11th November 1974, thereby enabling the residual stretch of the Beighton branch from Shirebrook North to Whaley Thorns to be closed. Goods facilities at Mansfield were withdrawn on 2nd June 1975, the remaining railways in the district now being entirely dependent on coal traffic for their survival.

In 1978-79 the infamous 'winter of discontent' saw all manner of industrial disputes and was a factor in the election of a new government determined to confront the more militant trade unions. This had far-reaching consequences for the Mansfield area over the next two decades. Some of the large late-Victorian collieries were now becoming life-expired, Langwith closing in February 1979 and Teversal in July 1980. Then came the disastrous miners' strike of 1984. By and large, Nottinghamshire pitmen continued to work and the breakaway Union of Democratic Mineworkers was founded in the Mansfield area, but that did not prevent a series of closures in the wake of the strike: Silverhill April 1985, Whitwell June 1986, Hucknall October 1986, Newstead March 1987, Mansfield Crown Farm March 1988, Linby July 1988. Annesley was merged with Bentinck in March 1988. To be fair, most of these pits were over a century old and had exhausted their reserves. However, the economy of the Leen Valley had been dealt a severe blow and the railway north of Bestwood Park was derelict.

On 27th October 1982, a meeting took place between the Railway Development Society and Mansfield District Council about the possibility of reinstating passenger trains to Mansfield, although British Rail and Nottinghamshire County Council declined to send representatives. Both parties were enthusiastic about the idea, despite the inevitable problem of funding. The local press were also in favour, but rightly stated that it would be difficult to provide an attractive service on the surviving line via Pye Bridge. There was spasmodic talk of rebuilding the Annesley-Kirkby link, but for over five years the scheme remained a dream. Meanwhile, future prospects for the Nottinghamshire coalfield were looking increasingly bleak and traffic congestion was becoming a real problem, especially in Nottingham. A single announcement succeeded in focusing the minds of all interested parties on the reopening. In February 1988, BR proposed the closure of the line from Mansfield Junction (near Nottingham) to Trowell in the Erewash Valley and no doubt the developer building houses next to the railway at Lenton would have been eager to take over the trackbed, thus severing access to the Leen Valley for ever.

In retrospect, 1988 proved a crucial year. During April, Nottinghamshire County Council commissioned two studies, one by Leeds University to assess potential patronage, the other by British Rail to examine the state of Kirkby Tunnel. The former concluded that there was a considerable demand for a service throughout the catchment area of 300,000 people, while the latter found that the 140 year old tunnel was in remarkably good condition. By August, the reopening campaign had become ferocious and BR agreed to safeguard the trackbed from Mansfield Junction to Newstead. Colliery closures continued unabated: Blidworth April 1989, Shirebrook and Pleasley July 1989, Sutton August 1989, Warsop November 1989, Markham February 1990, Steetley May 1990. The quest for Government and European money looked promising and an Act for the Newstead-Kirkby link was acquired by BR on 26th July 1990, the term 'Robin Hood Line' for proposed Nottingham-Retford services (the original intention), having been adopted the previous March. In 1991, the consortium of local authorities (by now, all of them along the route) gave the final go-ahead and work commenced.

Stage 1 involved upgrading the partially derelict line along the Leen Valley to Newstead; by this time BR had decided to retain the Mansfield Junction-Trowell link. The cost was £2.7 million and a Nottingham-Newstead service worked by Regional Railways began on 17th May 1993. On the single track section north of Bestwood Park, stations were provided at Hucknall and Newstead in the now familiar and highly distinctive Robin Hood style. Bulwell station, with two platforms, opened on 23rd May 1994. Work on Stage 2, from Newstead to Mansfield Woodhouse, commenced early in 1994 and was a huge undertaking costing £20 million. Kirkby Tunnel, together with its approach cuttings, had to be excavated and a new link built from just north of the tunnel to the Pye Bridge route south of Kirkby. Initially, this adopted a completely new alignment, but then briefly followed the course of the Great Central main line, albeit on an embankment 30ft above the original cutting floor! A new bridge spanned Lindleys

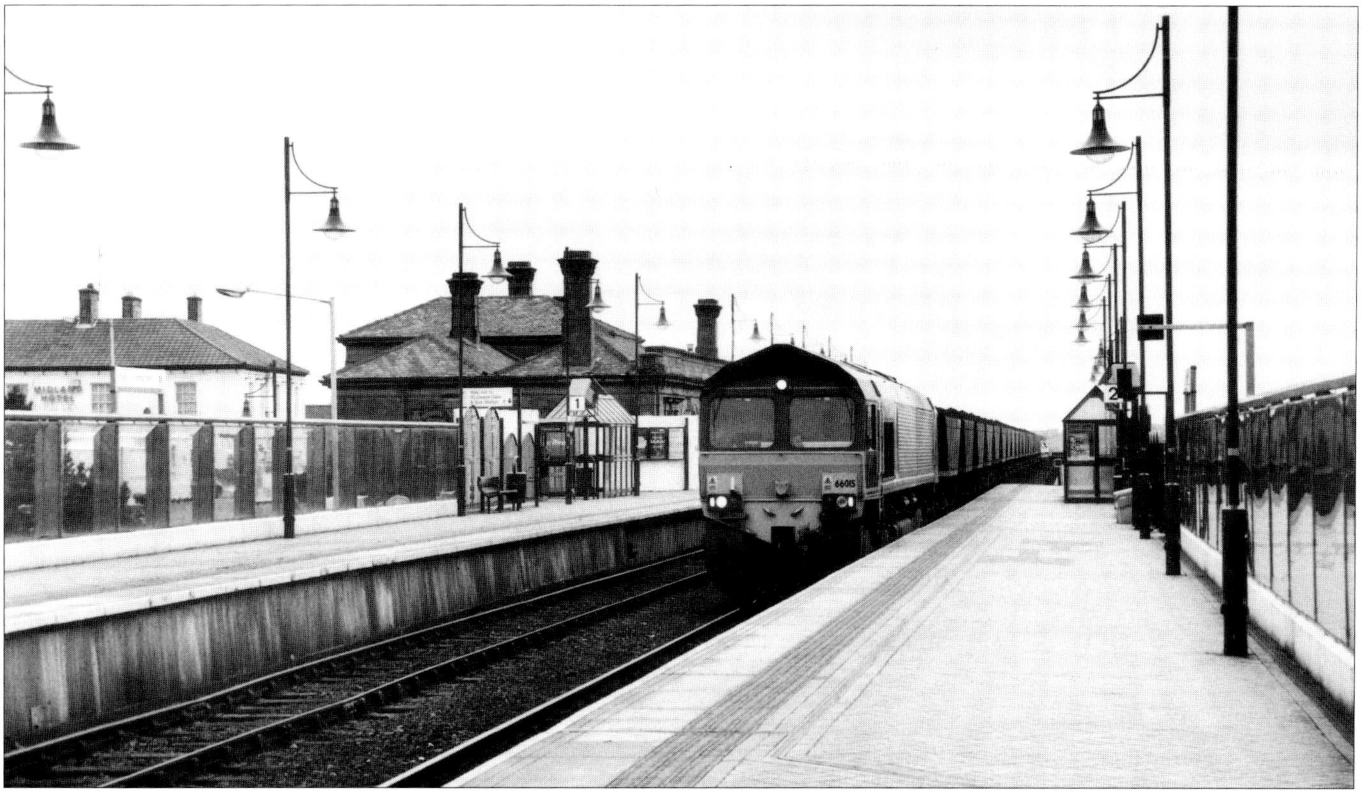

English Welsh & Scottish Railway class 66 No.66015, painted in the deep red and cream livery of the parent company, Wisconsin Central, heads the 10.10 merry-go-round from Welbeck Colliery to Didcot Power Station through Mansfield on 29th February 2000. These diesels represent the latest development in over 180 years of coal haulage by rail in the Mansfield area – from local horses to products of the General Motors factory at London, Ontario. Photograph Paul Anderson.

Lane at the precise point where there had once been a bridge over the railway. The Robin Hood line then descended into a cutting marking the course of the Leen Valley Extension, which had been ascending just here.

Passenger services from Nottingham to Mansfield Woodhouse were inaugurated on 20th November 1995, together with new stations at Sutton Parkway, Mansfield and Mansfield Woodhouse, with Kirkby in Ashfield joining them on 18th November 1996. The line was single from Newstead to just north of the tunnel, then double the rest of the way. Patronage reached a very encouraging 60,000 during December 1996, use of the trains being boosted by Christmas shopping trips to Nottingham. Later, a survey revealed that 40% of journeys from the Mansfield area had not been made at all prior to the line reopening, a clear indication of the principal aim of providing people with the means of travelling to employment elsewhere was being fulfilled. This was just as well, for colliery closures continued: Creswell September 1991, Sherwood January 1992, Rufford and Bevercotes April 1993 (the latter was a 'super pit' opened as recently as 1965), Ollerton April 1994, Bilsthorpe March 1997 and Calverton April 1999. The intention to close Clipstone during September 2000 was announced in September 1999, leaving just Thoresby and Welbeck to soldier on. Mining jobs in the Mansfield area declined from 41,000 in 1983 to just 1,230 in 2000.

Stage 3 from Mansfield Woodhouse to Worksop re-opened for passengers on 25th May 1998, with stations at Shirebrook, Langwith-Whaley Thorns, Creswell and Whitwell. The upgrading had cost £5 million, somewhat more than the £148,000 spent when the Mansfield-Worksop line was built in the 1870s. Following the privatisation of BR, engineering work was undertaken by Railtrack while Central Trains now operate the service. In 2000, Mansfield had eighteen departures for Nottingham (twenty-six on Saturdays) taking around thirty-three minutes. For comparison, there were ten trains (thirteen on Saturdays) taking forty minutes in summer 1964 and just six trains taking an hour in 1876.

It is well worth travelling on the Robin Hood line, if only for one reason. In the two miles of route from Kirkby Tunnel to Sutton Parkway, the train uses the following succession of trackbed: Midland 1848; Railtrack 1995; Manchester, Sheffield & Lincolnshire 1892 (but 30ft above it); Great Northern 1896 (partly above it); British Rail 1972; Mansfield & Pinxton 1819. At the beginning of the twenty-first century, there is nowhere else in Britain – or, indeed, the whole world – where one can travel over an amalgam of routes spanning almost two centuries of railway history in such a short distance. The story ranges from horse-drawn wagons during the times of George III to Turbostars well into the reign of Elizabeth II and all of it involves lines around Mansfield, in the heart of Robin Hood country.

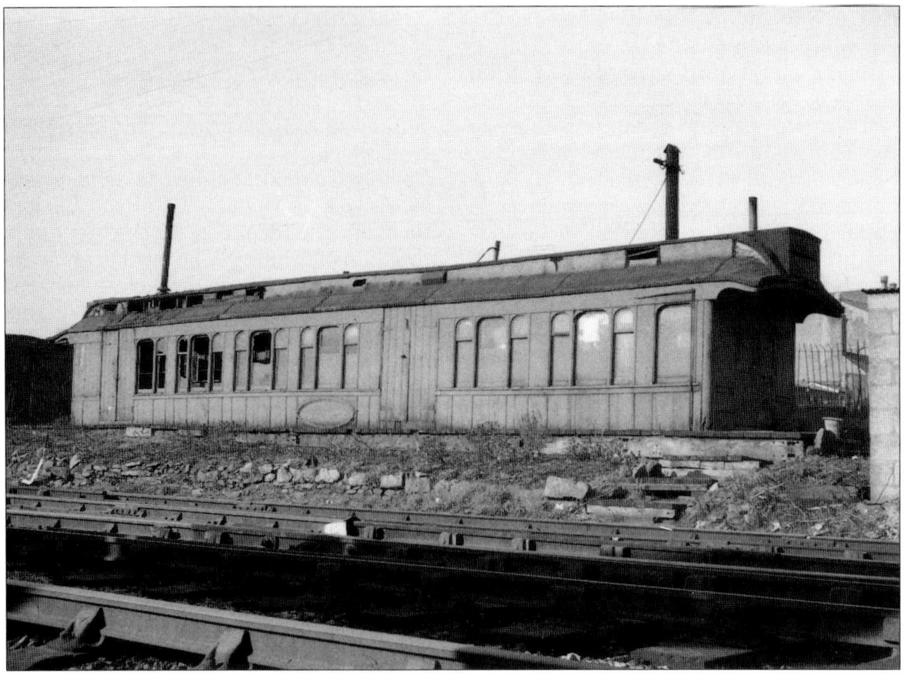

TAILPIECE 1. Considering the purely local nature of passenger services through Mansfield Town, this former Pullman car body grounded in the carriage sidings added an incongruous touch of faded splendour to the area. Although serving as a bothy for cleaners, the coach recalled the heady days of early Midland Anglo-Scottish expresses and had more than a hint of Jesse James and America's Mid-West about it, a far cry from humdrum Nottingham-Worksop trains! Sadly, the mutilated yet still venerable bodywork was ravaged by fire shortly after this view was taken on 18th February 1962. Photograph Jack Cupit.

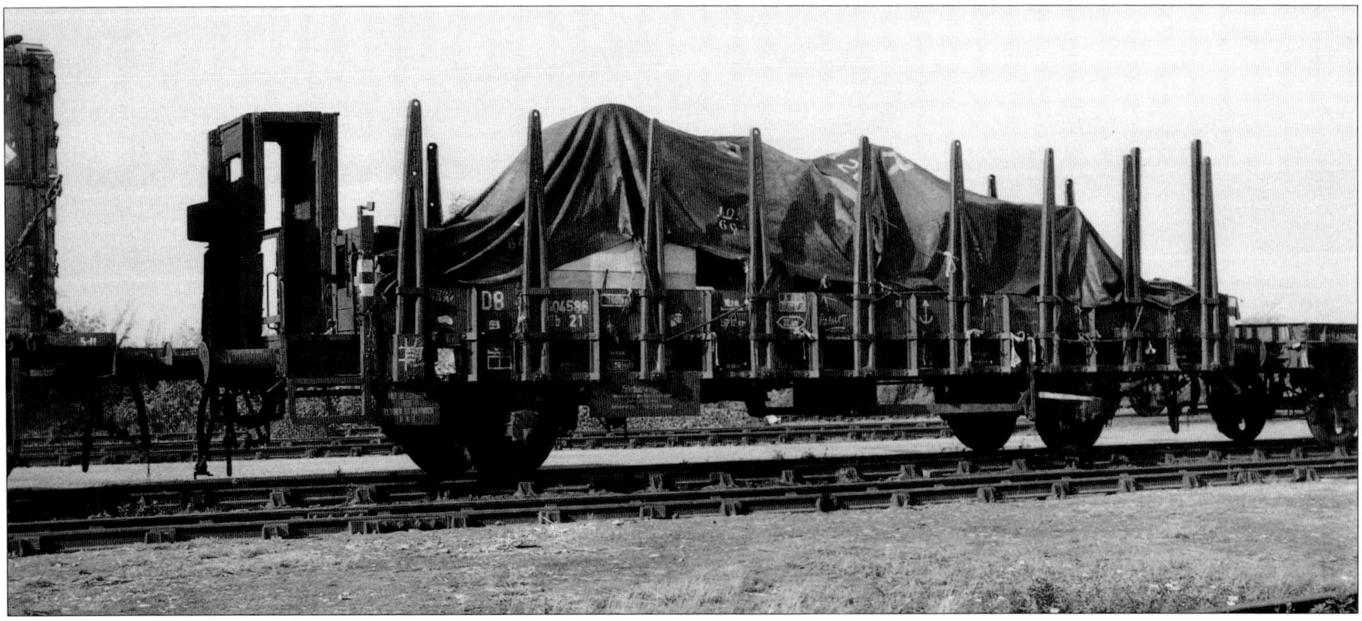

TAILPIECE 2. Although the Mansfield Railway was a regional and national link of some importance, it seems to have had continental connections as well! This DB (German State Railways) wagon with its long wheelbase and strange little brake cabin was a curiosity in Mansfield Central goods yard on 13th October 1963. The instruction *'Fährbootwagen Verwendbar für den Güterverkehr über Zeebrügge-Harwich zwischen dem Festland und Großbrittanien'* was probably not much help to local staff, although the gist of the message could be gleaned. Basically, it was 'Ferry wagon for working via Zeebrugge-Harwich between the mainland and Great Britain'. Photograph Jack Cupit.